BREAKING THE BOMBERS

Praise for Mark Shaw's previous books

'Mark Shaw's finger is on the trigger. Target: the complex criminal economy. And Shaw is a deadly marksman. So enthralling you would be forgiven if you thought time had stopped.'

– **VUSUMZI PIKOLI**, former head of the National Prosecuting Authority

'With his unique insight, Mark Shaw has thrown a spotlight onto the underworld, exposing the commercialisation of murder in South Africa. I have interviewed a fair number of hitmen as a journalist, but this book still shocked me from cover to cover.'

– **MANDY WIENER**, author of *Killing Kebble* and *The Whistleblowers*

'While Shaw might be an academic, his book is engrossing and highly readable. If you can get past the shock of the first 40 pages or so you will begin to see the pieces of the vast mosaic of crime, violence, politics and money that operates all around us, all of the time.'

– **MARIANNE THAMM**, author of *Hitler, Verwoerd, Mandela and Me*

'The man understands the terrain and quotes hundreds of interviews and conversations with key figures across the spectrum from police generals to assassins.'

– **JOHANN KRIEGLER,** former judge of the Constitutional Court

BREAKING THE BOMBERS

How the hunt for pagad created a crack police unit

MARK SHAW

Jonathan Ball Publishers
Johannesburg & Cape Town

Published in South Africa in 2023 by
JONATHAN BALL PUBLISHERS
A division of Media24 (Pty) Ltd
PO Box 33977
Jeppestown
2043

ISBN 978-1-77619-151-2
ebook ISBN 978-1-77619-152-9
audiobook ISBN: 978-1-77619-326-4

Every effort has been made to trace the copyright holders and to obtain their permission for the use of copyright material. The publishers apologise for any errors or omissions and would be grateful to be notified of any corrections that should be incorporated in future editions of this book.

www.jonathanball.co.za
www.twitter.com/JonathanBallPub
www.facebook.com/JonathanBallPublishers

Cover by Rudi Louw
Map by Liezel Bohdanowicz
Design and typesetting by MR Design
Set in Sabon

BREAKING THE BOMBERS

How the hunt for pagad created a crack police unit

MARK SHAW

Jonathan Ball Publishers
Johannesburg & Cape Town

Published in South Africa in 2023 by
JONATHAN BALL PUBLISHERS
A division of Media24 (Pty) Ltd
PO Box 33977
Jeppestown
2043

ISBN 978-1-77619-151-2
ebook ISBN 978-1-77619-152-9
audiobook ISBN: 978-1-77619-326-4

Every effort has been made to trace the copyright holders and to obtain their permission for the use of copyright material. The publishers apologise for any errors or omissions and would be grateful to be notified of any corrections that should be incorporated in future editions of this book.

www.jonathanball.co.za
www.twitter.com/JonathanBallPub
www.facebook.com/JonathanBallPublishers

Cover by Rudi Louw
Map by Liezel Bohdanowicz
Design and typesetting by MR Design
Set in Sabon

To the survivors

In memory of
Peter Spargo, 1937–2021

'Eventually, I came to understand the lesson that had been taught to me from the beginning: information is neither good nor evil; information is what information is. The people providing the information have their reasons and motives, many of them impure. What matters is the purity of the information, not the person.'

Jake Adelstein, *Tokyo Vice: An American Reporter on the Police Beat in Japan*, New York: Vintage, 2009, p. 101

'When police or military force is applied it is vital that it follow the rule of law. Miscreants should be brought to justice, evidence presented, and judgement rendered. The value of this approach is that it reinforces the notion that civil society should be respected and that the insurgent forces are the lawless ones.'

Mark Juergensmeyer, *When God Stops Fighting: How Religious Violence Ends*, Oakland: University of California Press, 2022, p. 134

CONTENTS

DRAMATIS PERSONAE

People Against Gangsterism and Drugs (Pagad)

Abdus-Salaam Ebrahim, central figure in the formation and leadership of Pagad. Imprisoned from December 1999 to September 2008.

Ali 'Phantom' Parker, earlier leader of Pagad. Survived an attempted assassination.

Abdurazak Ebrahim, spiritual leader of Pagad who appeared at early rallies with his face covered. Displaced by Abdus-Salaam Ebrahim.

Achmad Cassiem, charismatic leader and founder of Qibla. Active in Pagad before quietly withdrawing.

Aslam Toefy, once Pagad's leader and still active in the organisation. Sometimes described as the presentable face of the group.

Haroon Orrie, current Pagad coordinator. Arrested for an attempted bombing in November 2000 and imprisoned, but charges were dropped in 2003.

Yusuf Williams, aka 'Boeta Yu', widely respected older figure in Pagad who played a crucial role in delivering messages from the leadership to the cells. Later fell out with Abdus-Salaam Ebrahim and died in 2022.

Ebrahim Jeneker, by reputation one of the most practised killers in the Pagad movement, who became a thorn in the side of the state. Convicted for multiple murders in December 2002 and released in November 2020. Imprisoned again in June 2022 for violating parole conditions.

Moegsien Barendse, leader of Pagad's Grassy Park cell at the height of the violence. Part of the group that broke away to form the G-Force post 2010, which he now leads.

Ayob Mungalee, leader of Pagad in Gauteng and an informer for the National Intelligence Agency. Spent several years in prison after being arrested in February 1999. Assassinated in February 2023.

Politicians

Sydney Mufamadi and **Steve Tshwete**, ministers for safety and security from 1994 to 1999 and 1999 to 2002, respectively.

Hennie Bester, provincial minister for community safety in the Western Cape during the final phase of the state's response in 2001.

The police

George Fivaz, first national police commissioner of the South African Police Service (1995–1999), central to the initial police response to Pagad.

Jackie Selebi, commissioner after Fivaz (2000–2008), played a key role in galvanising the police response, although he sought to undercut the Scorpions.

Arno Lamoer, senior police officer – widely seen as a reformer and potential national commissioner – who played a key role against Pagad. He was later convicted of corruption.

Leonard Knipe, legendary apartheid-era detective and head of the Serious & Violent Crime unit in the Western Cape. He led the initial response to Pagad but was later sidelined.

Riaan Booysen, head of the Western Cape Serious & Violent Crime unit from 2000. Working closely with the Scorpions, he was essential in building cohesion in the Pagad response.

Bennie Lategan, detective working on Pagad cases. He was threatened by Ebrahim Jeneker and assassinated in January 1999.

Frank Gentle, leading member of the Cape Town bomb squad who disarmed a 'live' device outside the Keg and Swan in Bellville in November 2000.

Mzwandile Petros, head of the undercover operations unit that played a critical, if controversial, part in the response to Pagad.

David Africa and **Anwar Dramat**, members of the undercover operations unit, who played key roles in the response. Africa, in particular, was engaged throughout the campaign.

Intelligence

Arthur Fraser, head of the National Intelligence Agency (NIA) in the Western Cape from 1998 to 2004, when he led its efforts against Pagad.

Barry Gilder, deputy director-general of the NIA who led the 'peace discussions' with Pagad.

The Scorpions

Bulelani Ngcuka, director of the National Prosecuting Authority (1998–2004), founder of the Scorpions and key player in the state's strategic response to Pagad.

Percy Sonn, founder and head of the Investigative Directorate for Organised Crime in the Western Cape. He was convinced that a more effective and strategic response against Pagad was required.

Willie Viljoen and **Eunice Gray**, lead prosecutors on Pagad-related cases at the Scorpions.

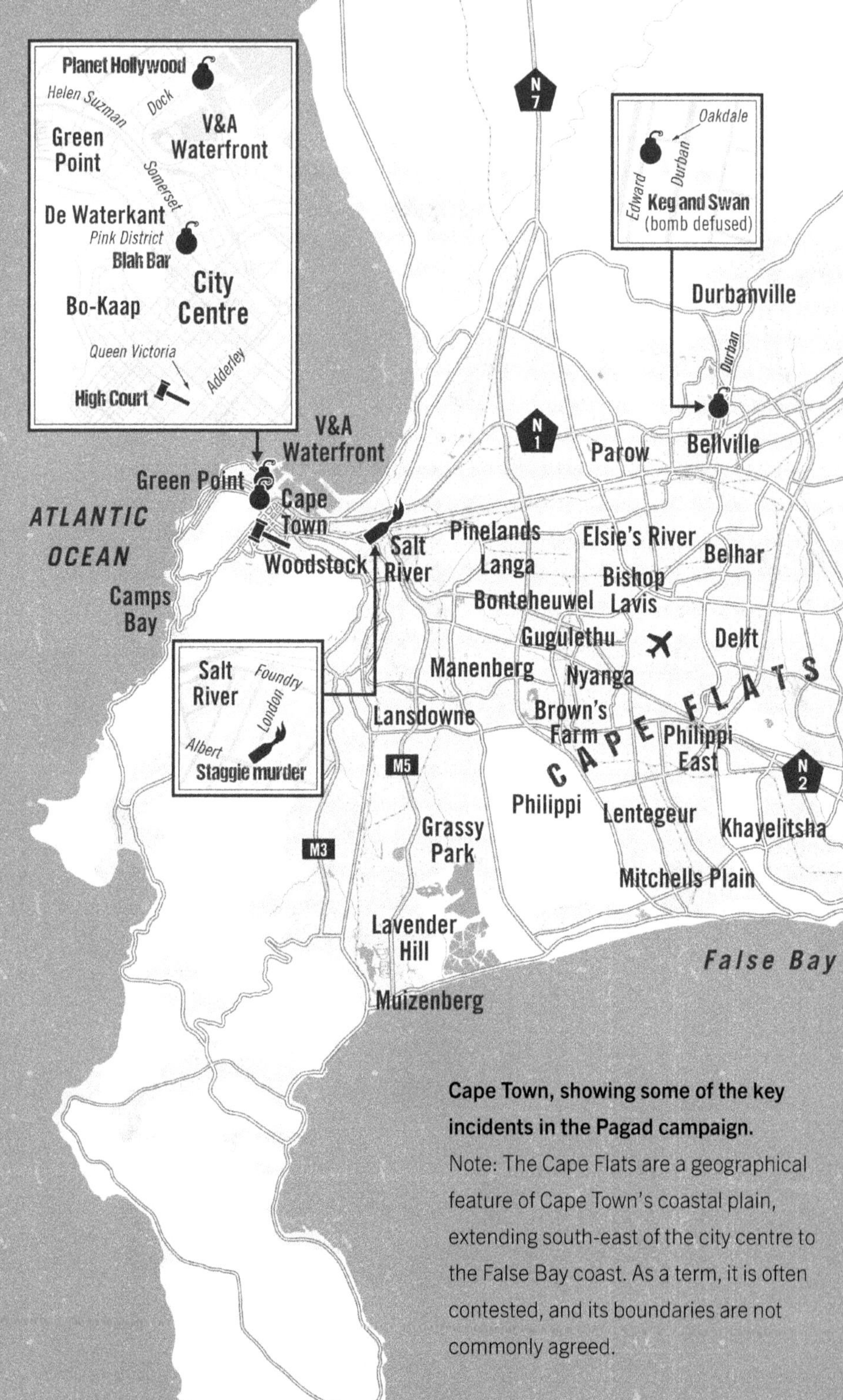

Cape Town, showing some of the key incidents in the Pagad campaign.

Note: The Cape Flats are a geographical feature of Cape Town's coastal plain, extending south-east of the city centre to the False Bay coast. As a term, it is often contested, and its boundaries are not commonly agreed.

PREFACE

THE BLACK WIDOW

I had to gulp for breath as I examined police photos of what was left of Mogamat Lakay, the bomber who became the bombed. A pipe bomb is a basic enough device but no less lethal for that. This makeshift bomb is constructed from a piece of ordinary metal piping that is packed with an explosive substance and sealed at both ends, usually by welding on two plates. The average bomb is about 30 centimetres long, and if you stand it upright with the fuse protruding from the top it looks a bit like an oversized Roman candle. When detonated, pressure builds up inside the sealed container, shattering the device and triggering immense shock waves of compressed air that rocket outwards from the core of the explosion, causing serious injuries to anyone in the vicinity (and often ripping off their clothes). The body of the pipe sprays lethal shrapnel but the imaginative bomb maker usually adds nails or ball bearings to the cocktail for additional deadly effect. It is a home-made device designed to shred human flesh.

Timing is everything. For the bomber, delaying the moment of detonation is crucial to allow him to put critical space between himself and the blast, between life and death. People who have used pipe bombs regularly say it is heart-in-your-mouth stuff: ignite, throw, escape. The timing between ignition and detonation can go badly wrong, which is why the basic pipe bomb has come to be known, darkly, as the black widow:[1] it makes widows of bombers' wives, at least the less fortunate ones.

Another occupational hazard is that these crudely constructed bombs are unstable, particularly if they are poorly assembled. They can go off when they are being moved, with devastating results. In August 2021, a pipe bomb accidentally detonated in a car as it was being transported to a target in Grassy Park, a gang-afflicted area of Cape Town. The bombers were out to kill a local gang boss, Desmond Swartz of the innocuously named Six Bobs, and they had packed the bomb with nails and screws to ensure maximum lethality. The three occupants of the vehicle were either members of, or contracted to, the once-powerful vigilante group People Against Gangsterism and Drugs, widely known as Pagad. The rickety white Mazda hijacked for the job struck a pothole and the jolt detonated the bomb.

The black widow was at the feet of the bomber, Mogamat Lackay, a drug user undergoing rehabilitation at a Pagad-linked facility. The plan was that he would pitch the device at the druglord, then speed off with his two companions as fast as the creaking Mazda would go. Things didn't turn out as planned. Lakay was torn apart. One leg ended up outside the car like a large wooden peg crushed by a hammer. His head was blown backwards to expose a ring of teeth, a macabre death mask but with the face removed. His torso was ripped apart. The blast left a gaping hole in the car roof. Lakay never stood a chance.

The gang boss he aimed to kill that day was luckier. Swartz escaped, again. This was the second attempt on his life and there would be a third, also unsuccessful. Local police intelligence had on several occasions warned Swartz he was under threat – not out of any particular affection for the gang boss, far from it, but perhaps out of basic human decency – and he had started to keep a low profile, making sure he was always surrounded by his heavies.

Swartz was a stereotypical new Cape gang boss: brash, youngish and violent. Drug distribution was his game, and it was a ruthless one that meant gunning down the opposition. He had been pushing the boundaries of his territory and police thought he might soon be the only boss in town. Ironically, Swartz escaped the bombs and the bullets only to die of a heart attack in his sleep on 9 August 2022. A serene picture of him on his deathbed, propped up on colourful pillows and in tartan pyjamas, circulated on social media.

Mobile death squads

The accident that killed Lakay was one in a long line of pipe bomb explosions in Cape Town and it barely made the news. But when I stumbled on the incident while researching this book, it transported me back to a series of events two and a half decades earlier. A string of seemingly isolated bomb incidents, like the one in which Lakay was killed and which still occur sporadically in Cape Town, were part of a wider war targeting the city's hardcore gangs. Such incidents are the legacy of Pagad.

Gangs had been present in South Africa for many years but the transition to democracy, the removal of international sanctions and the opening of borders to global trade coincided with a surge in domestic drug markets and the violent armed gangs that controlled them. Pagad began as a movement to oppose gangs and drugs soon after the first democratic elections in 1994. It would develop into a well-organised and popular vigilante-style movement before seemingly mutating into a hardcore violent outfit responsible for assassinations, including of state officials, and a plethora of bombings of high-profile civilian targets. It curated a mysterious aura around itself, with its operatives masking their faces, and the organisation seldom taking credit for violent acts. It denies its involvement in the bombing of civilian targets to this day.

A Pagad march with faces covered in Rylands in the early days of the organisation. Pagad was highly proficient at attracting wide public support while promoting an image of mystery and menace. PICTURE: Benny Gool

If Pagad seemed then to begin as a widely supported community protest movement to counter the gangs, it rapidly became something altogether more sinister, and before long Cape Town was at the mercy of hardcore terrorist violence coloured by radical Islamic ideology.

Between 1996 and 2001, about 400 bombs exploded in the city, with the bulk evenly spread across 1998 and 1999. There were 168 detonations recorded in 1998, and 166 in 1999.These figures come from police records, although nobody knows the real number.[2] The bombers say they produced many more devices than 400. There were also countless targeted killings: a coördinated programme of assassinations aimed at druglords and gang bosses. It was an orgy of death of such intensity that police investigators and the bomb disposal unit in Cape Town worked beyond the point of exhaustion. At the very dawn of democracy, Cape Town was at war.

The violence was at its most intense in the Cape ganglands but it spilled over to major commercial targets, including the popular Victoria & Alfred Waterfront, restaurants and entertainment venues in nearby Sea Point, and the city centre. Cape Town became pockmarked by bombings, sometimes several in a day. Bomb squad officers raced from crater to crater. Investigators hurriedly looked for clues before being called to the next blast or the next body.

While emerging crime strongman Desmond Swartz may have escaped death three times in late 2021, his cousins in crime from two decades before were less lucky. They fell in their droves. Small death squads moved around gangland, shooting and bombing, proficient and ruthless in their execution. Surveillance applied, team deployed, car drawing up, running men, shots to the head. It is impossible to know how many gangsters were killed, but safe to say it was in the hundreds.

Unprecedentedly, the gangs – generally at each other's throats but now under serious threat from an external enemy – formed themselves into a counter-organisation and attempted to fight back against the vigilantes. They may have been hardened killers on their own turf but they lacked a clear strategy in the face of the rapidly accumulating expertise of the death squads, partly because they did not know whom to kill.

The state response

The vigilantes' bombing and shooting campaign initially elicited contradictory responses from the state. Many police officers welcomed the fact that gang bosses were being slaughtered by a third party and quietly pointed the death squads in their direction. The police tried to negotiate with Pagad, but things spiralled out of control as the group became stronger and more organised, adopted a radical Islamic agenda and began to pull away from its community roots.

As the killing and bombing became more widespread and innocent people began to be targeted, the state labelled the violence 'urban terrorism'. A home-grown protection campaign that started with hits on gang bosses seemed to be spiralling out of control. The institutions of the state itself – the police, judges, the military – were also attacked under the pretext that they were defending gangsters. The state *was* in some cases defending gangsters: partly out of old connections forged in the 1980s when gang bosses were allies or enemies in politics, and partly out of an attempt to protect lives – even if they were the beating hearts of crime lords.

As the situation deteriorated, first President Nelson Mandela then his successor, Thabo Mbeki, called together the nascent security establishment and demanded action. Progress was slow, however; even the hard men of the apartheid state's security establishment had never encountered a threat like this. The killers seemed to operate with impunity, and often with public support.

Then, remarkably, the story took a game-changing turn. A few good men and women stepped forward, South African style: former apartheid-era detectives and intelligence personnel formed a combined force with newly integrated liberation struggle cadres and guerrilla fighters. They represented the full spectrum of the new rainbow nation and had widely divergent political views, but after a period of squabbling they began to work together.

Until then, security force integration had been halting and mistrustful. Finger-pointing characterised the first state responses until a series of decisions defined a way forward. It wasn't an instant fix but slowly, then more steadily, the emerging security establishment put old differences aside and argued with one voice that Pagad's campaign was endangering the very fabric of the new democracy. They were not wrong. Business and tourism were badly hit, police stations were attacked, police officers and judicial officers were assassinated. A group of what seemed like Islamic terror cells menacingly stalked the Cape. The city was a war zone, the crump of explosions answering in a deadly chorus the familiar sound of the noonday gun on Signal Hill.

Lessons of history

It seems remarkable that this story has never been told in full. But it was not possible until recently, when many were released after serving long prison sentences or retired and became willing to talk openly. It is a story of direct relevance for South Africa's response to the threat of organised crime today. Sadly, the state's success against Pagad was not sustained in the face of later threats; the promising post-apartheid security state fractured and fell apart, much of the innovation, drive and key personnel of this short but critical period lost.

I have set out to piece together what happened between 1995 and 2002 by talking to key individuals on all sides in the conflict. I wanted to recount the actions and motives of participants in the killing and bombing squads, and tell the story of the few good men and women who rallied together to construct a response. I have spoken to as many of them as would speak to me, in kitchens and coffee shops, in parked cars and on slow walks. Some told me how they killed, others how they investigated the killers. They told me about their 'enemies', naming them, often with grudging respect, and they whistled slowly as they recalled the war on the streets of Cape Town. Tears rolled down their cheeks, hands trembled, and many admitted they still live in fear and sleep badly.

Yet, despite all the interviews I conducted, mysteries remain: What compromises did the shaky transitional security state make to end the violence and the bombing of civilian targets? Did the leadership of Pagad negotiate with the state in prison and reach a secret deal to end the violence? Is the campaign over, or do the likes of bomber Mogamat Lakay signal the prospect of more attacks to come? Drawing on what I have been told, I have tried to assess these and other claims.

The story of Pagad and the state's response to an existential threat is important for other reasons, too, in contemporary South Africa. Pagad's strategy – driven, as we will see, by a small and radicalised group – drew on public fears about mounting crime and the state's inability to control it. Speak to people in the affected areas and the same concerns emerge time and again: 'We were worried about our children,' 'We had to do something,' 'We felt the state had given up on us and didn't care about us.' From the perspective of these communities, 'the few good men' were not the state's detectives but those who did the killing and served time.

Within these same communities, some reflect ruefully on how the killing went on for so long. They express their distress over how they developed into killing machines, hooked on adrenalin. 'I have read about serial killers,' one reminisced, 'and I think we had become that.' Others, more hardened, thrived on the bloodshed – brutal men who still express no remorse.

In this violent mix, too, were the unarmed heroes, the peacemakers. These are the community leaders who tried to reach out to the gangs and Pagad, seeking to stem the bloodshed and find a peaceful, sustainable solution to gangsterism. Their efforts may have been limited, but nonetheless they were beacons of sanity in an otherwise dark storm of violence. Many were threatened and some moved away, their dreams of the new democracy shattered.

For the state, and those charged with designing a new system of security, the experience of investigating and responding to Pagad laid the foundation for the systems and ideas that gave birth to the successful Scorpions unit, with its three-pronged focus on intelligence collection, investigation and prosecution. It was a war with consequence. It made a generation of law enforcement and intelligence officials who went on to influence South Africa in many ways. But what at first seemed like an enormous success in state law enforcement and intelligence ultimately heralded long-term failure. In this sense, often forgotten in the Pagad episode is the impact the group had on South Africa's gangs. A generation of gang bosses were literally blown away, their brains scattered on their driveways or in the street by bullets to the head. But these deaths did not terminate the gangs or even weaken them in the longer term. They merely spawned a new generation of virulent leaders, the likes of Desmond Swartz, who as a young gang member witnessed the targeted killings. Twenty-five years on, these gangsters still prey on their communities.

We must not forget the victims, the quieter, stoic citizens affected by the events I describe. These were the children and mothers caught in the crossfire and many other innocent people for whom the violence has had lifelong consequences. Many lost limbs and often still nurse terrible injuries, physical and psychological. Not one whom I spoke to sought vengeance, focusing instead on their struggles and their fears, the love of their families and the slow and difficult quest for recovery. This is their story.

But why a book on Pagad a quarter of a century after the carnage? There are many reasons, but two in particular: South Africans forget how destabilising crime may be politically, and the book is a reminder – in a new age when state institutions are more fragile and corrupted – of how dangerous an armed, organised and violent militia can be, no matter how well intentioned some of its members. And we forget quickly how in the immediate aftermath of the negotiated end to white rule, the state came together to face an enormous challenge because there was political will to do so. This suggests that with the right mix of people and support, the country can overcome today's challenges no matter how dire they seem. That is a central message of the book.

There is a final reason, one that is more personal and must surely mark the path of most authors: I was there too, in this case as an official in the national secretariat for safety and security, tasked to monitor progress in the response. Most did not remember me, and nor should they, given my minor role, but my periodic trips to Cape Town at the time gave me an outsider's feel for the urgency of the struggle and the desperation of those involved. It is quite simply a story that should be told.

Note on the research

The book is based on interviews with more than 60 people who were involved in Pagad as well as the community and state response. Several were kind enough to make themselves available for multiple discussions. The interviews were conducted in 2020, 2021 and the first part of 2022. Some of the key players were open and happy to be quoted. Unsurprisingly, given the sensitive nature of the topic, many people were not prepared to speak on the record, fearing the consequences of their past actions or the vengeance of Pagad. In a few cases, people answered questions through intermediaries. Some I approached for information cited official secrecy requirements, the sensitivity of their roles or possible threats to their safety, and refused to discuss matters. They are small in number and I am confident I have the main elements of the story.

There is an enormous volume of documentation available on Pagad and the state response, although not all of it is in the public domain. I have been provided with, or been able to read, internal state documents that proved useful in shaping the story. I have also had access to hundreds of pages of court records (although many case files are not locatable or are restricted to prevent the identity of witnesses being made public), which have been an essential guide to the actions of the protagonists and the failures and then success of the response. There is also a growing body of academic literature on Pagad that has been useful to frame the context, as well as a couple of published personal accounts of former security officials.

To help the reader orient themselves as the story unfolds, a detailed overview of key events can be found at the end of the book.

PROLOGUE

BOMBING THE DWARF STAR

It was the day of the celebrations marking Guy Fawkes's gunpowder plot, which in hindsight seems portentous. Friday 5 November 1999, a comfortable early summer evening in Cape Town with a light south-westerly breeze blowing as the sun slipped below the horizon at 7.30 pm. South Africa had been a democratic state for five and a half years.

A kilometre or two away from parliament, the seat of this fledgling democracy, was the Blah Bar, another venue that in the conception of its owners – and as its name suggested – was also meant for talking, even if only for friendlier exchanges. The Blah Bar was as much a testimony to the new democratic order as the transformed parliamentary precinct, located as it was in an area known as Cape Town's 'pink district'. Green Point was an increasingly safe and welcoming space for the gay community. The new constitution promised equality for all and the pink district was a vibrant manifestation of that.

On that Friday evening, as the weekend beckoned punters to the district, a young man gingerly entered the Blah Bar, where he had been told homosexual men hung out. It was elegant and tastefully lit, steps leading to a raised seating area at the back. The man's surveillance team had told him the bar would be quiet and that in the absence of moonlight he would be able to get in and out of this place of 'iniquity' discreetly. But the timing still had to be right: before the bar became crowded but not so early as to attract undue attention. Enter, deposit the bomb bag, linger for a moment, then leave – act like someone who has changed his mind and decided to go somewhere else.

The barman was not there. Slipping in unnoticed, the man probably sat at the back, hiding his blue kitbag under a table where its dark form merged into the shadows. 'Make sure it's at the back where it can cause more damage,' he had been advised. Having deposited his device, he left, walking briskly to a waiting car. It pulled away from the curb and sped into Cape Town's evening traffic. A perfect operation.

The pink district was the product of a group of irrepressible gay Cape Town entrepreneurs. Café Manhattan, a block from the Blah Bar, was the first establishment to open its doors, in August 1994, four months into the new democracy. Founder and owner Russell Shapiro, a veteran of the city's restaurant and entertainment industry, told me he had found the area promising for a venue even though there was nothing there at the time other than a panel beater. He negotiated the rent with a city property mogul and signed the contract on a torn-off scrap of paper. Shapiro's inkling was right – Café Manhattan drew crowds of young men who often spilled outside onto the pavement.[1]

The pink district quickly became a magnet for young gay men from all over South Africa, many of whom had not yet come out to their families. 'All of a sudden, and well before the days of dating apps, this was the place to go to meet people,' said Ian McMahon, the energetic local councillor, a prominent figure in the gay community and the owner of an establishment in the pink district.[2] By 1999, the area had changed beyond recognition and punters flooded in. Kevin Engelbrecht, a quietly spoken interior designer who grew up in a conservative household in Port Elizabeth (his father was a retired sergeant major) and who was at the Blah Bar that November evening, told me: 'Cape Town was amazing. To me, it was like New York – very different from Port Elizabeth. I came out quite young and I lived my life. It was just amazing and I wouldn't have changed it for anything. It was just happiness and meeting new people.'[3]

The late 1990s was still a time of uncertainty, however. One young man who was there that fateful November evening said he wondered whether the scantily dressed partygoers who overflowed from the clubs onto Somerset Road would be seen as a threat by some, the object for an attack.[4] For others, such as Engelbrecht, the gay district was a refuge but not necessarily one they told their parents about. 'Imagine being caught in a bomb blast, widely reported in the news, in a gay bar in a gay district when your parents don't know you're gay,' he mused.[5]

The BAD triangle

Today, there are gay-friendly venues across Cape Town and the once tightly clustered gay district is largely gone, overtaken by the development of a fancy shopping complex, the Cape Quarter. Dating apps now mean that men looking to hook up can meet anywhere.[6] If free enterprise, and freedoms, in the swinging new 'rainbow' order created the pink district, the combined forces of wider economic development and electronic communication have eroded it. The pink district, like the events of this story, marked a particular historical moment: the first years of the 'rainbow nation's' tempestuous early childhood. But in what could be a monument to that era, the building that housed the Blah Bar is still there, its facade painted bright pink.

In 1999, however, the district was in its ascendancy. The end of apartheid had led to the rapid relaxation of normative sexual behaviours that had been strictly enforced. Gay men were one of the first groups to enjoy the fruits of the new democracy. As gay activist Jack Lewis explained to a *New York Times* journalist in December 1994, just as Café Manhattan was starting to rock, it had become 'seriously politically incorrect' to restrict people's right to self-expression.[7] The young men who began to gather in the pink district may not have seen themselves as activists but they were in the vanguard of political and social change. Set against South Africa's more visible social movements and seismic political shifts, the gay and lesbian community's emergence and influence were described neatly by academic Sheila Croucher as a 'dwarf star' (a term borrowed from a study of comparative social movements): a small but vocal and powerful change agent, as opposed to a wider mass movement.[8] For some, though, the burgeoning conspicuously gay community captured the disorder of the present as set against the order of the past.

The gay district has been criticised for being predominantly white and middle class and leveraged to promote the city as a gay-friendly tourist destination.[9] But there is little doubt that it took off fast, had high visibility and created business opportunities. Several people who frequented the district also contest the view that it was an all-white affair. Whatever the case, there can be little doubt that its presence was connected to the freedoms of the new order – a base for a group whose existence had previously been unlawful and clandestine. It was also defined as a 'safe space' for the gay community.[10] Not that safe, as it would turn out: it was conspicuous, and the high degree of visibility of a like-minded group clustering in a clearly identifiable area also made the pink district a target.

The Blah Bar was the brainchild of Glyn Delaney, one of the early investors in the district. Delaney was a 'fag hag', in gay community parlance. She wore her hair red and her dresses short, and pretended she was younger than she was. She was the kind of irrepressible figure that the easy atmosphere of newly democratic Cape Town attracted.[11] The Blah Bar was close to a triangle of gay clubs known, appropriately enough to some, as BAD. There was Bronx, a hardcore, anything-goes kind of place, known for drugs and dancing on the bar; next door was Detour, a pulsing dance club; the third in the trio was Angels, a club favoured more by Coloured men. The idea of Delaney and her partners was that among the pulsating dance clubs, a place for a quiet conversation – 'blah blah' – was needed.[12]

Ian Martin, who was studying advertising and worked at the bar, told me it was tastefully decorated: 'It was beautiful inside – the sort of place you go for drinks when you are dressed up before hitting the town, a place where you would want to be seen.'[13] The concept was a combination of cocktail bar and bistro tables.

Demons and an angel

On 5 November 1999, the pink district had been simmering in the early summer heat. By 9 pm, Bronx was beginning to shake itself loose for action, while at the Blah Bar across the road the atmosphere was quieter. There were about ten customers inside and the place looked rather empty. A couple were sitting on stools next to where the dark blue bag had been placed. Kevin Engelbrecht and his then partner, whom I will refer to as Brian (he asked not to be named), debated whether to go out that night. Brian said it was a good way to end the week, so they set off from their flat in Green Point, not imagining their lives were about to be irrevocably changed. There was to be life before the bomb and life after it.

There is still some doubt as to the precise time the Blah Bar bomb exploded. By some accounts it was 9 pm, which could explain the small number of people in the bar, but by others it was around 11 pm or shortly after midnight. I could not locate the police file and interviews were contradictory, but in the end it does not really matter.

The pipe bomb lay innocuously under the table waiting to be activated by a cellphone. The young man who had carried the bag inside would have been nervous, as cellphone-activated bombs are notoriously unstable. When phone contact was made with the detonator, the explosion caused a deadly shock wave followed almost instantaneously by particles of lethal shrapnel. A large fish tank on the bar shattered, sending water, fish and shards of glass flying across the room.

Ian Martin was standing at the top of the short flight of stairs at the back, commenting to some customers how quiet the bar seemed to be for a Friday night. He remembers a loud crack, 'then it was a bit of a blur'. He was only about a metre from the bomb and was buffeted by the shock wave: 'I don't know how long I was out but it could not have been long. It was one of those things that felt like an eternity but was probably seconds. I came to and it was pandemonium, with fire, blood, glass and flames. Total, utter hysteria.'[14]

Martin was badly injured. A large piece of metal entered his leg, fracturing his tibia. It left a large, bloody hole. Another piece of shrapnel cut clean through an Achilles tendon. He could not walk. 'There was a shitload of blood,' he told me calmly.[15]

As the smoke and dust cleared, he looked around the shattered room: 'In the midst of all the chaos – and it sits with me as one of the strangest things in that situation of sheer trauma – all the faces looked like demons. It was like watching a horror film, with special effects making everyone's faces demonic – whether that was out of my own fear or whether they looked like that out of sheer terror.'[16]

Kevin Engelbrecht said the explosion was deafening and the shock wave was like nothing he had ever experienced: it picked him up and threw him three or four metres across the room. 'I remember getting up, and the sights and smell. It was smoky and my ears were ringing. I remember staggering to get out the front door.[17] I ran up the road and people were staring at me weirdly, and I didn't know why. When I got to Bronx, the doorman said, "What happened to you, where are your clothes?"' The shock wave had torn off most of Engelbrecht's clothes except for his shirt and what remained of his jacket. His hair was singed and he was covered in blood. In panic, he ran back to the Blah Bar to look for his partner.

Brian, who was sitting next to Engelbrecht, took the full force of the blast and the deadly shrapnel that followed milliseconds later. He had sustained multiple injuries but was still conscious. He recalled how three people picked him up and placed him by the door. As he lay there for what seemed like a few minutes, Engelbrecht reappeared and began singing to him, slowly and unsteadily at first but then more clearly as they waited for help.

Brian spoke at length about the bombing and his injuries. It's hard to fathom how people whose lives have been so dramatically transformed by the trauma of an explosion, followed by months of debilitation and pain, conveyed no bitterness, no desire for revenge. Brian felt only gratitude for being alive and for how the incident brought him and his family closer. Those sentiments all came later, though. In the moments after the bombing, he understood the consequences of what had happened. He also knew he would not be able to stand up. But he was resolute: 'Now that I am alive, I am going to survive,' he told himself.[18] A fire had started and Brian could feel its heat. His arm was hanging off to one side, his leg badly damaged, and he had multiple shrapnel wounds in his abdomen. He recalled how three came into the bar – he does not know who they were – gently lifted him away from the fire and placed him near the door.

Then, as several survivors recalled, an angel emerged. To this day, it is not clear who he was, and although none of the victims can describe him in detail they agree he was a doctor. He appears to have been driving past and stopped to assist the injured. The ambulances took an age to come, something like 45 minutes. In the interim, the doctor stepped in.

Ian Martin recalled: 'I was crawling across the floor surrounded by people running, with the sprinklers going off and the fire around me. The glass was cutting my chest while I was dragging myself across the floor to get out. And then this guy came in, a big man who was a doctor. He picked me up, took me outside and put me on a table. He took his T-shirt off and put it against the hole in my leg, which was gushing blood, and told me to hold it while I waited for the ambulance.'[19]

Brian also remembers the doctor. 'It was an Indian guy,' he said. 'He looked at me, went to his car and came back with a silver foil rescue blanket. I was really cold and in shock. I felt much better then.'[20] Then Engelbrecht heard the ambulance sirens. 'I said to the doctor to look after Brian and make sure that he didn't go to sleep or close his eyes. I ran to the ambulance, grabbed the guy and told them to take one person and one person only, and that was Brian because he was injured the worst.'[21]

The 'angel' then disappeared, as quietly as he had arrived.

1

PUBLIC BOMBINGS, PRIVATE TRAUMAS

Glyn Delaney, the founder of the Blah Bar, was inconsolable after the bombing. She was also angry. 'I am expecting more bombs in Cape Town,' she told the *Los Angeles Times*. 'The police don't know what they are doing or even who they are looking for.'[1] Desperate to show some progress, the police arrested a 26-year-old man, Deon Mostert. They claimed he was linked to 200 bombings, several of which had been aimed at civilian targets, that had been happening across the city since 1997; the Blah Bar attack was just the latest.

Mostert had a propensity for bending the truth, according to several people in my underworld network who bumped into him in prison in the late 1990s and early 2000s. He was believed to be a police informant and a small-time crook but certainly not a bomb mastermind. The *Los Angeles Times* reporter, perhaps with a journalist's eye for the absurd, deadpanned that Mostert was a 'chronic liar and a thief of household appliances'.[2]

His arrest seemed to confirm to many at the time that the police did not have a good handle on the bombings. The then national police commissioner, George Fivaz, held a press conference at which he dismissed any link between Mostert and the bombing, contradicting his provincial police chief. If confusion reigned supreme, it only worsened when Fivaz's spokesperson later retracted that statement and said Mostert was still a suspect.[3]

Fivaz, whose term as commissioner ended in January 2000, spent 1998 and 1999 under enormous political pressure. The South African Police Service (SAPS) had shown little progress in solving the bombings that had terrorised Cape Town for more than two years. UK diplomatic cables reported on a message passed to Fivaz offering assistance from the Metropolitan Police anti-terrorist branch. Fivaz, defending the performance of the SAPS through gritted teeth, politely declined.[4]

When I met Fivaz almost a quarter of a century later in a Pretoria cafe, I asked him about Mostert and he snorted, saying he had been embarrassed and frustrated by the incident.[5] At the time, he was deeply engaged in responding to the bombings, pushing hard for change, and making decisions about restructuring the nascent SAPS that would have long-term consequences. In August 1998, a year before the bombing of the Blah Bar, he had visited the scene of the explosion at the Planet Hollywood restaurant in Cape Town's popular V&A Waterfront, stepping over layers of shattered glass and debris and around the pools of blood. Fivaz said he had been determined to solve the cases but frustrated with the pace of investigations. He was acutely conscious of the devastating human costs of the bombing campaign. All indications pointed to Pagad as the source of the bombings, an allegation the organisation vigorously denied.

Many were killed and injured in the targeted shootings and explosions. Although the total number of fatalities is impossible to determine accurately, there were certainly hundreds. Gangs and gang bosses were initially targeted but when the bombing campaign moved to parts of the city relatively unaffected by organised crime and targeted the public, it drew much greater press scrutiny. While these numbers are also hard to confirm, more than 20 bomb attacks occurred in Cape Town city centre, and over time they showed an increasing level of sophistication.

The Planet Hollywood attack, in which two people were killed and 24 injured, attracted global media attention. It was one of the first Pagad attacks to target the public. The popular venue, co-owned by Hollywood stars Sylvester Stallone, Bruce Willis and Arnold Schwarzenegger, was packed with mainly British tourists when a bomb placed under the bar exploded. Eight British nationals were injured in the blast, some of them seriously. The incident occurred just days after the 7 August 1998 bombing attacks by al-Qaeda on the US embassies in Nairobi and Dar es Salaam, in which 224 people died. There was speculation as to whether there was a connection between the perpetrators.

Bruce Walsh was one of the survivors of the Planet Hollywood attack, losing both his legs. He was at the bar with two colleagues ordering drinks when the explosion went off, and he was the sole survivor of the three.[6] 'I felt my body being thrown upwards towards the rafters,' he told me. 'My shirt was gone and I felt I was floating – then I blacked out.'[7] Walsh told me that in October, just as he was beginning the long road to recovery, he saw a TV news announcement in which a police investigating officer announced a breakthrough in the investigation. Fragments of a blue and white shirt had been found in the rafters – with the brand Soviet, which seemed to arouse the police's suspicions – which they believed to be that of the bomber. It was Walsh's shirt, he said, and he contacted the police to tell them – he had to produce a credit card bill to prove it.

October 1998 cable traffic between the British consulate in Cape Town and the high commission in Pretoria, as well as communication with London, gives a flavour of the response.[8] While consulate staff worked hard to ascertain the nature and extent of the injuries sustained by British nationals, they also sought urgent answers from the SAPS about the identity of the bombers. Local police said they had an idea who the perpetrators were but no evidence tying them to the crime. A fax from the consulate to higher-ups in the diplomatic corps in Pretoria, and copied to London, stated: 'The police are being more guarded about who they believe to be responsible. But it is clear that they believe the bombing to be the work of a group linked to Pagad, not least because the design of the pipe bomb used matches those used in early attacks that have received less publicity.'[9]

The bombing campaign was relentless and the increasing focus on high-profile targets resulted in civilian casualties. In August 1998, a street vendor was killed by a time-delayed pipe bomb outside the Bellville office of the police unit investigating Pagad; in the same month, Planet Hollywood was attacked. In January 1999, the V&A Waterfront was targeted again, this time with a car bomb. This was followed by the blast at the Blah Bar in November and a few weeks later by an attack that injured 48 people at the popular St Elmo's pizzeria in well-heeled Camps Bay. The attacks continued in 2000, targeting public areas including shopping centres, restaurants, cafes and nightclubs. By August 2000 there had been six explosions targeting civilians in the city centre. Elsewhere, many other bombings were aimed mainly at drug dealers and gang bosses. It seemed the whole of Cape Town was under siege.

The victims of this urban terror campaign were innumerable. As for the survivors, their lives were changed forever and, unaware of the state's struggle against the bombers, they suffered in silence. For them, the proverbial hand of fate played a role in some way: what if they had been killed?

One I spoke with was Olivia Milner, who as a 16-year-old waitress was maimed in the 1999 St Elmo's bombing. Milner, who had been desperate to find a job, was proud to have landed this one. It was her first night working at the restaurant, and she spoke of how her life irrevocably changed after the attack, how her family had moved home, and how losing her leg had plagued her ever since. When we spoke she was in a wheelchair, unable to wear her prosthesis because of an infection. The bombing may have been many years ago but she said it was still 'something that I live with every day'. She ultimately reconciled herself to the challenges she faced, she said matter-of-factly, because, given the randomness of it, she was aware that she had not been targeted personally, that she was just 'an unfortunate casualty'.[10] Bruce Walsh told me something remarkably similar: that while he had been initially deeply angry, he had resolved that the bombing had not been targeted at him, and that he must live his life or be eaten by bitterness. He would go on to reach out to, and be contacted by, many other bombing and accident survivors, in particular amputees.

You need serious courage to remake your existence after such trauma, acknowledging the chance that life brings with it and a removal of the certainty of outcomes on which so many of us depend – all the while determining to make the best of what you have. Milner told me about the long time she spent in hospital, how she wept when she discovered the extent of her injuries, and how other bomb victims, including Brian from the Blah Bar and Bruce Walsh, reached out to her for mutual support.

Milner's mother, Elana Newman, an elegant and energetic woman who was part of Cape Town's classical music scene, told me how she encouraged her daughter to find work closer to home in Camps Bay rather than take a job in the city. On the day of the bombing, Newman had coffee in Kloof Street, where she bumped into some of Milner's friends. They asked her how her daughter was doing. 'Olivia was the person assigned at the pizzeria to take the phone orders for takeout pizzas, and I was just thinking about making a prank call to her with a Russian accent and asking for a ridiculous kind of pizza. Then I heard the blast,' she said.[11]

Newman raced there. 'There were police at the scene. As I was frantically trying to enter to look for Olivia, a police officer grabbed me and held me back. I could see Olivia on a stretcher with a blanket over her.'[12] Milner was rushed to hospital, her life hanging by a thread. Unsurprisingly, it was a life-changing moment for Elana, and she went on a quest to find out who planted the bomb. (She begged me to put her in touch with the suspected bomber, something I attempted through an intermediary. He refused to speak to her.)

A police officer, Natasha Pillay, also lost her leg a few weeks later in another bomb incident. She responded after a Green Point restaurant received a bomb threat. The bomb, placed in a dustbin, exploded while the police were searching for it and Pillay took the full impact of the blast. 'You are trained for this sort of thing but you can never be prepared. You never think it can happen to you,' she said.[13]

Stick that in your pipe bomb

While the police were struggling to find the perpetrators behind the string of attacks, something of a defiant response to the bombs set in among the South African public and the media. A popular women's magazine, *Femina*, launched an awareness campaign featuring portraits of the injured, with words taking the place of missing or severed limbs. The police emergency number was given next to the portraits. Bruce Walsh was photographed on a stool; characteristically, he said that he was embarrassed by the attention he received and did not want to be seen as a victim.

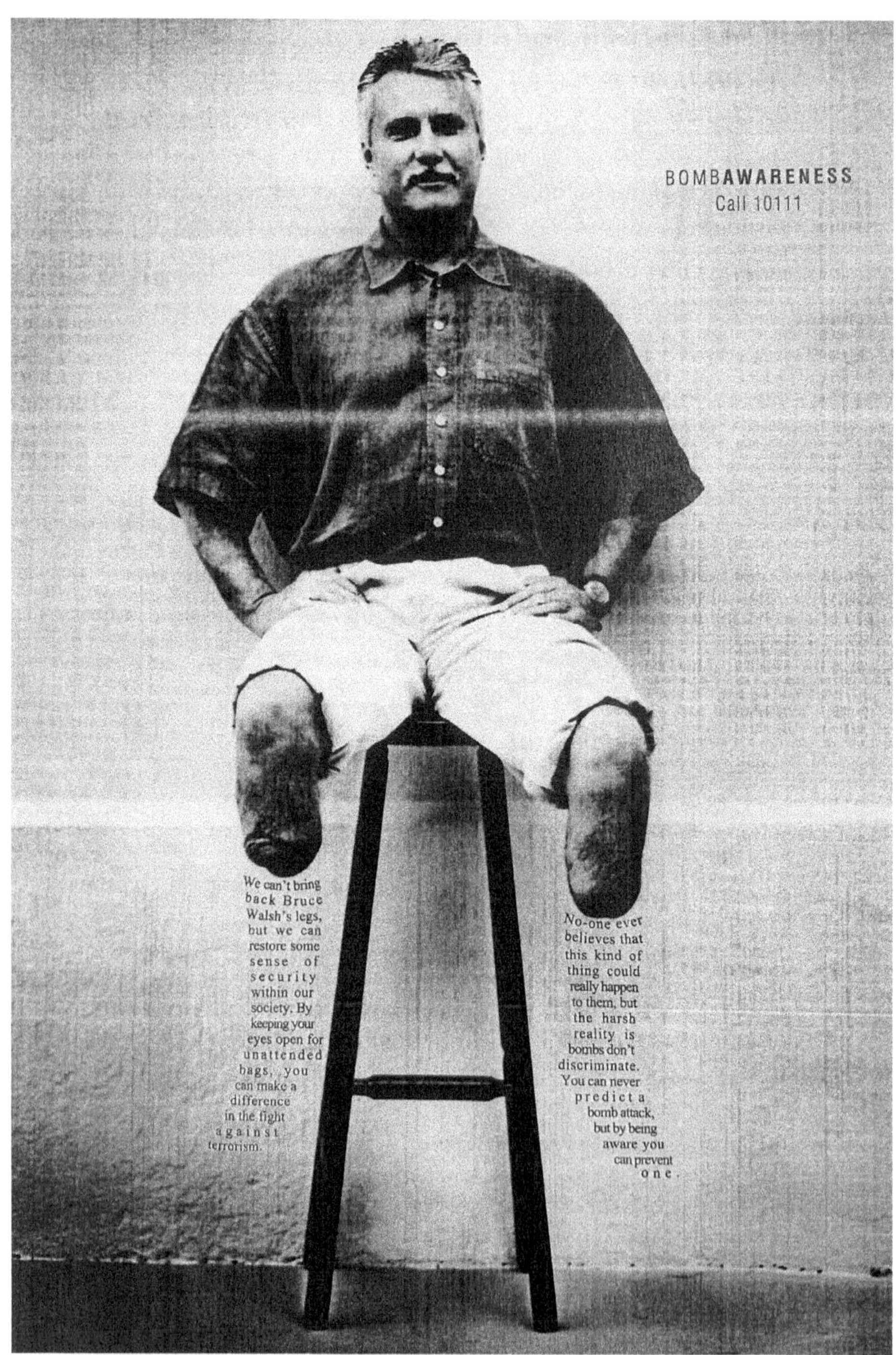
BOMBAWARENESS
Call 10111
We can't bring back Bruce Walsh's legs, but we can restore some sense of security within our society. By keeping your eyes open for unattended bags, you can make a difference in the fight against terrorism.
No-one ever believes that this kind of thing could really happen to them, but the harsh reality is bombs don't discriminate. You can never predict a bomb attack, but by being aware you can prevent one.

An editorial in *Femina* by Jane Raphaely, a prominent magazine publisher and public figure, concluded: 'What we like about the whole [awareness campaign] is that it sends a message to the bombers that they cannot win a war against people who refuse to give in.' It ended with a note of defiance: 'Stick that in your pipe bomb.'[14]

In another creative response to the bombings, artist Dorothee Kreutzfeldt prepared a montage of photographs combined with recordings of survivors' voices and it was displayed at the South African National Gallery in Cape Town. The installation did not sensationalise the bombings, contain pictures of the bomb sites or speculate as to the perpetrators.[15] An accompanying commentary said: 'There is a lack of resolution to the bombings. No one has been charged. Situated by other perceptions about the city, situated by the media's reportage of events surrounding each of the bombings, the narrative is without conclusion.' Then the statement: 'The nature of urban terror – and of bomb blasts in particular – is that they are public events and media spectacles. But they are also private traumas that profoundly affect the lives of individuals and their families.'[16]

Some survivors declined to take part in Kreutzfeldt's work because they felt the project might 'further the objectives of the bombers by giving them more attention' or because it was too painful to revisit the event in detail.[17] For the most part, the stories of survivors, often out of their own volition, seldom reached the public. Most struggled on in silence despite serious afflictions and endless visits to hospitals and doctors over many years. If the known survivors did not speak out, there was an even quieter category of affected people: the anonymous victims. The street hawker killed outside police offices in Bellville has

OPPOSITE: The photo of Bruce Walsh used in Femina's bomb awareness campaign. Walsh was reported by several survivors to be a quiet source of strength and support. The following words replace his missing left limb: 'No-one ever believes that this kind of thing could really happen to them, but the harsh reality is bombs don't discriminate. You can never predict a bomb attack, but by being aware you can prevent one.'[18] **PICTURE:** Bester Burke

not been named. And across the Cape Flats, the bombings and shootings affected untold numbers of unknown families and children.

For the survivors, the bombings often led to years of uncertainty and fear. 'It's like I'm waiting for the next bomb to go off. I'm afraid of people because I can't put a face to the bomber. It could be anyone. I don't know who to trust,' said Michelle Hunter, a police officer caught in the same blast as her colleague Natasha Pillay in Green Point.[19]

Of all the accounts, most touching perhaps are those of victims who helped and supported one another, turning up in hospital wards and at survivors' homes to console and share their experiences of losing limbs. Bruce Walsh was referred to recurringly as a quiet hero who did much hidden work behind the scenes. Several survivors also spoke of people who had had limbs amputated in other accidents; they shared their experiences with the bomb survivors and explained how their lives would still be liveable. One amputee, a former ballet dancer, was said to dance on tables with her prosthetic limbs, bringing laughter and hope to bomb survivors.

Despite the defiance and mutual support, however, there was also an atmosphere of fear. The identity of the bombers remained shrouded in mystery. Several survivors interviewed in 2007 hinted at but would not name the perpetrators out of fear.[20]

Most suspected Pagad, but stories also did the rounds that the bombing campaign was the work of prominent underworld figures attempting to extort money from businesses. Seeking clarity but convinced Pagad was to blame, Elana Newman remembers confronting Safety and Security minister Steve Tshwete at a private meeting: 'I said, "We're under siege by these bombers, whoever they are: nameless, faceless, who don't claim anything." And you know what, what was there to claim? We have the most democratic constitution in the world, so what did they want? What the hell did they want – Pagad or whoever it was?'[21] Tshwete, a minister for whom I had worked, was a gruff and tough-talking man. He quietly listened to Newman. But later in public, and unlike his predecessors who had been reluctant to lay blame, he raged against the bombers and said they belonged to Pagad.

The victims of bombings targeting popular public venues were overwhelmingly white, in part a stark reflection of the city's strongly demarcated georacial divide (the legacy of apartheid), which defines the civilian places that were bombed. Those who experienced the bombings who were not white had a different outlook: 'I don't know if it's [about] race,' one woman told a researcher. 'We as Coloured people are used to these things ... the gangsters fighting every day ... if they shoot it's normal that these things happen. Innocent people could get hurt.'[22] The bomb she experienced was not a disruptive event, concluded the study for which she was interviewed, because it was a single incident that formed part of 'a [continual] experience of varying degrees of violence in the city' that the woman was exposed to.[23]

The bombing campaign is now only a distant memory for most. The Centre for Popular Memory at the University of Cape Town (UCT) taped survivors and others reflecting on the period. While most of these recordings have been lost, those that remain provide an insight into the time and people's responses to it. One young man, Thabo Manetsi, said he moved to Cape Town to explore opportunities but the bombings changed the way he behaved, adding a layer of fear to everyday life. After one of the V&A Waterfront bombings, Manetsi said his family tried to get hold of him to ask if he was all right. Ordinary people like him seemed to have little doubt that Pagad was to blame.[24] A study of the period based on survivors' testimony concluded: 'Capetonians generally witnessed these events with the sobering knowledge that they themselves could have been the victims.'[25]

What is remarkable is how little reach the attacks had; several bombs at the V&A Waterfront today would be a massive global story. Was this because South Africa had recently emerged from a period of political transition which, despite the 'miracle' mantra placed on it, also featured significant violence? Was there just too much going on nationally for an exclusive focus on a Western Cape bombing campaign? Interviews with several people in the security establishment highlighted the degree to which other simultaneous threats dominated their thinking and competed for attention: violence in KwaZulu-Natal, the threat of the white right wing and a surge in taxi-related violence. The bombings were confined to the Western Cape, and the fact that hundreds of the explosions occurred in the Cape Flats and gang areas, places already characterised by abnormally high levels of violence, meant they often did not make it into mainstream media reporting.

That does not make the story or the collective suffering any less important – even from a distance of almost a quarter of a century. But its wider impact (and media appeal) could have been very different if just one of the many blasts had succeeded in being truly massive in scale. The bombers certainly hoped they could achieve this, and it would only have been a question of time before they did.

The bomb that failed to detonate

If the Blah Bar was designed for conversations over a quiet drink, Bronx in Green Point was the ultimate party venue. According to Russell Shapiro of Café Manhattan,[26] it was the essential apex to the BAD triangle, and it rocked. The bar attracted the keen interest of Cape Town's gay community and did not escape the notice of the bombers.

When you see photos of Bronx in police files, it looks, through the lens of time (and the eye of a crime scene photographer), like a jaded kind of place. It occupied the corner of Somerset Road and Napier Street, with pillars set against a green awning, 1930s style. There were curtains at the entrance and a stool for the bouncer. A sign above the door read 'The Action Bar', and it meant what it said, everyone I spoke to assured me. Of the three BAD venues, Bronx was the busiest.

The club had a manic atmosphere but it was also famed for its Monday evening karaoke. And it was a money-printing machine, said several of the entrepreneurs who watched enviously from the sidelines. Drinks were served so quickly that bar staff simply threw cash into a box and balanced up later. According to some, the absence of tills meant money was often siphoned off.[27]

Bronx had a reputation for drugs in the versions provided to me by partygoers and the police. All kinds of illicit substances were available there at a time when the local drug economy was taking off alongside the opened-up economy. For all that, though, it remained a remarkably friendly and violence-free kind of place, open and future-facing – a dwarf star on steroids.

By the time Bronx was targeted in mid-2000, the Pagad bomb makers had honed their skills and were turning out more sophisticated devices. A pipe bomb, while deadly, is limited in its impact by the amount of explosives that can be packed inside a small tubular container. Car bombs offer much more destructive potential, and by late 1999 and early 2000 they were being used in Cape Town. 'It was a natural step,' explained a former SAPS bomb disposal expert. 'A car provides space for explosives, it's mobile, and there are lots of them on the roads.'[28] For Pagad, car bombs meant a significant escalation of its terror campaign.

'Vehicle bombs', concludes urban theorist Mike Davis in his classic study of the car bomb, *Buda's Wagon*, 'offer extraordinary sociopolitical leverage to small, even ad hoc groups without significant constituencies or mass political legitimacy. Poorly equipped and unpopular conspiracies ... now possess a simple and reliable DIY arsenal for wreaking spectacular destruction.'[29] Davis points to the multiple advantages of car bombs: they are weapons of stealth; they give out a politically

The remains of a car in which a bomb was placed in Heerengracht, central Cape Town, on 29 August 2000. PICTURE: Author collection

powerful message because their level of destructiveness is huge; and they are remarkably cheap, operationally simple and indiscriminate. As Davis's work indicates, car bombs also allow the enfranchisement of marginal actors.[30]

At the time of the Pagad campaign, car bombs were not new to South Africa. Far-right-wing groups had attempted to disrupt the new order in 1995 with a series of car bombs in Johannesburg, Pretoria and elsewhere. The ANC also experimented with car bombs in the 1980s but their use led to considerable disagreement and controversy within the movement.[31] For reasons we will explore later, no such ethical qualms affected the Cape Town bombers. I spoke with one of the drivers who parked a car bomb in this period and he described the fear he experienced as he drove. What was interesting, however, was his anger; he said he thought his comrades were trying to kill him by detonating the bomb while he was still close by. It was a sign of the paranoia that developed among the bombers.

About a year after the pipe-bombing of the Blah Bar, the Pagad bombers plotted a much bigger attack. On Saturday 19 August 2000, a car packed with explosives was parked outside Bronx. By that time, the city was on the alert for suspicious packages, and Bronx doorman Brian Abrahams said he checked parked vehicles for strange parcels. He noticed a light-green Nissan Sentra outside the main entrance and inspected it twice, but could not identify anything conspicuously out of place about the vehicle. He then turned his back on the car to concentrate on the club DJ, who was unloading kit from his nearby vehicle. In a news report at the time, Abrahams said: 'Seconds later there was a thunderous crash. I ran a few metres to get away. I felt no pain and didn't at first realise that I was hurt.'[32]

It is unclear at precisely what time the car was parked outside the club. The rudimentary timing device was an alarm clock, which by its design would have allowed exactly one hour for the bomber to make his escape. Working backwards, the car must have been left there around 9 pm, before the club was crowded, with the timer set for the bomb to detonate at 10 pm. A few minutes before the explosion, a man telephoned CapeTalk, a local radio station, and warned the producer that a bomb was about to go off. The same man had phoned with a warning a few weeks earlier, and several hours later a car parked at the upmarket Constantia Village shopping centre detonated, injuring two, including a ten-year-old boy.

The boot of the car outside Bronx was packed with ammonium nitrate, derived from commercial fertiliser. I don't know the exact amount but a boot of that size would be able to take around 200 kilograms of explosives. 'It was the biggest bomb we had ever seen,' said a bomb technician who experienced Pagad's Cape Town campaign.[33] To provide some idea of the impact of a bomb that size, the recommended evacuation distance would have been a radius of about 500 metres.[34] The explosion would have destroyed an enormous area around the pink district.

In terms of the damage that could have been caused, the bomb would have had a lethal air blast range of about 30 metres, easily reaching Bronx and causing the building to collapse – something that was 'highly likely', an experienced police bomb technician told me.[35]

The Nissan Sentra used in the bomb attack on Bronx on 19 August 2000. The white powder around the scene is ammonium nitrate that had been packed in the boot. Had the detonation occurred as planned, there would likely have been great loss of life. PICTURE: Author collection

What actually happened when doorman Brian Abrahams heard the loud crash? It was not reported at the time, but the device did not activate properly. The blast was what bomb disposal experts call a 'low order initiation', a limited explosion of a bomb that has not been set up correctly. In fact it was the explosion of a small one-kilogram pipe bomb, which was meant to detonate the ammonium nitrate, but the bombers got the mix wrong. Bystanders reported a strong smell of sulphur, and fertiliser debris was scattered around the ruined car. I have been asked to skip the details on why the device didn't go off properly, so as not to provide technical information to other would-be bombers, but the bomb makers missed a crucial link. Had the attack gone to plan, the explosion would have left many dead and hundreds injured. It would have gone down as the worst bombing in South African history.

As it turned out, the failed bomb caused little damage and injury. Abrahams, who was standing next to the car, had shrapnel surgically removed from his foot.[36] One woman's arm was broken and three other people were treated in hospital for minor injuries. Perhaps surprisingly, the other clubs in the BAD triangle continued to operate normally. Bronx opened the next day and its clientele partied on. Owner Martin Hogan paid tribute to the 'incredible support' of his customers. Bronx closed down later, but due to the effect of market forces rather than explosive ones.

2

THE LIQUID POLICE

The liberalised new order that provided the opportunity for venues such as the Blah Bar and Bronx to open inherited the old law enforcement and security architecture to protect revellers who frequented them.

After 1994, the police and intelligence services began to transform their systems and reform their ideology and approach. But this was still work in progress when urban terror emerged, and the state security sector was ill-prepared for the sudden new threat. The police needed to get tough on Pagad, and to be seen to be doing so, but they also had to adhere to the new constitution and the constraints of a public service under a democratic dispensation.[1] The challenges facing the SAPS became glaringly apparent in its counter-campaign against Pagad.

For one thing, there were operational constraints. Security agents could no longer deploy shoot-to-kill tactics to suppress riots, or detain suspects longer than permitted by human rights laws, as they had done during apartheid. There were also fundamentally different political seas to navigate, especially for George Fivaz, the man tasked to manage the transformation of the authoritarian South African Police (SAP) into the democratised SAPS.

Fivaz was appointed more for what he was not than for what he was. He had not been a member of the old Security Branch, so he was untainted by the past. He was at the time the head of the SAP's Orwellian-sounding Efficiency Services, an outfit that looked for management and workflow improvements. This gave him the advantage of knowing the ins and outs of the institution and how it operated in theory and practice. In that function, he was appointed to a transitional structure that included government and ANC representatives as well as independent experts. He was plucked from there to be national police commissioner.

In many respects, Fivaz was not a policeman's policeman: he had not done the hard yards that were a prerequisite for the top job under the old system – no riot control, no secret policing or time spent on 'the border'. 'It was strange to the then police generals that I had been selected,' Fivaz told me. 'I was not really the most senior guy in the hierarchy to become commissioner.'[2]

Fivaz had been a station-level detective before moving into management, so he was not a total outsider. But almost all national commissioners before him had come up through the security police apparatus, and those who made key decisions, particularly as civil strife intensified in the 1980s, were from the secret side of the organisation. Having said that, Fivaz would not have risen through the ranks without an acute sense of intelligence and an ability to read people. He was adept at building personal relationships and had the skills to manoeuvre around the factions in the old order. He also understood that power had seeped from his office into the hands of his new political overseers.

Pictured here in October 1995 shortly after his appointment, George Fivaz was a compromise candidate to steer police reform under the democratic government. Without the Security Branch background that had been a prerequisite for apartheid-era police chiefs, Fivaz was seen as a more neutral figure. PICTURE: Juda Ngwenya, Reuters

Reformers in the house

The focus of police and wider security reform in the first years of democracy was largely on making the state's instruments of enforcement legitimate to the now enfranchised majority. There was emphasis on 'community policing' in the belief that if communities regained trust in the police they would support them and the police would be more effective. Although the overall outcome was meant to be greater security for citizens, the issue of crime figured much less in debates than it should have. The first step was to reform the police, and among politicians at least the idea was that once the legitimacy of the SAPS had been established, crime would decline. It was a model that can be criticised in retrospect, but given the notorieties of apartheid policing it made sense. For the most part, and exhausted by the long struggle of the 1980s, the police went grudgingly along the new path.[3]

Of course, to see the old SAP as a homogeneous repressive instrument would be wrong. Several young reformers emerged in the force during the late 1980s and 1990s. On the Cape Flats, gang-ridden Manenberg – a place that often took centre stage in the Pagad story – was a fulcrum for change, bringing together police and civil society reformers. The police commander there in the early 1990s was Arno Lamoer, a thoughtful and widely respected officer who was convinced change was needed.

Lamoer, who grew up in Riviersonderend in the Overberg, has the persona of an amiable uncle rather than a hardcore cop. He chuckles easily but thinks strategically and politically. The small-town boy later rocketed up the police hierarchy and was identified in corridor gossip as a possible national commissioner. He served as divisional commissioner for operational services, one of the most senior policing posts in the country, and later as provincial commissioner for the Western Cape, but his career crashed and burned when he was convicted of corruption. Although acquitted of charges of racketeering and money laundering, he served several years in prison. It was the end of his police career.

In 1995, though, Lamoer was still a rising star. At a conference co-organised by the new Safety and Security ministry in September 1995, he gave a presentation entitled, 'Creating a human rights culture in the SAPS'. The conference was a watershed moment in the police reform process and highlighted the ANC government's approach.

Sydney Mufamadi, the new Safety and Security minister, opened the gathering with a keynote speech, saying: 'Confronting crime is not the responsibility of the state alone, but a responsibility shared between government and civil society.'[4] The notion of security as a shared responsibility in society was a point taken literally later by Pagad, but for the moment Mufamadi's comments highlighted the general thrust of post-apartheid policing policy: building legitimacy and partnerships with the public.

It was not insignificant that such an auspicious gathering on police reform took place in Cape Town. The city had in many respects been at the forefront of a drive to reform the police and build engagement with the public.[5]

Senior reformist officers such as Lamoer, who were committed to reaching across the divide between the old and new orders, understood what would be needed. At a meeting where newly constituted community police forums and the police were to present their plans, station commanders rose to address the audience. When it came to Manenberg, only the community representatives got up to speak. Lamoer's point in agreeing to this approach with local activists was that the community owned the police, not the other way around. It went down like a lead balloon among senior police management present.

Dismantling the security state

Defending the apartheid state had required an extensive intelligence apparatus. While coverage of death squads and other special operations rightly caught public attention worldwide as the transition to democracy proceeded falteringly, much of the secret work of the state was done in the background by bureaucrats. The country was divided into geographic segments where the local Security Branch closely monitored goings-on.[6]

Violence escalated in the final days of the old order and the Security Branch faced strong accusations that it had promoted and not countered this. The dawn of democracy therefore spelt great uncertainty for the personnel of the Security Branch. They had, after all, spied on the ANC, and many had little doubt they would be dispensed with. As it turned out, policing expediency trumped political expectations. George Fivaz explained to me what happened: 'I had a couple of sessions with the old security police. I had an agreement with Mandela that we would accommodate the people. He asked me to convey to them that if they go with the new structure of the police service there would be no reason to fear: They don't have to go. They can stay on.'[7]

Fivaz made sure his consultations with Security Branch people were well covered in the media. 'I wanted to show an open hand. It was not supposed to be a secret that we would like people to remain and to be incorporated – as long as they went with our new strategy.'[8]

Unexpectedly, Fivaz received a call from FW de Klerk, then deputy president, who wanted to meet the commissioner. De Klerk was upset that Security Branch officers were particularly critical of him. Fivaz told De Klerk they felt betrayed because they had done things of which he was aware but which he now denied. 'I told FW they were bitterly disappointed.'[9] Fivaz asked De Klerk to address the officers. He agreed, but in the end never arranged the meeting.

This suggests that the mood in the post-1994 secret police was more complicated than a simple old order/new order divide. Many officers, suspicious of the new system and disillusioned at being sold out by De Klerk, took financial packages and left.[10] That said, some competent officers stayed on and were integrated into the new intelligence environment, which morphed from the Security Branch into the Crime Information Service and later became Crime Intelligence.

While police intelligence structures were transforming, the same did not apply to the cohort of old detectives who emerged from a system that produced a storied group of investigators. Think Suiker Britz, Bushie Engelbrecht, or the hard-drinking, chain-smoking serial killer hunter Piet Byleveld. There are others, such as the modest and mild-mannered Frank Dutton, who acted outside the police's institutional interest in solving cases that implicated fellow officers. He was the first head of the elite crime-fighting unit, the Scorpions.[11]

The system that bred these big-name detectives relied on a process of filtered recruitment. Station detectives were selected from the wider force and earned their spurs investigating petty crimes such as burglary and car theft. Those who were competent (or, as cynics have suggested, who had contacts) were elevated to specialist units. The best were selected to work in elite outfits, the most famous (or notorious, depending on your point of view) being the Murder & Robbery units in each of the main cities.

In understanding their later response to Pagad and the terror threat in the Western Cape, it is worth highlighting the challenges these units faced. The idea of the units, under the old dispensation, had been to ensure a specialised detective capacity. They became involved only when white people were victims, or if the victim was a state official. The units would then work as a team to solve cases. The lead detectives were all white, with a limited number of black and Coloured officers assisting.

Murder & Robbery units were at their most effective in the early 1980s. Crimes with white victims were still relatively few and the civil unrest of the mid to late 1980s had not yet begun. Murder & Robbery units were largely focused on crime and were not political in the same way as the Security Branch. Nevertheless, they developed a reputation for violence and extracting confessions from suspects.

By the late 1980s, however, Murder & Robbery units were coming under severe strain. The number of homicides, including of white people, was increasing dramatically while the targeting of black councillors for assassination (they fell into the category of state officials for which the unit had a mandate) greatly added to the caseload and politicised the units. More detectives were recruited to meet the demands but the overall number remained small. As tensions mounted countrywide, several former members told me, the pressures on the units became intense. One said the attitude of senior police leaders was to 'shit on them', demanding more rapid and more successful investigations.[12] That added to the level of violence used in their investigations.

This ratcheting-up of conflict led to tension between the Security Branch and Murder & Robbery units – something that was also seen between detectives and Crime Intelligence at the time of Pagad.

Detectives complained that the intelligence they received could not be used in court; the security police, meanwhile, claimed that detectives did not consider how intelligence could be used to shape their investigations. It was clear who was the senior partner.

After 1994, the specialist units continued to function but not without lingering suspicion among the new political masters. As wider police reforms focused on a community policing mandate began to gain traction, Murder & Robbery units and other specialist outfits were still sceptically seen as the preserve of whites. One officer told me: 'Murder & Robbery was essentially a small group of guys that were not ready for change. What happened is that the system changed around them.'[13] Once the elite, by the late 1990s they faced increasing political pressure and suspicion – and when Pagad came along, their flaws became exposed for all to see.

Top detectives came across as celebrities in the press – and some even courted publicity, rather than working as collective, cohesive units. This reflected how the work of investigation, with its piles of dockets requiring attention, seldom allowed a more strategic, proactive focus. Their ethos of elitist specialism, combined with a sense that the detective units were racial holdouts, contrasted with the philosophy so clearly spelt out in the 1995 Cape Town policing conference: that community and station-based policing was the key if all citizens' interests were to be served.

A good illustration of how the units were regarded with suspicion is an exchange between a senior detective and Jackie Selebi, who succeeded Fivaz as national police commissioner. Selebi, a senior member of the ANC who had previously been a diplomat, was clearly a political appointment. When confronted at a meeting about why he was dismantling the specialist units, the notoriously blunt Selebi replied: 'Because you guys in Murder & Robbery will take over the country.'[14] Even if that were untrue, the curt reply perfectly captured the political sentiment.

Specialist police officers were subsequently made available to bolster local skills and service delivery at station level. 'Selebi just didn't understand,' one former Murder & Robbery officer told me. 'He didn't get that everything we did was going to go to defence attorneys, so he weakened the system.'[15] That was certainly the case, but it was also true that the specialist detectives did not fight their cause well internally. Part of the problem was that they came across as arrogant, so they had enemies in the house who moaned that they were a 'glory-hunting' clique.

Pagad's first responder

If Johannesburg's serious crimes and the hard knocks of KwaZulu-Natal bred some widely known detectives, the Cape detective cadre had its own high-profile officers.[16] Emerging from the province was a man who would play a key and contested role against Pagad: Leonard Knipe.

Knipe is an intriguing figure. At the time Pagad struck he was at the peak of his operational career as commander of the Serious & Violent Crimes unit in Cape Town, of which Murder & Robbery was a part.

In a fascinating exchange at a Truth and Reconciliation Commission (TRC) hearing in February 1997, just as Pagad's campaign of violence was scaling up, Knipe outlined some of the difficulties he had experienced in the old SAP. The hearing was about the Gugulethu Seven, a group of young men who were killed by the apartheid police in March 1986. It later emerged that the men, who were not ANC guerrillas, died in a Security Branch entrapment operation which was then covered up. Knipe was one of the Murder & Robbery investigators called to the scene.

His point was that he was not implicated in the case but appeared to have left or been forced out of Murder & Robbery as a result: 'I have a clean departmental record but I was suspended for expressing my opinion,' he said.[17]

Knipe's evidence suggests a good deal of enmity between him and the Security Branch. 'I had fallen foul during my career with the security police. There was a dossier held on me by the security police. The security police and I did not work in close relationship with each other.'[18] Not getting along with the security police in the 1980s was indeed something to be lauded, and Knipe rightly presented it as a badge of honour.

Knipe was involved in numerous complex investigations. One of the most prominent followed the attack on St James Church in Kenilworth, Cape Town, in July 1993, less than a year before the first democratic elections. The perpetrators were members of the Azanian

People's Liberation Army (Apla), the armed wing of the Pan Africanist Congress (PAC).

A very senior police officer with no connections to or sympathy for the Security Branch told me: 'I don't think Leonard is a team player. I always summed him up as a person who had his own way of doing things. He's a complicated guy. He is moody and he has his own mind-set. It would be difficult to convince him that there could be an alternative. It's like, "I'm right, to hell with the rest. It's impossible for me to be wrong".'[19]

As democracy dawned, the hard-pressed Cape Town Murder & Robbery detectives under Knipe turned to new challenges. The requirement to investigate cases involving serious violent crime committed only against white people (something that had disgusted him, Knipe told the TRC) was dropped, and the number of cases that needed attention increased. The group of informers that Murder & Robbery had across the peninsula included the usual criminal and gang suspects but they did not include people from Pagad, who had not had any contact with the state's crime-fighting or political control instruments. That was to prove a serious blind spot. The hypersensitive and difficult Knipe and what some described as the insular group of detectives around him were about to be sorely tested by the formation and, later, escalating violence of Pagad.

The new arrivals

The ANC wanted to ensure it had members within the new police service, but that was a challenge in terms of capacity. Unlike the integration of the military and intelligence services, where the ANC had higher numbers of trained personnel because of the protracted conflict of the 1980s and 1990s, the same did not apply to the police: there had been no ANC police force, so there were no new police officers to bring on board.

The solution was to select a group of ANC cadres, mainly from the intelligence environment, and insert them into the police. In some cases, these prospective police officers were rushed through military or intelligence training to bolster the numbers. In the end, only a tiny number

– fewer than 50 – were integrated into the SAPS (an organisation of more than 100 000 members), and since all of them came from an intelligence background, Crime Intelligence (in effect the old Security Branch) was where they would go.

'With no clear programme of action from the ANC to direct us,' recalled Jeremy Vearey, Mandela's former bodyguard and an outspoken member of this group, 'we had to raft this whitewater without any paddles'.[20] The 'whitewater' was a none too subtle reference to new colleagues.

The new arrivals were a diverse group. The most senior was Tim Williams, who assumed the leadership of Crime Intelligence as the Pagad threat emerged. Williams was a wizened and quiet veteran of the liberation organisation's spooks, the Department of Intelligence and Security. In many ways he was a good choice. Unassuming and unobtrusive, his appointment and management style created few waves.[21]

Another ANC entry who rose to senior levels was Raymond Lalla, who headed the police's secret apparatus as the Pagad crisis abated. Lalla's background was Umkhonto we Sizwe (MK) military intelligence. His non-threatening exterior masks a man with a shrewd judgement of people. Lalla made it clear he was now a police professional, not a political actor.

Anwar Dramat, who also went on to play a key role against Pagad, was a former underground operative from the Western Cape and one of the last ANC members to be released from Robben Island. Considered, principled and inclined to avoid the limelight, he later rose to high office as the deputy national commissioner in charge of the specialised police unit, the Hawks.[22]

Another key appointment was an ANC Department of Intelligence and Security operative from Paarl in the Western Cape, Mzwandile Petros. A former teacher, Petros was integrated as a constable and rapidly promoted to major. He played a key, albeit controversial, role in the secret war against Pagad and later became provincial commissioner for both the Western Cape and Gauteng.[23]

One of the most intriguing of the new arrivals, a man destined to play a crucial role against Pagad, was a quietly spoken but determined individual called David Africa. Africa was an unnatural fit for the aggressive, macho world of policing in South Africa. Hailing from gang-ridden Manenberg, he had joined the liberation struggle as a schoolboy. Never comfortable in a bureaucracy, Africa left the police shortly after engaging with Pagad.

As Vearey's 'whitewater' reference suggests, the ANC newcomers to the police service did not always have it easy. A strong sense of mistrust pervaded SAPS corridors. The new arrivals were excluded from meetings and information flows, and meetings were conducted in Afrikaans. The ANC group met and strategised together, fuelling the suspicions of former Security Branch members. A former SAP officer told me they searched Africa's office when he was away, convinced the new ANC appointments were keeping information out of the system. They found nothing suspicious. Bonds did form, however, as the new arrivals ascended the ranks. A senior SAP police intelligence officer who is still serving told me that even though several of the ANC recruits had earlier been arrested and tortured, this was never once raised.

The secret system of policing was changing too. The old bonds of trust and ethnicity which characterised the fight against the liberation movements in the late 1980s broke down. White officers were now worried about their future, and a new and often ugly careerism emerged as people struggled to move up the greasy promotional pole. People on both sides were quick to undermine former colleagues in arms.[24]

The former ANC cadres, uncomfortable in their new blue uniforms or ill-fitting suits, were termed the 'plastic police'; but they were themselves floating in a wider sea of change. This eclectic crew, operating amid the uncertainties and constraints of a police service in the process of transforming, and lacking expertise for a democratic era, would shortly face a highly organised terrorist network. And few in the new Crime Intelligence apparatus had ever systematically collected or analysed intelligence on criminals.

3

BIRTHING PAGAD

In mid-1996, in the early days of Pagad, before it was officially launched or its campaign had turned violent, a furtive meeting took place in Pretoria.

The encounter was between one of the founders of Pagad and the national police commissioner, George Fivaz.[1] The Pagad man did not make an appointment to meet the country's most senior police officer. Wearing a blue hoodie against the early-morning winter chill and with a cap pulled low over his eyes, he waited for Fivaz at the entrance to the car park of police headquarters at the Wachthuis building. The man seemed to know something of the commissioner's movements, including what time he usually arrived. He had driven from Cape Town and had every intention of speaking to him.

Fivaz remembers that the cap wearer approached his car before the police officer on guard moved quickly to restrain him. 'It was at about seven o'clock one morning,' Fivaz recalled. He gestured to the guard to back off and the man approached the car uneasily. 'I need to meet with you,' he told Fivaz. 'But you don't have an appointment,' Fivaz replied, winding down his window. 'I can't make an appointment,' retorted the Pagad man. He paused. 'They will kill me.'

It says something about Fivaz's openness that he told the stranger to get into the car. They took the lift to his office and talked for an hour. The Pagad man told Fivaz he had been involved in the formation of the organisation and that things would shortly turn bad. What had started as a peaceful mass movement, he said, was about to turn extremely violent and there would be a campaign of assassinations. The man explained that the radical Islamic group Qibla, which had always been in the background, was seizing control of the anti-gang and anti-drugs campaign. He was emphatic: things would not turn out well, and the police urgently needed to understand this and act. He explained how Qibla operatives had been planning things behind the backs of the wider Pagad leadership from the beginning.

Contacting the national commissioner of the SAPS was a courageous act. Some members of the original Pagad committee were later attacked or killed, and the threat the capped man spoke about was real. He was under no illusions about the future and told Fivaz as much.[2] Fivaz told me he was shocked by the encounter, and while the man's warning matched the intelligence he was receiving, the in-person appeal left him with a sense of foreboding.

Pagad's midwife

There is little doubt that Pagad left a decisive imprint on the emerging politics of Cape Town in the first years of democracy but there is some dispute as to the origins of the movement. There are two broad hypotheses about the events that gave rise to the group, and about who sought to shape them.

The first, largely reflecting the views of certain security officials who worked over the years on the Pagad file, is that the organisation was a creation of Qibla. In this telling, Pagad was a cleverly designed front for the radical movement, which used it to mobilise wider community support. The second theory, more widely held, is that Pagad began as a mass movement of ordinary people concerned about gangs and drugs and was later hijacked by Qibla in pursuit of a more radical agenda. The common denominator in both explanations is, of course, Qibla.

As far as I have been able to ascertain, the truth includes elements of both accounts. There is strong evidence to suggest Qibla shaped and managed the creation of Pagad to bolster its own aims and agenda. At the same time, however, Pagad in its embryonic phase garnered considerable local support, particularly from the Muslim middle-class community who were devastated by the impact of drugs and gangs on the Cape Flats.

Qibla was formed in 1980, 16 years before the birth of Pagad and in a completely different era, as part of a wider political awakening in the Muslim community. South Africa's 'brand' of Islam was far from uniform. For some, the teachings of the Prophet were of more importance than the need for sociopolitical reform; others were more politically conscious and believed religious orthodoxy should not preclude their involvement in the liberation struggle or the transition to democracy.[3]

This awakening began in the 1970s with the establishment of the Muslim Youth Movement (MYM), which challenged the established religious leadership. While it was a new contender in an older and established order, the MYM did not promote wider societal change but focused on individual spiritual Islamic values and learning. In doing so, however, it raised important issues about how the Muslim community should respond to the oppression of the apartheid state. Muslim religious leaders had generally adopted a non-ideological approach to opposing white rule, arguing that Muslims need not have a quibble with the authorities if they could still practise their religion. But in 1984, a new organisation, the Call of Islam, was formed as conflict in South Africa mounted. It aligned itself with the wider liberation movement and joined the United Democratic Front (UDF), a broad coalition of anti-apartheid forces.[4]

Inspired by the success of the 1979 Iranian revolution and in response to the narrow outlook of the MYM, Qibla, like the Call of Islam, was also a response to increasing political conflict. More radical, less compromising and narrower in outlook, Qibla initially aligned itself with the PAC and operatives from the two organisations trained together in Libya.[5] 'Qibla discourse', notes a study of political Islam, was a 'fusion' of Islamic principles, Iranian revolutionary slogans and anti-apartheid messaging.[6]

The founder of Qibla was Achmad Cassiem, a charismatic former teacher who had been incarcerated on Robben Island. Cassiem positioned himself as the heir to the legacy of Imam Abdullah Haron, an anti-apartheid activist and leader who died in police detention in 1969. Cassiem, who resided in Cape Town until his death in July 2023, is an enigmatic figure. Inspired by the Iranian revolution, he believed an Islamic revolution was also possible in South Africa.[7] He gathered around him a core group of fellow believers.

While Qibla often appeared dogmatic and unstrategic, Cassiem was described in the late 1980s as 'the most serious theoretician in the ranks of the Islamists opposing apartheid'.[8] Qibla's slogan was 'One solution: Islamic revolution' and its leadership saw themselves as a vanguard for the creation of an Islamic state. How this focus on religion fitted in with the PAC's agenda was never quite clear,[9] and relations between the two organisations later deteriorated.[10]

In his writings, Cassiem says Muslims have a religious obligation to eliminate elements deemed non-beneficial to their communities.[11] There were at least two contradictions in this philosophy. The first was that while Cassiem believed Qibla must remain an Islamic organisation, he also saw the organisation as a 'mass movement'. That seemed something of a non-starter, as Qibla regarded South Africa as a 'community of infidels' and believed 'Muslims must not work with them'.[12] The second and related problem was the flawed idea that a minority within a minority – Muslims were at the time only about 2 per cent of the population – could achieve the numbers to be a mass movement.

Such practical challenges did not make Qibla any more compromising. Cassiem and his acolytes believed that only a revolution could establish an Islamic state in South Africa. The organisation thus opposed the negotiations between the ANC and the National Party government designed to lead to the end of white rule; it was to be an Islamic revolution for South Africa or nothing, in Qibla's way of thinking. A religious revolution precluded a political one. Dogmatic as ever, Qibla called on Muslims to boycott the democratic elections of 1994 and 1999. This political orientation ensured that Qibla always had limited support in the Muslim community, the vast majority of whom were eager for the creation of a democratic order in which they could play an active and committed part.[13] Under Qibla's influence, Pagad lost its popular support.

A senior police intelligence officer from the old SAP told me that briefings he saw at the time suggested individuals associated with Qibla were sent out of the country for training 'to prepare themselves for an Islamic state', which would be achieved through jihad. 'There were serious activities in the Western Cape at that time,' he said. Another serving officer confirmed this, and while it is difficult to verify the information I regard both sources as reliable.[14]

Achmad Cassiem, the leader and founder of Qibla and a former prisoner on Robben Island, leading a march in the period just before the formation of Pagad. PICTURE: Benny Gool

Democratic gangsters

At the same time as a social and religious renaissance was happening in the Muslim community and movements, new gangs were gestating in Cape Town, partly in response to forced removals of Coloured people by the authorities in the 1970s and 1980s. The street gangs, already present for many years, emerged stronger from a period of upheaval in which old community, social and family ties were torn apart, and they were instrumental in the development of new forms of social ordering.[15]

The spiralling state violence of the 1980s that was the hallmark of apartheid South Africa was decisive in shaping this emerging criminal economy. In the fraught and conflict-ridden Cape Town of the time, gangs and their leaders became enmeshed in the political struggle. Some aligned themselves with the apartheid government and its security forces while others positioned themselves closer to the liberation movements. These alliances were a function of a struggle for survival on both sides, and winning was more important than the political leanings of your allies.

There were also profound shifts under way in how the gangs resourced themselves. Gangsters had long been involved in the drug economy. Cannabis and Mandrax (methaqualone) were two of their staples, but the end of apartheid and the opening up of South Africa to the global economy – including the globalised *illicit* economy – saw drug imports swell dramatically. 'Drugs poured into the country and the criminal justice system could offer little resistance,' noted Wilfried Schärf, one of the country's most respected criminologists.[16] Hungry for profits, gang bosses bought and distributed new drugs from emerging suppliers. The availability and diversity of drugs in the clubs and on the streets seemed to surge. In particular, consumption of crystal methamphetamine, commonly known in South Africa as 'tik', increased dramatically, as did access to heroin and cocaine.[17]

Violent competition over drug turf, marked by bloody conflict between gangs, escalated in the months before the 1994 elections. The reported surge in drug availability was also matched by harder data. Prices of drugs on the streets, a reliable measure of supply levels, declined. Levels of reported drug use and addiction increased from this period, as did the number of people seeking treatment for addiction.[18]

Meanwhile, a web of contacts linked the gangs and the police. A former police intelligence officer active in the 1990s handed me, through an intermediary, a document detailing how 'at the time allegations of police corruption were frowned upon and victims or witnesses who reported such heinous relationships between only a handful of SAPS members and gang bosses were either ignored or the information given back to the prominent gang bosses'.[19] Schärf notes that the police regularly used gangs as paid informers to monitor liberation activists and local politics, so they were protected.[20]

A fundamental recalibration of the constellation of criminal power ensued in the Western Cape. In anticipation of political change and opportunities for influence, criminal bosses formed 'The Firm' in 1994. This was in effect a criminal cartel of some of the most prominent Cape gangs.[21] The Firm was rumoured to have been pulled together by a slick business-minded gang boss, Colin Stanfield, leader of the up-and-coming 28s.[22] In Schärf's words, gang leaders who became part of The Firm 'realised that there were enormous opportunities for increased business. By that stage they had also realised that when the borders opened and foreign criminal syndicates had access to these new markets, they stood to lose if the gangs did not stand together.'[23]

While drug use had been largely confined to excluded communities, it began to spread into Muslim middle-class neighbourhoods. Discussing the formation of Pagad with people in the Cape Town Muslim community, I repeatedly heard that suddenly, 'drugs were everywhere' and 'we needed to do this for our children'.[24] Muslim middle-class areas tended to neighbour those where drug use was already widespread, and as gangs sought new markets these communities were obvious targets: 'Relatively better-off bored youth have moved on from dagga to other kinds of dope,' said a local assessment of Pagad's rise.[25]

As the turf-linked shootouts just before the elections foretold, surges in drug markets led to more violent competition between gangs. An expanding drug economy accentuated the need to control and defend turf where drugs could be sold.

Gangs and the associated problem of drug use on the Cape Flats were concerns for the new democratic government but were largely viewed as the social consequences of exclusion and white rule. As recounted in the previous chapter, the primary focus of the ANC's law enforcement agenda was on making the police legitimate, with the assumption that effective policing would naturally follow. They were missing a trick. Several analysts suggested that what were known colloquially as 'Coloured gangs' were in some cases developing into hardcore organised crime outfits. In 2000, Irvin Kinnes, a well-connected anti-crime activist (and now a professor at UCT) published an analysis of the changing face of gangs in the Western Cape. The title captured what had been occurring since the early 1990s: 'From Urban Street Gangs to Criminal Empires'.[26]

To some extent, the intense focus on the final exhausting but exhilarating steps towards democracy masked the horrors of escalating gang violence and booming drug use. Nevertheless, communities had begun to mobilise against drugs and crime. The Salt River Anti-Drug Committee was formed, followed by the establishment of similar formations in Bo-Kaap, Surrey Estate, Athlone and Wynberg, all affected by the expanding drug economy. Neighbourhood watches, largely in middle-class Muslim areas, also began to pop up. Clearly, communities felt there was a growing problem that needed to be addressed. 'Many people living outside of the townships simply have no concept of the real horror of gangsterism and the power that gangsters wield,' noted a Roman Catholic priest, Father Christopher Clohessy, who later openly supported Pagad.[27]

Who governs?

Apartheid rule also wrought a longer-term, and perhaps more worrying, trend than the drug mobsters themselves: 'gang governance'. Poor communities on the Cape Flats became susceptible to criminal governance as the apartheid state excluded non-white communities from legitimate forms of state support and security. Politics abhors a vacuum and the gangs stepped in to fill the governance space.

Criminal governance (as it is known in the academic literature) came about because of two seismic shifts in South Africa during the transition period. First, as mentioned, the profound political shake-up resulted in a move from authoritarian to democratic policing, with the assumption that this would solve deeply embedded forms of structural alienation and disorder. Second, the criminal economy expanded and diversified rapidly as drug markets became connected to globalised illicit supply chains. It was a combustible mix.

The stereotype of the Coloured gangster, common currency around the braais of white Capetonians, hid a darker reality: marginalised Capetonians looked to gangs for leadership and support because all they received from the state was harassment and coercion. In that sense, gangs can be seen as an extension of the prevailing hierarchy of white governance. Democracy shook that hierarchy, allowing gang bosses to manoeuvre for influence in the community by distributing food, dispensing cash and providing protection. In exchange, communities were compelled to live under the spectre of governance by criminals, resisting attempts by the police to get cooperation or information on the gangs, and compromising themselves and their children by hiding drugs and weapons from the police. This form of criminal governance was key to the rise of Pagad and highlighted the degree to which the state seemed to have lost local control.

Gangs also had political ambitions and The Firm began publicly discussing the establishment of a political party to contest Western Cape elections in March 1996. There was talk of disbanding the cartel and seeking amnesty,[28] and it is possible that gangsters used the threat of political participation as leverage for obtaining immunity from prosecution. Whether or not that is true, underworld actors were clearly trying to reposition themselves as the tectonic plates of politics shifted.

In Qibla's way of thinking, these developments reinforced the view that far from closing off the space for criminal elements who were destroying the community, democracy had considerably opened it up. But it also suggested a period of profound opportunity for a radical movement looking for an in. Discussions on the growing impact of drugs and gangs had been reverberating around mosques across Cape Town. It is important to note that Qibla's external reference point was

Shia Iran and the Islamic Revolution, but while drawing on Iranian revolutionary and anti-imperialist reference points, it was strongly rooted in South Africa. This was despite attacks on it from 'a fierce anti-Shia lobby' in Cape Town, which on at least one occasion in the 1980s led to a shootout with supporters of the mainstream religious establishment.[29] Locally rooted meant finding an issue that would have wider appeal, bolstering the popularity and reach of a Leninist-style party in need of a mass following. It is hard to believe the charismatic Cassiem did not see these connections.

'We are people against gangsterism and drugs'

Pagad did not become a public phenomenon until 1996, but discussions about the establishment of a movement to oppose gangs and drugs began earlier. Aslam Toefy, a founder of Pagad who left but rejoined and now sits on the executive, told me he joined the campaign in its early days in about 1995. 'I decided to join Pagad because of the justice that it was involved in,' he said. 'Pagad people came from all parts of the community – bricklayers, carpenters – it was not some academic-style response. People simply did not have the courage to stand up to the violence of gangsters. They hoped that Pagad could counter this. It was the tears of the mothers that drove a lot of people into Pagad.'[30]

Discussions about a response to drugs and gangs drew in a wide array of actors, including members of the Christian community. At the time Clohessy, then the priest at St Timothy's in Mitchells Plain,[31] wrote unequivocally about his participation: 'As a Catholic priest, and without losing any of my Christian conviction, I am unashamedly pro-Pagad, having supported the movement from its inception and having been involved in its structures to a greater or lesser degree.' A non-confrontational approach to the problem of gangs and drugs was 'no longer a viable route', Clohessy concluded.[32]

Besides the intensification of gang governance and growing drug markets, it is worth asking why Pagad formed almost immediately after democracy was attained. Keith Gottschalk, then professor of politics at the University of the Western Cape, has made the important point that the period from just before the 1994 elections to the early 2000s saw the formation of several vigilante-style groups. 'This phenomenon,' he argues, 'peaked during the 1990s as the authority of white supremacy collapsed, while state transformation and the construction of new democratic authorities and institutions took a good decade to be consolidated.'[33] This emergence of self-policing institutions at a time when the state was weak or in transition has fascinating parallels with contemporary South Africa.

The advent of democracy created hopes that gangsterism, and crime in general, would now be properly addressed, that the new government would take note and act. For moderate Muslims, organising protests was a way of drawing attention to the challenge and their mounting frustration. Even if they did not all take to the streets, there was wide support for calls on the state to do something about gangs.

In line with a focus on holding the new leaders to account, one of the first anti-drug and anti-gang protests, in February 1996 (it was not a Pagad event, as the organisation had not yet been officially formed) was targeted at the new justice minister, Dullah Omar, a prominent activist from Rylands on the Cape Flats. Omar, a brave, compassionate and widely respected man, had to vacate his home, as his security detail feared for his safety. Qibla activists were implicated in the protest and Cassiem – disingenuously, several suggest – ordered a disciplinary inquiry into what had occurred.

Pressure continued to build. In early March 1996, hundreds of protesters converged on parliament in Cape Town, demanding action from the government against drugs and crime. 'Who are we?' the leaders shouted. 'We are people against gangsterism and drugs,' came the crowd's reply, thus bestowing a name on the organisation. Those who were present told me the gathering was attended mainly by Muslim people, although there was a smattering of non-Muslims.

Pagad moved quickly to retain the momentum. Another march on the parliamentary precinct took place a few weeks later in May 1996. This time, Pagad upped the ante by giving the authorities a 60-day ultimatum to rid the city of drugs and gangs. Abdus-Salaam Ebrahim, who was central to these events, told me that after delivering the ultimatum

Pagad members daubed on walls the phrase 'the deadly countdown'.[34] As far as the core group of Pagad operatives was concerned, the clock was ticking.

It is hard not to see Qibla's hand in this unfolding cycle of protest. First the robust gathering outside Dullah Omar's house, followed by the parliament protests, then the issuing of an ultimatum. Predictably, the deadline passed without an effective response from the state. The protesters had by that time also met Omar to discuss their grievances.

July 1996 saw the Pagad campaign grow, and its targets were clear: protests were held outside the homes of drug dealers. Gang bosses, while privately unsettled, largely chose to respond with outward defiance. In some cases, they exacerbated the hostility by reminding their opponents in profanity-laden exchanges that they also had contacts within the police.

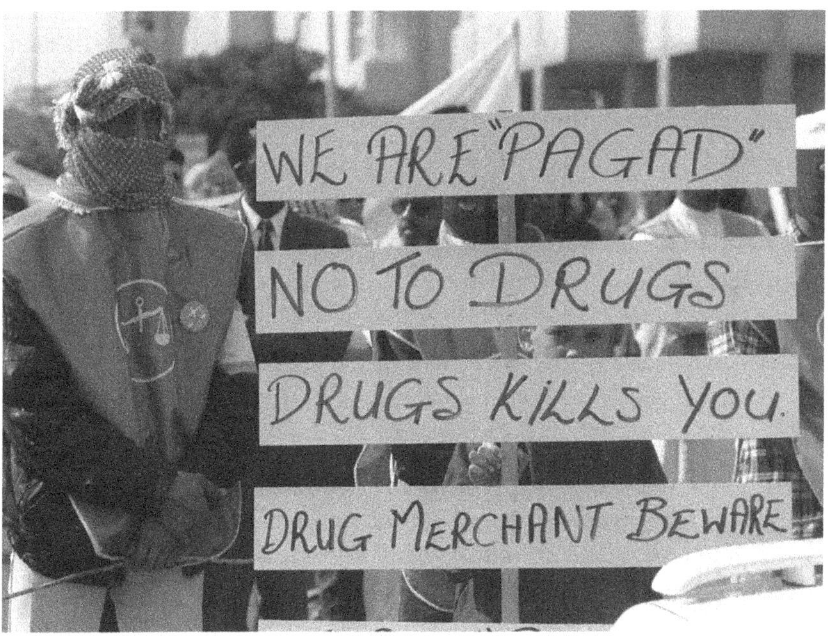

Pagad marched on Parliament twice in the first half of 1996. 'We are people against gangsterism and drugs,' the crowd chanted. In the May 1996 march, this sign warned drug merchants to beware. It was not a hollow threat. PICTURE: Benny Gool

As if choreographed, the gauntlet was thrown down and the stage was set for a significant escalation. It was only a matter of time, and tensions came to a head on 4 August 1996, a key date in the unfolding confrontation between Pagad, the gangs, and ultimately the state itself.

The human torch

Throughout the 1970s, the dominant criminal gang in Cape Town was the Americans. In the early 1980s, entrepreneurial twin brothers Rashied and Rashaad Staggie broke away from the Americans to form their own gang in the hardscrabble and gang-infested area of Manenberg. It is said that the brothers had tired of acting as intermediaries for the illegal transactions of others and decided to form their own operation. The evocatively named Hard Livings was the result, the new gang's name an etymologically vivid description of its leaders' world view.

By the 1990s, the Hard Livings had become notorious for liberally using violence – an essential part of their business model – to seize and hold drug territory, most notably from the sprawling criminal outfit that spawned them, the Americans. Manenberg became the theatre of a long-running war for control and the crack of gunshots is still a regular occurrence in the area today. The Staggies' strategy was two-pronged: flood the area with drugs to ensure profits, and win community support to protect the space for drug sales – an example of the gang governance described earlier. It was a playbook that was being developed across Cape Town, but the Staggies moved fast and they broke things.

In that sense, the brothers were criminal innovators, and by pushing the envelope they were central to the rapid expansion of drug distribution and use across the Cape. Partly because of the violence they dispensed, the brothers were seen as untouchable. Rashaad Staggie appeared fearless too, even in the face of Muslim mobilisation against him. I have it on record that he said, 'I fucked Allah' – or words to that effect – at a mosque. If that is indeed true, he seemed to have little idea that he was tempting fate. But he soon found out.

On 4 August 1996, an estimated 2000 Pagad members and supporters gathered at Gatesville Mosque in Rylands, not far from where

Rashaad Staggie, co-leader with his twin brother, Rashied, of the Hard Livings Gang, was a key criminal innovator in Cape Town's evolving underworld in the mid-1990s. Pictured here in January 1995 at a gang 'peace rally' in Manenberg, he was a highly visible and influential crime boss. His killing in August 1996 was a decisive turning point in Pagad's campaign against the gangs. PICTURE: Chae Kihn, I-Afrika/AFP via Getty Images

they had surrounded the Justice minister's house a few months earlier. Among the crowd, and unbeknown to Pagad, were several police intelligence officers dressed to blend in. As the winter night deepened, the group moved in procession about ten kilometres to the Staggie brothers' house in Salt River, widely thought to be used for drug storage and sales. They were heavily armed, guns sprouting from the windows of accompanying vehicles. The mood was at fever pitch; this crowd meant business.

When the convoy arrived at the Staggies' stronghold in London Road, only Rashied was at home. Shots were exchanged between occupants of the house and members of the crowd and several protesters were injured. A police unit that arrived on the scene was approached by Pagad's then head of internal security, Nadthmie Edries. He promised to call off the marchers after consulting Ali 'Phantom' Parker, then Pagad's chief commander, who was also there. The police withdrew to a position a short distance away.[35]

It was all to no avail. Rashaad Staggie had got word of what was happening and, perhaps as an indication of his belief in his own impunity, headed home in his white bakkie to confront the crowd and protect his brother. It was just after 1.30 am and the police allowed him through. In a green jacket with white sleeves, Staggie started to argue with someone as the crowd closed in around his vehicle.

Suddenly a shot rang out. Staggie was hit. A picture taken at the scene shows him slumped forward in his bakkie with blood pouring down the side of his face. Emergency paramedics, presumably on standby because of the authorities' concerns about violence, appeared to treat Staggie. As the paramedics moved off, someone in the crowd shouted, 'This is the man who kills our children,' and a firebomb was hurled at him. In a widely publicised series of photos, Staggie, now ablaze from the Molotov cocktail, is seen running towards the group that attacked him, like a human torch. He fell to the ground, writhing in agony as the flames consumed him.

The mob closed in, kicking and beating him before the flames were extinguished by the paramedics. One of Cape Town's most prominent gang kingpins was no more.[36]

4

KILLING THE BOSSES

The killing of Rashaad Staggie was a defining moment in the evolution of organised crime in South Africa. It catapulted Pagad onto the national scene and marked the beginning of a sustained campaign of violence. Staggie's murder also shook the gangs, which mobilised to demand that the state protect them. The criminal protectorate pleading for protection: it was a request that incensed the vigilantes, reinforcing in the minds of hardcore Pagad members their belief that the police were the gangs' minders rather than enforcers of the law.

On 11 August 1996, a week after Staggie's killing, Pagad members and supporters gathered once again in their thousands, this time at Vygieskraal Stadium in Rylands. At the same time, like enemy forces mustering for battle, hundreds of gang members converged on Manenberg.[1]

The Pagad rally was planned as a way of inaugurating the organisation. There were an estimated 10000 supporters in attendance. Significantly, Sheikh Nazeem Mohamed, leader of the Muslim Judicial Council (MJC), was present, lending legitimacy to the movement despite the violent killing of Staggie. Gregory Rockman, a well-known progressive former police officer who was the driving force behind the Police and Prisons Civil Rights Union, was also said to have been there, conferring additional credibility on the gathering.

Arno Lamoer was the senior police officer responsible for crime prevention in the part of Cape Town where both gatherings were taking place. Amazingly, under the circumstances, both Pagad and the gangs had made official applications to the authorities for their rallies. Police intelligence operatives sent urgent reports on the SAPS communications network that gang bosses were on the podium with Pagad members at the stadium,[2] and senior officers tried frantically to make sense of what was going on.

In Manenberg, the march, led by Rashied Staggie, made its way to the police station. The gangs had drafted a memo that they wanted to hand over to the Safety and Security minister, Sydney Mufamadi. He rightly refused to receive it and the responsibility for dealing with it was passed down the police chain of command until it landed in Lamoer's lap. 'I said that I would receive the memorandum on one condition, that the gangsters moved away from the police station and gathered in an area of open ground in Valhalla Park,' recounted Lamoer.[3] He wanted to ensure the gangsters could not attempt to confront the police or Pagad, and they agreed to this condition. The police were still smarting from criticism that they had failed to prevent the killing of Staggie, and with his twin brother now in the vanguard of the Manenberg gathering, one of Lamoer's key objectives was to keep the heavily armed groups well apart.

As befitted his strategically minded and democratic approach, Lamoer was keen to engage with leaders on both sides of the line and he shuttled between the two gatherings, which were about four kilometres apart.

In Valhalla Park, the gangsters made it clear that they did not want a strong police presence as they intended to hand over their memo peacefully. Lamoer switched off his radio and phone, told his officers to keep their distance and entered the gathering to receive the memorandum. The gangs asked him to address them and a sound system was rigged up. Lamoer began in English but was told to switch to Afrikaans. In their memorandum, the gangs demanded that attacks by Pagad be stopped and said gangsters should receive amnesty for their previous crimes. Ad-libbing to his audience, Lamoer said something to the effect that the police were responsible for the safety of all South Africans, including presumably hardcore and violent gangsters.

Meanwhile, at the stadium, Pagad supporters were vocal about the lack of an effective police response to the gangs. As the rally wound down, a sizable part of the crowd began to move towards the home of a drug dealer in nearby Hanover Park, an area with a strong gang presence. Although they could hardly have reacted otherwise, particularly after the publicity surrounding Staggie's death, police deployed teargas to disperse the crowd. For those present this was another demonstration that the state appeared to be protecting the gangs and not ordinary citizens.

At the gathering, Pagad presented a unified face. Under the surface, however, tensions were brewing. While the movement had enjoyed a period of public support, demonstrated most clearly by the Vygieskraal rally, rifts came to the fore in September 1996 as the public unity of the core group of founders began to crumble.

Internal enemies

Before the 11 August meeting at Vygieskraal there were signs that Pagad's strategy was to target gang bosses and drug merchants. Earlier that month, about 200 Pagad supporters had set fire to a minibus outside the Hanover Park home of Richard 'Pot' Stemmet, a drug dealer. Although this was technically an act of public violence and Stemmet was not harmed, the torching of the minibus was clearly a warning to him and other druglords.

The stadium event was orchestrated to rally community support for Pagad's cause and the next day the organisation issued an ultimatum to the gangs to stop dealing in drugs. The gangs responded by threatening to burn down mosques and disrupt schools – both issues a flashpoint for the Muslim middle class. The state, now shaken from its stupor, banned weapons at public gatherings. Edries, who had promised the police he would call off the march at Staggie's house, was arrested on the serious charge of sedition. This was grist to the mill of Pagad's core supporters, who blew the whistle once again on the authorities being swift to act against those who targeted the gangs but not against the gangs themselves.

Meanwhile, ominous signs were emerging of Pagad's international connection to Islamic radicalism. Much was made in the media of the group's links with Hamas and Hezbollah. These claims turned out to be fuelled by the inflated pronouncements of 'Phantom' Parker, who was eager to ensure Pagad punched above its weight.

In early August, Parker, who was shortly to be forced out of the group for being too tame, had called for a 'jihad' against gangsters. The Iranian embassy, sympathetic to the new democratic administration in Pretoria and eager not to damage ties, was quick to deny connections with Pagad. 'The Iranians clearly had no interest in getting involved despite attempts by Qibla's leaders to make the link,' a police intelligence analyst who was following developments told me.[4]

Throughout September 1996, a series of events crystallised the lines of the conflict. The first of these was within Pagad itself. Numerous reports began to surface that the leadership was divided and that Qibla figures were intent on seizing control from a more moderate group, which included some of the original founders. Parker, despite his statements quoted above, lacked the hard ideological bent of Qibla members such as Abdus-Salaam Ebrahim and privately expressed his concerns about the direction of the organisation. Edries and Parker may also have been sincere in their desire to constrain the crowd outside Staggie's home and, if so, this was a clear demonstration of their more moderate credentials. But both were increasingly being challenged as the movement radicalised.

A tense meeting on 22 September at the Habibia Soofie Mosque in Rylands resulted in the expulsion of three leading figures – Parker, Edries and Farouk Jaffer. The state, perhaps to counter the sentiment that it only targeted Pagad, had withdrawn charges against Edries five days earlier. Given the conspiratorial mood at the nerve centre of Pagad, such a move would have been regarded as suspicious by the hardcore faction. Jaffer, in particular, was viewed with distrust. He had become, in the words of two close observers, 'a loose cannon, flying around the world on unknown missions and issuing statements to the media without consulting the organisation he claimed to represent'.[5]

The immediate cause for the leadership split was Parker's repeated public accusation that Qibla wanted to take control of the movement. At the time, he said his expulsion was because of his 'discovery of Qibla's hidden agenda'. Remarkably, Parker and Jaffer went off and registered a Section 21 company in the name of Pagad, presumably with the idea of creating a legal framework for a more moderate form of the movement. By the end of September, the three outcasts had cut all ties with the original Pagad. Parker, whose life was then repeatedly threatened, survived an assassination attempt in October 1998.

Jaffer, who later turned out to have been working undercover for the state, was not so lucky. Before and after his expulsion he was seen in the company of senior police officers. And earlier, when Pagad supporters clashed with police at Cape Town airport in December 1996, he was reported to have been seen in a police helicopter. He was murdered in July 1999. An intelligence source at the time said: 'Jaffer started helping us a long time ago. But he also advertised his assistance. The hit could be linked to his role.'[6]

In late 1996, with the original more moderate leadership of the organisation now expelled, a radical faction associated with Qibla took charge of Pagad. The outspoken Ebrahim assumed overall control, and although he publicly denied the connection he was widely regarded as a Qibla man and an extremist. The suave and well-spoken businessman Aslam Toefy also took a leading role, as did Sharief Khan and Abdurazak Ebrahim, the latter emerging as a spiritual figure.

At this point the organisation developed a more formal structure, with a national executive, a secretariat and departments covering functional areas including social welfare, security, finance, media and education. What was formed as an 'organic populist movement' turned into a 'kind of vanguard party appealing to local Muslims', in the words of Shamil Jeppie, an academic and observer of events at the time.[7]

Although public expressions of support for Pagad among prominent members of the community declined from this point, it is likely that the group retained significant popular backing. In a survey published in November 1996, a sizable proportion (62%) of Muslim respondents in Cape Town expressed support for Pagad a few months after Staggie's lynching. This was particularly strong among the middle and lower-middle classes. Unsurprisingly, the survey showed much lower levels of support for Pagad among Christians, with a quarter of respondents saying it was a Muslim organisation.[8] Father Clohessy's view was unwavering, however: 'If, as is being claimed, Pagad was from its inception a Qibla initiative, this does not make the initiative any less noble or legitimate,' he said.[9] The statement may have been a genuine measure of his distaste for the harm being wrought by the gangs but it did nothing for his career as a priest; Clohessy was swiftly bundled off by the church to a post in the Vatican.

From late 1996, Pagad's rhetoric began to change. Where once it had used inclusive language appealing for community responses to drug trafficking and gangs, it now adopted more overtly Islamic extremist messaging. The organisation declared a 'jihad against drugs'; the now secret leader of Pagad (although this was presumably to create added mystique, as it was widely known that Ebrahim was in charge) was referred to as an 'emir'; Muslim opponents were labelled *munafiqs* (hypocrites) and non-Muslim opponents as *kaafiers*, or unbelievers. Within months of the Vygieskraal rally, a systematic campaign to assassinate Cape Town's criminal elite would unfold.

The information war

The gangs, too, were going through a period of introspection. If Pagad's new, more extremist approach meant less support in the community, should they not capitalise on this and seek to bolster their support base? At the same time as the early leadership cohort of Pagad was being expelled, gang bosses announced they were forming a united organisation. The grandiosely named Community Outreach Forum, or Core, was conceived by the gang collective as a 'community relations' drive.

Gangsters told journalists at the time that Core was an 'umbrella body' comprising leaders of the most powerful gangs in the province, as well as 'reformed gangsters' (a term used even when there was evidence that the 'reformed' elements remained attached to the criminal economy). Emulating Pagad, Core supporters marched on parliament. Remarkably, as they gathered and gyrated outside the people's legislature, the gangsters did not deny their involvement in the criminal economy. Rather, and without a hint of irony, they called on 'present and previous governments' to 'accept responsibility for them turning to crime'.[10]

Other surprising developments were in store. On 9 October, the Hard Livings and the Americans, the city's biggest criminal gangs, who continually clashed violently, said they were disbanding to embrace peace under the Core banner. The response to this public relations exercise, then and now, was general cynicism. No serious observer believed the gangs would lay down arms; there was too much money at stake. Most viewed it as an attempt to reconfigure their operations while seeking wider legitimacy with politicians and the public.

But the extent to which the gangs were willing to make public announcements like this, even if they were patently disingenuous, suggested the Pagad threat had hit the mark and led to some strategising about how organised crime needed to manoeuvre for survival. The gangs' strategy was perhaps surprising: by openly blaming the government for the fact that gangsters felt compelled to turn to crime, they were ironically reinforcing the Pagad narrative that the government was not doing enough to ensure societal security. But it also provided an opportunity to shift the blame for their criminal activities, like a court defence of bad parenting for a juvenile offender.

That the opposing parties both blamed the government says something about the nature of the new democracy and the institutional levers now controlled by the ANC. With so much responsibility placed on it, the government seemed stymied. The first target of state action was Pagad, again reinforcing the narrative that the state somehow cushioned the gangs – who were in any event showing little fear by turning up in front of parliament to blame the state for their plight.

The government also faced a growing sense in the press (and among a group of policy advisers in the Ministry of Safety and Security) that the state needed to signal it was in control, and foreign unease that Pagad reflected an Islamic terrorism threat emerging in South Africa (something the ANC was particularly keen to counter). One result of these emerging challenges was that the police could not be seen simply to allow armed marches to proceed. The government responded by banning firearms at public gatherings and the police no longer tolerated disguises or head-coverings at marches; offenders were arrested under apartheid-era legislation, the 1969 Prohibition of Disguises Act. That again fed the Pagad narrative that nothing much had changed in two years of democracy.

As 1996 ended, the conflict between Pagad and the state escalated. The police clashed openly with Pagad protesters at the V&A Waterfront. The brother of a Muslim cleric was fatally shot and allegations surfaced that the Qibla-led faction of Pagad had deliberately provoked the shooting (see Chapter 5). Angered at press coverage that labelled the organisation as fundamentalist, Pagad called for a boycott of the city's morning newspaper, the *Cape Times*.

Disagreements about the wearing of masks and the open carrying of firearms scuppered any attempts at mediation between state and Pagad representatives, with each side accusing the other of not wanting a resolution. In the midst of all of this, Ebrahim was arrested, souring relations further. On 16 December, a holiday designated as the Day of Reconciliation, Pagad staged an illegal protest outside Cape Town International Airport. Previously the group had applied to the authorities to conduct protests so the message was clear: no more would Pagad seek permission from the state to 'defend' the community.

The purpose of the airport protest was to draw attention to the government's responsibility to stem the flow of drugs through major entry points. (Cape Town airport, ironically, unlike Johannesburg, had never had a reputation as a drugs gateway.) Several Pagad members were arrested, and when these arrests were contested with another protest outside Bellville Magistrates' Court, five police officers were shot. The police then took off the gloves and let rip, accusing Pagad of being 'just another gang' and 'part of the crime problem'.[11] It is unlikely such statements would have been made without prior political approval.

Shifts were also occurring in the Muslim community, where there was growing unease about the violence and strong language emanating from Pagad. In August, as mentioned, the MJC had expressed support for Pagad and subsequently attended the Vygieskraal rally and, alongside Qibla, endorsed Pagad's objectives. But now it started to get cold feet. After the march at the V&A Waterfront and the subsequent shooting of the police, the MJC, the Call of Islam and the Islamic Council of South Africa called on Pagad to 'mobilise public awareness' but 'without violating any laws'.[12] It was a not-so-subtle signal that the MJC, under pressure from multiple sides – including the government – was beginning to step away from the movement.

All these pronouncements suggest just how important the information war was for Pagad, the gangs and the government itself. Each – although arguably the state at this stage was the clunkiest – was trying to shape a narrative explanation of the past and the present. Pagad, in particular, showed itself to be a sophisticated purveyor of messaging and each time the organisation was targeted, be it by the government or the gangs, it was turned into a news-ready opportunity to remind the public that the state was on the side of the gangsters, not the good.

Killing the merchants

Pagad's public marches and announcements were now matched by a more sinister turn to targeted and hidden violence. From January 1997 there was an uptick in the assassination of prominent criminal figures. Such underworld people go under multiple names in Cape Town – they are 'bosses', 'druglords' or, more respectfully, 'merchants', a nod to their entrepreneurial side. Whatever their label, they were now Pagad's targets. Over the next few years there was a regular drumbeat of ganglord killings; the old-school criminal elite, gang royalty and some newer ones were picked off by Pagad assassins.

Individuals involved in the shootings told me the killings reached a quick tempo as small assassination squads operated night after night at the height of the campaign in 1998 and 1999. I estimate that over two to three years, between 30 and 40 key gang bosses or senior gangsters were killed, and well over a hundred lower-ranking members. These numbers are speculative but the result was clear: a cohort of older, widely known gang figures, many of whom had risen through the ranks in the 1980s and early 1990s, were eliminated. Lower-level and emerging leaders were also targeted, so gang leadership responsibility in some cases fell to more violent and unruly young men.

From a strategic perspective, these assassinations served a few purposes. The killings were carried out in secret and Pagad never claimed responsibility, leaving it open to the interpretation that the ganglords might have been killing each other. Rumours also swirled – and still do – that the police were carrying out hits against gangsters. Pagad statements about the shootings were deliberately ambiguous, although it would have been clear enough to the communities affected who had done the work.

The who and the how of the killings were tightly guarded secrets in Pagad, but it is evident that they were carried out by a small number of hit squads, separate from the wider organisation. (I will examine this in more detail later in the book.) Assassinations were generally preceded by warnings, usually in the form of a telephone call from an unlisted number or a visit. If the threatened gangster did not halt his activities, as was inevitably the case – even though several claimed they had left the business – a hit squad was dispatched.

It's a woman's job

One of the first prominent gang bosses to die at the hands of Pagad was an unusual case. It was unorthodox because she was a woman in a distinctly male world and one of the few women at the top of the city's gang hierarchy. Katy-Ann Arendse and Faried 'Keusie' Davids had been movers and shakers in the formation of The Firm drug cartel and they managed a complex criminal operation encompassing extortion, drugs, prostitution and legal and illegal drinking houses, known as shebeens.

A police intelligence report compiled in 1996, two years before Arendse's death, listed her as a major drug distributor.[13] As a foundation for the business and a vehicle to launder money, she ran a network of shebeens. Upwardly mobile, she also owned property in the fancy suburb of Plattekloof.[14]

Like the handful of other powerful female gang leaders in Cape Town, Arendse rose on the shoulders of her husband, Chris 'Langkop' Arendse. Langkop was a notoriously violent gangland figure from Elsies River, a bleak and poverty-stricken housing settlement. After he was sent to prison (where he assumed the rank of general in the 26s Numbers gang), his wife stepped into his shoes and assumed his no-nonsense and violent disposition. (Unusually for a boss in the violent gangland environment of Cape Town, where not many in the business survive into old age, Langkop is still around, although dogged by health problems.)

Divorcing Langkop, Arendse hitched up with 'Keusie' Davids and the couple sold drugs in partnership with Colin Stanfield of the 28s. She also appeared to dabble in fraud, and like several other gang bosses who started out in Cape Town, by the 1990s she began to travel widely to expand her criminal interests. 'We looked up to her like you can't believe,' a general in the 27s told me. 'She went to Joburg all the time. Joburg for us was like a foreign country then. It was like going overseas.'[15]

In March 1998, Arendse and Davids were killed in a professional hit that caught them unawares in their car outside a relative's house in Heideveld. Hitting victims in their cars became something of a signature modus operandi for the Pagad death squads.

Given the large cast of VIP criminal figures in the city, why Arendse was singled out as one of the first to be targeted after Staggie's lynching is not clear. Perhaps she was viewed as an easy target, or her association with The Firm made her a justifiable one. In any case, her death was followed by the striking out of several others of the city's criminal elite.

By far the most prominent of these was Jackie Lonte, also known as Jakkals (the fox), whose real name was Neville Heroldt. Lonte was the father of the Americans gang, South Africa's largest, and a pioneer of the country's criminal economy. He grew his illegal business in the 1980s on the back of the dagga and Mandrax trade, and by the end of the decade he was an established criminal kingpin in the city, a Porsche-driving wheeler-dealer with a serious cocaine habit. When trade barriers were lifted after 1994, Lonte was behind the sourcing of exotic new drugs such as Ecstasy and acid to feed the country's burgeoning party scene.

Lonte's innovation lay in how he created the symbols that communicated the Americans' power. Even his backyard shed where the gang's strategy was mapped out was labelled the 'White House'. The Americans' strategy was to mark out gang territory across Cape Town and appoint local leaders, allowing a dispersed operation that raked in profits while ensuring the gang's tentacles reached into every suburb. Lonte was not shy of violence and under him the Americans gunned their way to a greater share of the drug market. The gang also worked to ensure operations were resilient in the face of police crackdowns through a strategic campaign to co-opt officers who were willing to be corrupted.

By the late 1990s, Lonte seemed to be reconsidering his way of life. In 1998 he announced his retirement from criminal activities, perhaps because he wanted to take the Pagad heat off him. The fox must have known he was being hunted. A few months earlier, Ferrel Human, described as Lonte's main lieutenant, was hit by ten bullets outside a hardware store in Manenberg. But Lonte also had cancer and word was that he wanted to put things right with his maker. Either way, there seemed little doubt he would also be targeted. He was too big a fish to be allowed to get away. The inevitable happened and he was gunned down outside his brother's house in Athlone in November 1998.

Dead dogs

Rashaad Staggie may have died in public, spontaneously set ablaze in front of a Pagad mob, but Lonte and Arendse died in targeted killings that bore all the features of well-planned professional hits. The way these murders were executed signified how the war against the gangs had shifted. They symbolised the end of one era and the beginning of something distinctly new.

A week after Lonte succumbed, and with the city's underworld still reeling in shock, Ernie 'Lapepa' Peters – leader of the 28s in Belhar – met his maker. With typical gangland humour, the diminutive Peters was nicknamed 'Big Man'. But what he lacked in size Peters made up for in the scale of his violence. He terrorised communities in areas where he managed drug outlets. With Rashied Staggie and Colin Stanfield, Peters was one of the founders of Core.[16] But his brand of community outreach had a twist: it was standard Lapepa practice to advance drugs to community members, then threaten violence to secure payment. Once, to send a message, he savagely beat to death a woman who owed him money. Peters was widely feared – a 'sociopath', as several of my contacts with memories of the period told me. Justice took its painful course: his assassination was not cleanly administered and Peters hung on for a week in a hospital intensive care unit.

If Jackie Lonte was all flash – fast cars, beautiful women and lines of cocaine – Bobby Mongrel (real name Ismail April) went everywhere with his dogs. The gang he led, the Mongrels, was a hardcore street outfit. It was also one of the longest-established gangs in Cape Town, originating in District Six in the 1960s as one of the so-called corner gangs, which were more like clubs operating in the grey economy than hardcore criminal operations. The Mongrels, like many gangs at the time, found new energy in the rough and tumble of the 1990s when they aggressively seized a segment of the drug market and defended it viciously.

Gang boss Ernie 'Lapepa' Peters's home turf was in Belhar, where he ran a drinking establishment widely known to be a drug house. Peters was influential in acting as a facilitator bringing opposing gangs together as Pagad's campaign of violence unfolded. No stranger to administering violence himself, Peters was killed in November 1998. PICTURE: Benny Gool

Bobby Mongrel, a criminal innovator in his own right, was key to managing these developments. Like Lonte, who used branding to build gang cohesion, he grasped the importance of portraying a widely recognisable criminal persona. He travelled around with his three large dogs, all carefully chosen mixed breeds to align with his gang's name. 'When there were gang fights and the dogs were on the field,' said a now ageing one-time gangster, 'then we knew Bobby Mongrel was around. The dogs would catch you and he would chop you up.'[17] 'Feral' is how two journalists described the Mongrels in the late 1990s.[18]

In Cape Town's gangland environment, where violence seemed to ooze from every pore, Mongrel developed a reputation for taking things to even higher levels. In one gruesome account, he used the serrated metal circumference of a tin can to carve the image of a dog into the flesh of a gang member who had committed some minor infraction. In another, in a dispute linked to the payment of a drug debt, he cut off his victim's penis, opened his belly, stuffed it in and had the incision sewn up. These sorts of stories circulated on the Cape Flats and Bobby Mongrel was – naturally – widely feared.[19]

Like most gang bosses, he blended violence with a certain amount of charm. He was tall, dark and handsome, with an impressive set of tattoos and a mouth full of gold teeth. And he had a following: his street creed emphasised that you need to stand alone, something that struck a chord among young men with few prospects on the violent edges of the city.[20]

Like Lonte, Mongrel was killed in November 1998, shot dead in a professional-style assassination outside his house in Grassy Park. After the killing his gang seemed to go wild and went through a period of bloodletting while contesting factions fought for control.

The Cisco Yakkies also started out as a corner gang, and the story of how it grew to become a widespread criminal organisation is a familiar one. During the 1980s, fuelled by the lucrative drugs and prostitution markets, the gang expanded, cementing its position first in Athlone then across the Cape Flats in Bonteheuwel, Delft, Elsies River, Mitchells Plain, Blue Downs, Belgravia and Parkwood. Reflecting the influx of a new generation of recruits, the gang is today known as the Junior Cisco Yakkies. Its influence stretches well beyond Cape Town to Boland towns including Worcester.[21]

Managing the growth of the gang over this period were three brothers, the Khans, and by the late 1990s they were established criminal figures (although they had stepped back from day-to-day management of the gang). Pagad seemed to have a particular beef with the Cisco Yakkies, and in late 1998 the gang's ranking leader, Achmat 'Amatie' Thomas, was gunned down outside a mosque. Thomas was considered to be a big-time drug dealer, aggressively clashing with other gangs over turf. But the real targets of the Pagad hit squads were the Khan trio, symbols of criminal success.

The eldest brother, Glen Khan, was widely known across the Cape Flats. A handsome man with the tattoos that characterised older-generation gangsters, Khan was a hit with women. 'A lot of ladies stayed with him and he had kids with many different women,' a community worker told me.[22]

He managed a string of drug houses and spaza shops, and pioneered the local extortion economy, forcing businesses to pay a toll in areas where he had muscle and dominated drug markets. While he used violence when necessary – 'He came across as a gentleman but was cruel-minded,' said the community worker[23] – Khan and his brothers also had a philanthropic side to their operations. In areas where the Yakkies sold drugs, the Khans took pains to garner community support by helping with cash handouts and other forms of support. This was perhaps one reason why Pagad viewed Glen Khan as an important target, despite his retirement from active gang life.

Khan was attacked in February 1999. He escaped with his life but Pagad killed his wife. Two months later, Khan was murdered while sitting in his car with three bodyguards. Pagad also dispatched his daughter, Chantine Veldsman, and her boyfriend, Jerome Petersen, a henchman for the Khans. Glen Khan and his immediate family ceased to exist.

When gang members refer to a leader's 'panel', they mean the crew close to him, his confidants, and these are often the men who do the dirty work of dispatching errant members or the opposition. Rashaad and Rashied Staggie's Hard Livings panel was whittled away in a series of assassinations. In April 1998, Leon 'Chippy' Achilles, the gang's second-in-command, met his end in Woodstock. Earlier in the year, Ivan Oliver, another Staggie panel member (and reputed hitman) was killed, shot in his car as per standard practice. Oliver's murder may have had revenge value, as he was said to have shot at Pagad members after Rashaad's murder.

Bookends

One of the first prominent gang leaders killed by Pagad was a woman, Katy-Ann Arendse, and the targeted assassination campaign began to wind down, symmetrically, with the murder of another powerful woman merchant. They formed female bookends in the vigilantes' campaign. Adiela 'Mama Africa' Davids was murdered in April 1999. Like Arendse, she challenged the notion that Cape gangsterism was a man's world. In the mythology of the Americans, women such as Davids were figures of liberty – a reference to the Statue of Liberty – who 'bear the fruit, keep the gang alive and protect its members'.[24]

Davids owned a hairdressing salon where she met her end (the blood-spattered walls discernible in court photographs a stark reminder of the violence with which she was dispatched). She also managed a network of drug houses and shebeens with her husband, the prominent Americans Hanover Park gang leader Sanie 'Oog'. (His real name was Igshaan Marcus and he was killed in December 2021 in a drug turf dispute with the Ghetto Kids gang.) Davids's status was also evident from the fact that she was referred to by a code name. She could call upon a network of hitmen to dispatch unruly Americans members or those affiliated to opposing gangs, and she did not have any qualms about procuring their services.

When it extracted revenge, as was the case with Glen Khan's family, Pagad not only killed Davids but also her daughter, Feroza Marcus, and her niece, Marlene Abrahams. In revenge, Igshaan Marcus, Davids's stepson, killed the son of a prominent Pagad member. Marcus then fled and went into hiding but he was killed in Athlone in 2019.

These killings all took their toll on Cape Town's gangland leadership. Ivan Waldeck, one-time leader of the Ugly Americans who later became a pastor, often acted as an intermediary between gang bosses and the outside world. He spoke publicly at the time of the assassination campaign: 'The gangsters are scared and that's what makes them so dangerous. Tell me a person who is not scared to die.'[25]

Gangsters could not necessarily even look to their families for support. Rashaad Staggie's mother had said she was not dissatisfied with her son's death 'but the manner [in which it was done]'.[26] That statement may have been an attempt to fend off other attacks on the family but it also highlighted the fears of many in gangland in the face of the cruelty and unpredictability of the death squads' campaign. The gangs were thrown into confusion by the intensity of the strikes in 1998 and 1999. No gang leader could behave any longer like Staggie had, defiantly swearing in mosques.

Several prominent gang bosses left town: Colin Stanfield relocated to Pretoria and Rashied Staggie to Durban. In reality, these 'highflyers' (a term regularly used in police reporting) were already building a national infrastructure, so Pagad's assassination campaign probably merely expedited this process.[27]

The seemingly random killing of elite gang figures across Cape Town was not random. It was the result of a specific form of politics developing within Pagad and a system of targeting kingpins that was both highly organised and reliant on the initiative of a network of ruthless killers.

5

THE POLITICS OF ASSASSINATION

After the killing of Rashaad Staggie in 1996 and the leadership split between Qibla hardliners and the more 'moderate' community vigilante faction that was expelled, Pagad's campaign took a more confrontational turn against the state. On the streets, anger about the impact of gangsterism and drugs in the Cape was still raw, and in a bid to take advantage of this sentiment and harness popular support Pagad turned to a man with wide legitimacy, Aslam Toefy, one of the organisation's founders.

At the time, the degree to which the old-order Pagad still held on to its support base is demonstrated by the efforts of ex-leader Ali 'Phantom' Parker to mobilise an alternative structure. Making one last bid for popular support, he organised a meeting of supporters in Kensington in the weeks after he was ejected. It was a courageous move. The original Pagad, the brand represented by Parker and his allies, was still widely seen as an organisation that could take down the gangs in a context where the state's enforcement agencies were regarded as compromised. But only 200 people showed up. Phantom's efforts were doomed to fail and he faced serious threats to his life for his impertinence. As for Pagad, now led by the radical Abdus-Salaam Ebrahim, a more ambitious and confrontational agenda was not long in arriving.

Toefy was now the public face of Pagad, and on 3 November 1996 he fronted a bold mass meeting to promote its anti-drug efforts in a highly public setting, the V&A Waterfront. Toefy was involved in Pagad's early days when it was a 'unifying force in a fractured Muslim community', in the words of a former police officer who worked in an intelligence capacity.[1] He was related by marriage to the MJC president and appeared to have broad support, so he was pushed upwards to provide a more acceptable face for the organisation. Later, as Pagad-inspired violence mounted, and under pressure from the MJC to leave, Toefy withdrew.[2]

Shrewd, well dressed and well spoken, Toefy has never struck me as an ideologue, nor was he a member of Qibla. Whereas others within the

Pagad networks were secretive and reluctant to speak, Toefy was open and forthcoming. Regardless, there is no disguising his hatred of gangs and drugs. Like many members and former members of Pagad, he expressed this loathing by providing an example of his own family's experience when his son was threatened by a gangster. 'We are not going to allow this to happen to our children,' he insisted. 'We are focused only on the truth and suffering of our people.'[3] By the time he was in a leadership position in late 1996, Toefy's statements had taken on a harder edge: 'We are fighting the police's inability to deal with the problem of drugs and will apply pressure on them. We will show them how to deal with crime.'[4]

The making of a martyr

In selecting a place to amplify Pagad's message to a wider audience, the V&A Waterfront was an inspired choice: it is the hub of the city's tourism economy and one of the most visited shopping precincts on the African continent. And it would become the setting for several key turning points in the Pagad story, including the Planet Hollywood bombing.

This meeting was one of the first occasions when Pagad mobilised beyond the Cape Flats and the authorities specifically asked members not to bring their guns. The rhetoric of the new leadership was clear and strongly supported by the crowd. The message they conveyed was that there was a drug problem in South Africa and the world should know, hence the venue; and that neither the government nor the police were interested in solving the problem. In fact, the police were an instrument of repression against law-abiding people.[5]

Things quickly got out of hand. The police used teargas and apparently charged the crowd to disperse it. Gunshots went off and several arrests were made. In the melee, Achmat Najaar, brother of Sheik Thafier Najaar of the Islamic Council of South Africa, was killed by a gunshot. The police were widely blamed and a huge funeral for Najaar was used to mobilise Pagad supporters. It was a defining and widely remembered moment in the history of the organisation. But the details about who discharged the gunshot that killed Najaar have never been established.

As Anneli Botha, a police intelligence analyst at the time, has noted, although Pagad blamed the police for his death, Najaar was shot by a 7.65 mm calibre firearm, whereas the police never resorted to live ammunition at this event, discharging only rubber bullets. (When the police did use live rounds, they were generally 9 mm.)[6]

There were also rumours, spelt out in a letter to the police that found its way to the media, that Pagad had killed one of their own and 'the death of Mr Najaar was well planned by several Muslim organisations to provide "them" with a martyr'.[7] Fivaz himself stated that 'undisciplined elements' within Pagad had killed Najaar.[8] Najaar was formally declared a martyr on his burial, which took place in a carefully choreographed and well-attended ceremony.

The killing of Najaar has remained shrouded in mystery. But one man who was at the centre of events at the time claimed to know the truth. Boeta Yu (real name Yusuf Williams) was one of the wizened veterans of

Masked members of Pagad fire into the air in a military-style salute at the funeral of Achmat Najaar on 4 November 1996. Najaar was shot dead during a Pagad protest at the V&A Waterfront the day before in a case that remains unresolved. PICTURE: Mike Hutchings, Reuters

Pagad's campaign of violence against the gangs. As befits his status in the veterans' group, I never heard Williams referred to by his real name. 'Boeta' means 'older brother' or 'uncle', denoting a widely respected older man who looks out for others. He died in July 2022, having lived into his eighties. When I met him, he retained a passion for countering gangs and drugs, the glint in his eyes a reminder that this old man's generous and open exterior concealed a heart of steel. It was he who was rumoured to have thrown the petrol bomb that set Rashaad Staggie alight.

Boeta Yu was Pagad's security coordinator when its campaign of violence against drug merchants was at its height, so he was right at the centre of events. That makes him an impeccable source as to the internal happenings in the organisation.

A former police intelligence officer told me that Boeta Yu was not particularly political and definitely not linked to Qibla. 'He was too old to be politicised. But, like others, he was attracted to the idea of striking at the gangs. He developed a close relationship with Abdus-Salaam [Ebrahim]. He was quite a charismatic person.'[9] Boeta Yu helped the combative and increasingly powerful Ebrahim to build a relationship with a network of younger people, and he was the intermediary between Ebrahim and the Pagad cells and wider networks.

As the state later scrambled to dismantle Pagad's violent capacity, Boeta Yu was arrested in December 1999. He was finally released in May 2005 after his conviction had been overturned. He recalled:

> When they arrested me, the NIA [Pagad members often said the NIA even when it may have been police conducting interrogations] tortured me to the point where they made me say a few things ... I said something like, maybe I was close by when something happened, or that I knew about something that happened, but I never mentioned anyone's names ... You understand they tortured me and threatened to hurt my wife and children while I was detained.[10]

He signed a statement, upon which Ebrahim declared him *munafiq* and various cells were ordered to kill him. It was another key character, Ebrahim Jeneker, whom we are shortly to encounter, who then stepped in, sending the message that anyone who touched Boeta Yu would themselves be killed with their wives and children.

Until the end, Boeta Yu decried Pagad's shift towards radicalism and the bombing of civilian targets. That did not mean he did not actively participate in the killing of gangsters and police (it is highly likely he was directly involved in the killing of a prominent detective[11]), but he remained deeply socially conservative and he was strongly opposed to the bombing of innocent civilians. He also became incensed by what Pagad operatives were being instructed to do:

> Pagad was bombing mosques and targeting our own members. I was asked to incite a slander campaign against the imam of the Gatesville mosque. They didn't like the imam because of his honesty and commitment to the ideals of the Quran.[12]

Boeta Yu had a speech impediment and was hard to understand but he was clear on one issue: the killing of Achmat Najaar at the V&A Waterfront in November 1996, he believed, was a Pagad operation all along:

> I was there when the hit was ordered ... [They] felt threatened by him maybe [because he was] someone who had strong leadership characteristics. Najaar's brother was an excellent speaker and he was rising up the ranks ... Many people really liked him and pegged him for a future leadership position. This was only one of the cracks that started to happen inside Pagad.[13]

Boeta Yu was central to the establishment of a breakaway group, also to be called G-Force, when Pagad members returned from prison from 2010 onwards after the state's campaign against the organisation.

A (shrinking) foot in every place

The death of Najaar signalled a new period of mobilisation. Pagad supporters were incensed that a prominent and inspirational member of the movement had been killed, with the finger being pointed at the police. But if it was a conspiratorial internally ordered killing, which seems to be the case from Boeta Yu's account, it showed the distorted and violent streak that was emerging. If Pagad, now increasingly under Qibla-aligned management, was to wage a low-level war with the state, it needed to become an organisation that would enable this. Indeed, as the Najaar killing and events around it suggested, two Pagads were taking shape simultaneously: a public-facing, seemingly well-organised and structured version, and a secret, violent and increasingly fragmenting core.

Pagad's formal structure presented an impressive system of organisation and representation. There was a national executive overseeing countrywide operations and a central coordination committee in the Western Cape that planned most activities. There were also functional departments, including a secretariat responsible for administration; a legal department providing support to arrested members and responding to police actions such as raids; a social welfare department which, among other tasks, educated community members about drugs; and a medical unit to assist members who sustained injuries. Crucially, too, a security and operations department was established to be responsible for activities and security in neighbourhoods where Pagad members lived. This reported to a grandly named 'security council'.[14]

On the face of it, Pagad seemed to be a professional organisation formed as a community response mechanism by a group of self-sufficient and committed people. But there was a darker side; at heart, it had evolved into an extremely violent organisation. While the formal structure was key to the movement's operations, the tasking and execution of violence fell to an underground network, which became known as the G-Force. The organisation had two faces.

In early 1998, a provincial Crime Intelligence report noted: 'Despite attempts within Pagad to formally structure the organisation and collectively control its support base to date, it is still primarily a fragmented collection of leadership and fiefdoms with individual leaders initiating the violent activities of the G-Force against drug dealers and gangsters impulsively.'[15] In short, the public-facing organisation belied a more complex, hidden reality: Pagad was riven with internal conflict. In the underbelly of the organisation, pressure from the police and internal disagreements and suspicions meant clear lines of command and control were never fully established. As a result, operatives dwindled to a small number of hardcore activists, and their targets and the ideological imprint of the organisation shifted.

Pagad's security capacity was originally founded on a broad-based appeal. A decision had been made that the organisation needed a wide geographic reach, so cells – small groups of members operating in specific areas – were established across Cape Town. They were meant to be clandestine so as not to attract attacks from gangs or the attention of the police. The cell network was also intended to ensure resilience: if one part of the organisation was compromised by the gangs or the state, others would be untouched.

While Pagad had thousands of rank-and-file members, its hardcore battalion of violent operatives probably never consisted of more than about 120 people. An active member of Pagad described how it worked: 'The cells together had a lot of people because there was one in each community ... but that does not mean that everyone in the cell was doing the type of work that we were doing. Everyone had a role. Many were there because they filled up the marches and they gave support in that way.'[16] Any cell might have 15 to 20 active members, of whom only three or four would be deployed in violent operations.

The Pagad security structure had a strong extremist imprint from the beginning. For example, I was told that cell leaders were chosen on the merit of possessing the strength of character within the paradigm of *mujahideen* – meaning those who fight on behalf of Allah. That meant these were people who would have to 'kill for the cause and be ready to give themselves to the cause without hesitation'.[17]

Pagad faced the challenge of any rapidly growing organisation. Cells grew, which led to security challenges. And because there were many people in the cells, it was difficult to establish who was trustworthy, say insiders.[18] There were the possibilities that cells would be penetrated by the state and that they would not always operate according to centrally imposed principles or ethical guidelines.

The most obvious temptation was money. Druglords often stashed substantial amounts of cash in their homes, providing a temptation for those on anti-gang operations. An former Pagad executive member said: 'It is difficult to know who was sincere, who was *mujahideen* ... some would rob the [gangs'] houses because it was a free ride, because the merchants all had money in their properties and lots of other things that you could take, like their cars and guns and bullets.'[19]

Many Pagad recruits, while enthusiastic, were middle-class men who were not prepared for the levels of violence and killing that began to occur. Understandably, they often shrank from the task. As a result the cell structure, building on the relatively few who proved themselves capable of violence, effectively morphed into a smaller number of harder-core and more reliable members, which became the G-Force. This killing unit operated in area-based cells, effectively replacing the wider organisation that had constituted Pagad's geographic footprint. While still within Pagad's overall command structure, the system became more secretive and the cells more independent, with greater capacity for initiating their own operations. In short, as Pagad's ideology changed under its emerging leadership, it contracted in size but grew in violent reach.

At its height, the G-Force operated in about 20 cells across the city, mainly taking direction from the secret Tuesday meetings of the security council. Decisions on whom to attack and when were left to individual cells, meaning different cells sometimes found they were targeting the same drug merchant or gang boss. An active member of the Grassy Park cell at the time said: 'We went to do surveillance on a target once and we found another team there doing the same thing. So we went up to them to find out what was happening, and then we left and let them do the job because they were there first.'[20]

Jeremy Vearey, then commander of police intelligence coordination in the Western Cape, noted at the time the direction cell structures would take: 'There is very little centralised control ... and the energy unleashed by the Pagad cause could reproduce itself in a pattern of militancy with a life of its own independent of direct structural ties to Pagad.'[21] It was a prescient observation.

Paranoia and fracture

Underground work breeds paranoia, and the G-Force was constantly on guard against the risk of being penetrated by external agents. Arrests in late 1997 seemed to indicate the state had a better handle on the membership of the force than many in Pagad had suspected. Worryingly for Pagad, around this time the gang umbrella organisation Core had compiled a list containing the personal particulars of 40 G-Force operatives and other prominent members of Pagad. This list fell into Pagad's hands.

Great care had been taken to keep the secret operational side of Pagad under wraps, so the fact that the gangs had a better knowledge of who was active in Pagad than many within the movement itself was deeply unsettling. It suggested the sophistication of the gangs' intelligence systems, raising the distinct possibility that the movement, specifically its supposedly secret cell structure, had been penetrated by the gangs – or, worse, that the state was passing information to the gangs.

This development, combined with the movement's internal ideological tensions and conflict, meant the capacity of the G-Force shrank. Perhaps more importantly, it meant the organisation's systems of oversight and governance of its violent capacity became even more eroded.

Pagad's leadership was slowly losing control of the movement, and making matters worse was the factionalism caused by the rift between Abdus-Salaam Ebrahim, Pagad's operational head, and Abdurazak Ebrahim, its spiritual emir. The security council, under whose command the G-Force was meant to act, became dysfunctional and stopped meeting. Pagad effectively splintered into two centres of power. On one side was Abdus-Salaam and a small group that included Aslam Toefy; and on the other was Abdurazak. The reason for the split hinged on the deployment of the G-Force, with Abdurazak accusing Abdus-Salaam of using the armed wing to go after targets without proper consultation.

Abdurazak Ebrahim was a widely respected and charismatic leader. A deeply religious man, he also had a sharp eye for the symbolic aspects of building a brand. He covered his face in public, giving his persona a mysterious, otherworldly feel. He arrived at meetings in an expensive Mercedes-Benz surrounded by bodyguards, like a dignitary. 'Whenever he spoke at rallies,' said a long-time member of Pagad, 'he commanded everyone's attention and spoke with passion about Islam and society's ideals. … He was never a man for ego because his face was always covered, but women would swoon over him because of his voice and the content of his speeches.'[22]

Abdurazak was uncompromising about who should be the strategic targets of Pagad's operations. In a video shot before Rashaad Staggie's murder in 1996, he stated: 'We saw what happened in Afghanistan and Russia, where a military superpower was defeated by a handful of *mujahideen* … so let us embark on this programme with full commitment to the cause of Allah. They [the drug dealers] are destroying our communities. They are running rampant in our societies. The time is over. The time for talk is over. Now is the time for us to do. The time for us to move into actions. Time for us to wipe this scum from our earth and from our society.'[23] At the same time, he was appalled by how the focus of the campaign had been widened to include civilian targets.

Pagad members say Abdurazak Ebrahim did not resign as much as simply disappear from the scene. The man he fell out with, Abdus-Salaam, emerges as a complicated and highly flawed figure in the history of Pagad. Ideologically 'less coherent' than Qibla founder and leader Achmad Cassiem, Abdus-Salaam was regarded as 'a good orator and organiser' and had, like Cassiem, undergone military training during the liberation struggle.[24] But his personality seemed to warp as Pagad's struggle became more extremist with the targeting of state officials and civilians, and he took greater control: 'He was not necessarily like that when he was younger because he started off as a nice guy,' said an insider who knows him well.[25]

Yet there is little doubt that he had the ability to mobilise and influence people. When I met him, during a discussion with a group of Pagad's executive committee in September 2021, he commanded the room. Many would have readily empathised with Pagad representatives in settings like this – they were, after all, passionately vociferous about the damage drugs and gangs had wrought on their communities, while artfully sidestepping questions about violence or suggesting that Pagad had not in fact been violent. As the meeting warmed up, Ebrahim, who had been sitting quietly, took the floor. A small, compact man whose body seems to exude pent-up energy, he expounded on the ideology and activities of Pagad. As he held forth, the rest of the committee fell silent. It was clear how his personality could exert a wide influence.

There can be little doubt that Ebrahim was a fast-talking, though not always coherent, ideologue who began to shape the activities of Pagad from 1997, a period that aligned with the ramping up of its violence; but he was also a highly divisive figure. 'Abdus does not keep guys around him for long: he finds fault with you, and if he doesn't he will scratch until he does, especially if you outshine him or think of something that he could not think of, then you are a big problem to him,' said a member who worked closely with him.[26] A senior member of the post-2010 G-Force described him as 'a cancer' eating away at the institutional cohesion of Pagad.[27] (For their part, the current Pagad leadership describe the breakaway G-Force members as criminals now involved in drug trafficking and extortion.)

Abdus-Salaam Ebrahim, the charismatic and fast-talking leader of Pagad, who did the most to shape the organisation. He was later to fall out with many of Pagad's key violent operatives. PICTURE: Esa Alexander, Media24

Ebrahim's corrosive influence was initially masked because he commanded genuine respect. Finally, some within Pagad made an active break with him but that took many years, including the period when the core group of violent actors were imprisoned together. Indeed, prison seemed to be a defining moment for many Pagad operatives in their relationship with Ebrahim. In confinement he seemed to lose his gloss, becoming a weak and vulnerable old man longing for the comforts of home. The killers he recruited were a tougher and more resilient crowd and they expected the same from their leader. When that turned out not to be the case, many expressed genuine shock.

One of the casualties of Ebrahim's leadership style appeared to be Achmad Cassiem, a development that undercut explanations that Pagad was simply a tool of Qibla. A member of the post-2010 G-Force said: 'There were Qibla members who were part of Pagad, in fact many of them started Pagad with us. But many of them left after their leader, Imam Cassiem, and Abdus-Salaam had a falling out … It was Abdus's paranoia that destroyed his relationship with Imam Cassiem and Qibla as a whole.'[28]

Inevitably, too, money was a source of conflict. Frontline operatives were told to hand in the money and drugs they seized. What rankled was that there was no transparency about how these resources were used. 'Abdus-Salaam wanted all the money himself,' claimed an original G-Force member from the late 1990s. 'Only he could decide how it was going to be disbursed. We would send the money back into the Muslim community because we wanted to build the communities, and we also sent the money to our fallen brothers in prison so that we could help them, because they worked for the struggle and gave their lives and family lives to the cause … so we had to help them. But,' he emphasised, gesticulating, 'Abdus-Salaam did not want that. He wanted all the money to himself.'[29]

I have no doubt that money was a motivating factor for at least some Pagad members, and that the prerogative of economic self-gain led to the later targeting of businessmen for extortion. It also underlies the accusation made by what is left of mainstream Pagad that the breakaway groups were just criminals motivated by material gain. Over time, Pagad activities targeting a local drugs economy awash with cash seemed to descend into a sordid, profit-driven business.

A 'third force'

All that was in the future, however. In 1997 Ebrahim commanded respect, many hiding their misgivings out of fear or the general threat they felt as the campaign intensified. As Pagad's violent activities unspooled, several things happened at the same time.

The group deployed to carry out the violent attacks and hits diminished in size but commitment increased among those who remained. They became trapped in a cage of their own justification, increasingly seeing the state as a threat, particularly state actors who were seen to act in a murky conspiracy with the gangs. Ebrahim was central to this way of thinking, which made its mark on naive, often impressionable young men eager to help the cause. As a newspaper opinion piece at the time concluded: 'While Pagad's leaders are perversely intelligent individuals with a hard core of defiant supporters who are normally a few chromosomes short of being garden furniture, most of them are driven by a blind rage and are clueless about the subtleties of religious discourse.'[30]

That was written in August 1998 at the height of the bombing campaign and shortly after the Planet Hollywood attack, so the angle is entirely understandable (and, it should be said, it was a brave article to publish at the time). However, my experience of trying to talk to the 'hardcore' group is that they were considerably brighter than garden furniture and many (though not all) have come to regret their actions. One of the bombers, who went on to get a psychology degree in prison, confessed that he no longer sleeps very well. While they may not have been ideologically grounded, there can be little doubt (whether or not you agree with them, and I do not) that they were a formidable group: clever, organised, almost insanely brave. Ideologically misdirected as they were, there was much to fear from them.

This smaller group who began the bombing campaign against state and civilian targets remain the most shadowy Pagad operatives to this day and those least likely to talk. For the most part, they retained a link to or sympathy for Qibla.

The internal rifts did not hamper the campaign of violence but reinforced it. The wider community, the explanation ran, did not always know what was good for them. Ideological and religious explanations in effect trumped the need for community support. A violent vanguard would decide what was best for the rest.

The dual structure described above also allowed a degree of plausible deniability around attacks – whether on gangsters or other targets; Pagad executive members claim to this day that the bombings were not the work of Pagad. It also allowed Pagad to attack the state while ostensibly talking to it. As the same police intelligence report quoted earlier noted, 'Abdus-Salaam's impulsive and unilateral control over some elements of the G-Force, and the fact that Pagad has not publicly pledged to cease its armed attacks on druglords and gangsters, creates space for parallel dualism in its strategy and the continuation of armed attacks while negotiating with the government.'[31]

By the mid-1990s, the idea of a third force that disrupted politics and stoked violence was part and parcel of the South African discussion. During the last decade of white rule, in particular, government agents disseminated weapons and arranged the abductions and killings of liberation struggle operatives. The notion that there was a third force lingered long after the democratic transition, so blaming the attacks and bombings on this unseen enemy of the state was a convenient way to shift the blame while fostering a general sense of unease.

Perhaps most distressing for many members of the violent core was how Pagad's capacity for violence was increasingly directed internally towards three targets. The first were those whom a paranoid leadership saw as threatening to their own position – the killing of the brother of Sheik Thafier Najaar may be a case in point. The second included dissenters within the Muslim community and past members of Pagad. Ali Parker, for example, received many threats and survived an attempt on his life. The slander campaign that was ordered against the imam of the Gatesville mosque out of enmity is another case in point.[32] One operative was told to throw rotten eggs at the imam, and while this may have been a mild form of attack, many others faced bullets. The third involved broader sections of the Muslim community, and, as noted earlier, these attacks were designed to suggest the community as a whole was under attack. Pagad's role as the defender of community interests was then reinforced.

One of the most intriguing – and without a doubt most dangerous – men in the Pagad network had no interest in internal targets, however. The team led by Ebrahim Jeneker, an intelligent, complicated and wily character, were responsible for an inordinate amount of violence aimed at drug merchants and probably also the police. They also became a considerable danger and embarrassment to the state. Given his violent role in this story, Jeneker deserves a chapter of his own.

6

THE SERIAL OFFENDER

Ebrahim Jeneker was on his way to school one morning. It was 1987. His home was in Sherwood Park, a Cape Flats suburb neighbouring gang-infested Manenberg, and he attended Manenberg High. Walking to school and back each day, Jeneker ran the gauntlet of street violence, crossing the lines from the comparative peace of lower-middle-class Sherwood Park to gang central.

That morning, the schoolboy found himself surrounded by gangsters hanging out near Manenberg library. The young Ebrahim was snacking on a packet of NikNaks that a thug called Cisko apparently decided was going to be his. Jeneker refused to hand over the chips, an understandable if ill-judged and petulant decision. 'He hated those gangsters so much he didn't want to give them the satisfaction of handing over his packet of NikNaks', said a friend.[1] A knife appeared and the gangsters did their damage. According to a friend, Jeneker's guts were left hanging out, like a tortured sinner in Dante's *Inferno*.[2]

In the late 1980s, Manenberg was a spawning ground for gangs, including the hard-talking and heavy-shooting Hard Livings birthed by the Staggies. Even at its margins it was not an easy place to grow up; a young boy adopted by his mother was stabbed to death by a gang, greatly affecting Jeneker's family and his mother in particular. Jeneker was one of seven children whom his mother raised on her own; he is a compact, fit and handsome man, highly intelligent and with an arrogant streak. He was also an obdurate, determined character from a young age. Those who know him say he is almost unnaturally fearless.

Ebrahim Jeneker despised the gangs. That encounter on the way to school and the death of his adopted brother seem to have triggered a deep-seated desire to wreak havoc on the local ganglords. If those gangsters had any idea which schoolboy they were disembowelling that morning, they probably would have left him well alone. While he has his detractors in the febrile world of Pagad politics, Jeneker commanded an almost godlike status among a small group of operatives, exerting a talismanic power over the trusted men who went out with him to assassinate gangsters.

Although Jeneker was widely revered, he occupied an unorthodox position within the Pagad firmament: a classic insider-outsider is perhaps the best way to describe him. Acting independently of the organisation, according to those around him, he embarked on what would become a mass killing spree of his own initiative before being brought under the umbrella of the group – and even then he proudly maintained an independent outlook in his operations.

Whether he was operating as part of the organisation or outside it, there is little doubt that Jeneker was one of the most prolific killers during Pagad's entire campaign. The police investigating him, whom he had in his sights as targets, became terrified of him.[3] Jeneker transformed how Pagad came to be regarded. Without him and his hitmen, Pagad would have been a considerably tamer organisation. How a single individual came to be responsible for so much violence is a story in itself, and it undercuts the narrative created by Pagad and several commentators.

To understand Jeneker's story, it is important to consider his background and world view, and how these drove his actions. He was born in 1970, and like many South Africans of a similar age he was deeply shaped by the events of the political transition early in their adult lives. Democracy promised a future full of opportunities and free of crime, an era in which gangsters would not rule neighbourhoods by terror and ordinary people could make a good living free from fear. Growing up in Sherwood Park during the 1980s, Jeneker was deeply perturbed by the increasing presence of gangs in Manenberg. This environment and events during and after the transition were key in shaping his violent outlook.[4]

The stabbing incident as a schoolboy seemed to profoundly unsettle the young Ebrahim. He became obsessively angry about the area's gangs. Growing listless at school, he dropped out and went to work in the family landscaping and plant business. Servicing gardens and buying and selling plants may have provided a therapeutic outlet for a quietly simmering rage but Jeneker continued to nurture a burning need for revenge, the abdominal scars a perpetual reminder of his tormentors.

He applied dogged determination as a door-to-door plant salesman. Jeneker and his siblings had targets set by their mother, whom he worshipped. Difficult, unbending customers, vicious dogs baring their fangs, unflinching rejections did not deter him: they were all merely obstacles to be overcome. Street by street, the plant sales crew worked its way across the Cape Flats to grow the business.

These challenges may have paved the way for Jeneker's later more deadly activities. What emerges from accounts is that the family business steadily moulded his personality. He became self-reliant, streetwise and entrepreneurial, characteristics that shaped him into a perfect embodiment of violence. As several people who know him told me, in a less unequal and more 'normal' country Jeneker's personality type would have made him ideal for the military. Unobtrusive, smart and focused, his attributes would certainly be right for a man of action, but I have my doubts whether Jeneker, who struggled with authority, could work within the confines of a large organisation. Pagad found this out for itself.

In 1989, two years after the stabbing, and as South Africa was gripped by spasms of political violence and uncertainty before the formal beginning of the transition, Jeneker left Cape Town to source tropical plants in Tzaneen, in what was then the Northern Transvaal. But his hatred of the gangs welled up whenever he returned to sell the stock, just as a new democracy full of promise beckoned.

Self-appointed killers join the fold

For all the violence that Jeneker perpetrated in its name, he was not involved in the establishment of Pagad, nor its marches and protests. But he observed them from a distance with a morbid fascination. The Staggies and the Hard Livings had stamped their violent and bloody imprint on Manenberg, and by implication on the life of Jeneker and his family. Several people said the lynching of Rashaad Staggie in 1996, a milestone in Pagad's history, was also a defining moment for Jeneker. As he watched the gang boss burning to death in TV news footage, it no doubt brought him some satisfaction. For self-sufficient Jeneker, it was also a reminder that individuals could make a difference. If the powerful

Staggie, the maker of one of Cape Town's biggest and most violent gangs, could be brought down by ordinary people, then there was more work to do. It was in effect a spur to action.

Jeneker watched and waited for months before he made his first move, in early 1997. One of the former members of his killing squad explained the decision: 'You had mass action, where there are so many people responding that it often became undisciplined and chaotic ... and this was also the time that the gangs retaliated with all their energy.'[5]

Jeneker believed angry mob violence played into the hands of the gangsters, and that element of chaos in Pagad's activities kept him away from the group. He decided something more clinical was needed. The Pagad campaign was now going at top speed and gang responses intensified throughout 1997 in the form of general intimidation and outright violence. Jeneker, now 26 and in his physical prime, decided to act.

He had watched with concern as hostilities mounted on both sides, but it was the disproportion of the gang response that seemed to pique him intensely. The gang bosses and their flunkies were responding with violence to what were, in his mind, the rightful actions of a community under threat – a community that wanted something better in the first light of democracy. A close family member said: 'His whole heart was believing that [ordinary people] were protecting society and that it was really the government's task and that they have the power to do it, but they are just not doing it. So he has to take his own initiative.'[6]

In November 1996, Jeneker came across Pagad at the V&A Waterfront, a place now clearly connected to the rise of the movement. Jeneker was with his wife, Saudicka, an attractive, self-assured woman with whom he was close (they split for a period while he was in prison but reunited on his release), and they stumbled across a Pagad protest. It was the meeting that degenerated into chaos when shots were fired and Achmat Najaar was killed. The speakers, Aslam Toefy and Abdus-Salaam Ebrahim, were revving up the crowd but Jeneker paid more attention to the men providing security. They were from his own community and he knew many of them. He was shocked. It struck Jeneker that these individuals were not up to the task. They could 'never challenge these gangsters, not even in conversation', said one of his former crew members. With such men as their self-appointed guardians, Jeneker felt the community was staring defeat in the face. Something different was needed.

Jeneker was not a particularly religious man. Unlike other members of Pagad he did not dress in overtly Islamic clothing. Later, he clearly told the court of his religious affiliation, but it was perhaps not so much religious piety that fired him as a strong belief in a community which he felt needed to be self-reliant to survive. 'I belong to the Muslim faith, your honour,' he told the judge during his trial. 'As I understand it, the faith rests on five principles ... [and] if someone needs help then the other one must, so to speak, break his legs to assist him.'[7]

For Jeneker, the Pagad members and leaders he encountered at the Waterfront meeting 'would not be able to finish the job or fulfil the journey that they started', in the words of Boeta Yu.[8] He was convinced this rabble would not be able to deal with the gangsters properly. There is some irony here. This was the point when Pagad was perhaps at its strongest – it had enormous community support and a state falling over itself to accommodate it. Yet Jeneker saw it as a disorganised mob, unqualified and unable to respond to gang violence. It was an uninvited and very personal call to arms.

Given the public narrative that Pagad had created, and to some extent the state too, it seems remarkable that the organisation's most deadly killing squad operated autonomously, independent of the movement. Jeneker was not ordered to kill by Pagad leaders. He was not even a member of Pagad at the time. He selected his own targets with a small group of men who were close to him, often on a whim. Those who know Jeneker are adamant on this point.

Later, it is true, Jeneker consulted Pagad's leadership, notably Abdus-Salaam Ebrahim, and he was eventually brought into the Pagad stable and supported by the organisation, acting on instructions while seemingly retaining a degree of independence. But at the beginning Jeneker's crew were a self-appointed killing squad. And they came onto the state's radar only when they made direct contact with Pagad. It is a brutal but remarkable story.

By this time, Jeneker was no longer working for the family plant business. He was employed by a small sewing machine business owned by the Orrie brothers, Phadiel and Haroon, both of whom feature in later events. Jeneker's brother-in-law, Anees Adams, also seemed to have worked closely with him. Later, Ismail Edwards – a tough, thick-set character nicknamed Miley – served as a getaway driver. Edwards, who seemed to have operated on the fringes of the law, believed the gangsters had gone beyond the pale and needed reining in.

Two rifles were sourced, apparently from gangs in Mitchells Plain. Jeneker started to hunt down the gang bosses. He was a man transformed. There was no question of consulting with Pagad – he was clear what needed to be done and he had a vocation: 'There was all this pent-up hatred looking for a way out. It was like he had been prepared for this role. He wanted to do what the government seemed to refuse to do and what Pagad seemed incapable of,' Boeta Yu told me.[9]

The ghost squad

Based on their own information, the vigilante hit squad targeted gang bosses. Their mission was not to take out low-level drug dealers but to get the kingpins. From late 1997 to 1999, a string of high-profile ganglords died in targeted assassinations. Detailed intelligence was collected on their movements before they were killed execution-style. At first, though, an approach would be made to order them to stop their activities. Perhaps there was a Pagad link here earlier on, and it certainly developed later, but at the beginning Jeneker seemed to operate undirected.

An important addition was Zain Cornelsen, a hard-boiled operator with external training. Cornelsen is an interesting figure who later crossed between different Pagad camps. A muscled man with street smarts, he was reputed to be completely calm under pressure.[10] Boeta Yu joined the hit squad for some jobs.

Edwards, the driver, was quietly competent, unflustered under pressure when the others entered a house. I met him at his home with his wheelchair-bound wife and he talked quietly and guardedly about his days of action. Others said Edwards had been accused of lacking the courage to be a shooter. Jeneker defended him, Edwards explained, because it took a particular brand of courage to wait patiently, exposed in the street, and not race off at the first sign of trouble.

The skills Jeneker learnt from his work selling plants were put to the test. When a salesman or intruder rings the doorbell, there is a 'golden moment' when the occupant opening the door is momentarily disorientated as he processes details about the caller. The person waiting to be let in is armed and ready with a rehearsed sales pitch – or a gun. In the sales game, those first few seconds are psychologically crucial if the door isn't to be slammed in your face. In the shooting business, they deliver maximum disorientation for the victim, maximum advantage for the attacker. In the case of unsuspecting gang bosses they were often fatal.

Jeneker's squad also struck while their victims were in cars, which provided other advantages. If the target was pulling into the drive of his home, his guard would be down, and a driver often lacks all-round vision and can easily be surprised from the rear.

When they started out, the crew had no formal training in the use of guns and were unaware of some of the basics of the assassination business. As one member explained, it was a steep learning curve and the details were crucial: 'One empty casing on the floor brought almost all of us to court because someone was using a pistol instead of a revolver, which retains the bullet casings.'[11] Only later, when they were brought under the Pagad umbrella, did they encounter professional military-trained instructors. They were then taught how to use and maintain their weapons, and trained in bomb construction.

Out on a hit, the group disguised themselves with T-shirts pulled over their heads. It was a bizarre yet effective tactic – holes for the eyes and sleeves flapping like ears, which gave a menacing guise, exactly what the team wanted to achieve. Boeta Yu remembers: 'Jeneker wanted the same reaction from whomever we hit. They would take the T-shirt off afterwards and wear it like a normal shirt.'[12] The element of surprise extended the 'golden moment' in doorstep killings by a few valuable seconds.

One way Jeneker sent a warning to gang bosses was by taking their cars. On one occasion he is said to have seen a vehicle belonging to the notorious Jackie Lonte, a BMW 525i. The driver was a woman. The car was halted and the driver ejected at gunpoint. Jeneker told the shaken woman to tell Lonte his car had been taken and he would not be getting it back. 'He did this a couple of times to say that we have had enough of their nonsense and they have to stop selling drugs in their communities,' said Edwards.[13] Their thinking was that once the warning had been given, the boss became fair game.

The activities and the targets of the squad ranged far and wide. On several occasions they killed taxi bosses who supplied drugs to gangs. In one case the hit occurred in the plush suburb of Constantia. In the tightly knit communities in which they operated, assassinations were sometimes carried out on the spur of the moment. If a target was seen, the team gave chase. A good example was the murder of Hard Livings boss Moeneeb 'Bowtie' Abrahams in January 1998.

Bowtie, so named because of a tattoo on his neck, was a big-time and long-standing gang boss, a high-ranking member of the 26s prison gang and second in charge of the Hard Livings. He cut a distinctive figure because he was confined to a wheelchair, the consequence of a shooting outside a club which left him paralysed. While no stranger to the proactive use of violence, Bowtie had a certain charm; he was something of a ladies' man and had a reputation for coercing young boys into carrying out criminal activities. His main area of operation was Woodstock, a working-class suburb at the foot of Table Mountain that is gradually being gentrified.

The previous year, Pagad arrived at Abrahams's house to warn him to stop dealing in drugs. The gang boss was characteristically defiant. 'He came out in his wheelchair and told them all to fuck off, that nobody could touch him and that they should never come back,' Boeta Yu said.[14] Despite the abuse, several Pagad members spoke of Bowtie with grudging respect. 'In the underworld, Bowtie was one of the few guys that was really shrewd, a sharp, intelligent guy but also pretty brazen and very arrogant,' a senior Pagad man with a long history of violence told me.[15] Wheeling himself around, he was a popular figure in a place where gang bosses commanded respect and handed out goodies.

On this summer's day, the intended target for Jeneker's crew was Rashied Staggie, who would have been prime quarry in the bag after the killing of his brother. Their information was that Staggie would be visiting a barber shop in Manenberg. Staggie feared little on his home turf, even if in this case the barber shop was on the boundary of Hard Livings territory. He had a vain streak and was a regular at Salon Avalon on the town's main throughfare, where he had his hair trimmed and his beard dyed. For Jeneker it was an ideal opportunity to catch Staggie out in the open. The team hung around near the shop. It turned out the intelligence provided had got the timing wrong, and the freshly coiffured Rashied Staggie had already departed. Instead, the loitering gunmen saw Bowtie's car, an expensive and conspicuous BMW, cruising past Salon Avalon, and gave chase in a less edifying green and white Ford Granada. (The Granada had one number plate on it, as Edwards felt it would be suspicious if it had no plates at all.)

Gang bosses would have been acutely aware of the dangers of being targeted and, as mentioned, Bowtie was regarded as a smart operator. But that day he seemed oblivious to the danger, or perhaps confident that nobody would dare attack him in daylight in the centre of Manenberg. The Granada drew up alongside the BMW and Bowtie was killed with a handgun. Jeneker recognised the man in the back of the car, as he had gone to school with him, but he didn't regard him as a gangster, just someone who enjoyed a drink with Bowtie. For that reason his life was spared by the hit squad, even though the man shot back. People streamed out of their houses to see what had happened. To disperse the crowd, the crew fired an R1 assault rifle into the air.

It is ironic that Jeneker and his team were later arrested at Bowtie's funeral in possession of weapons. They were acquitted of the killing for lack of evidence. It was Jeneker's second arrest, and by this time he was well and truly on the state's radar.

At what point this autonomous, self-appointed killing crew reached out to Pagad is not entirely clear, but it was probably in late 1997. Haroon Orrie, who employed Jeneker in the sewing machine business, already had contacts in the movement and Pagad may have had an inkling of what the off-the-books cell was doing, even if they were not instructing them and perhaps were not even sure who they were. In any event, it was Orrie who suggested that Jeneker make contact with Pagad.

Jeneker contacted the ubiquitous Boeta Yu and an individual called Faizel Waggie, both of whom later participated in some operations. Waggie is described as a complex, intelligent man and a key tactical thinker for the organisation. He later earned a psychology degree in prison and post-2010 G-Force members suggest he suffered from post-traumatic stress disorder (PTSD). But that was in the future; for now, the challenge was to bring the unpredictable Jeneker into the fold.

Boeta Yu suggested that they meet representatives of Pagad at a mosque in Grassy Park. Given what they had been up to, it should have been a happy union and comparing of notes. Instead, plagued with suspicions that were compounded by Jeneker's personality, the encounter did not go well.

Jeneker is a stickler for punctuality, and when he and his men arrived at the mosque the intermediaries – Boeta Yu and Waggie – were not yet there. The mosque was full of G-Force members who became suspicious of the new arrivals. 'Things escalated quickly,' one of Jeneker's group said. 'There were five of us who had entered the mosque and we sat down. These G-Force members demanded to know who we were and why we were at the meeting.'[16] Given Jeneker's scepticism about G-Force members' commitment to action, this was an inauspicious start. As someone who had been doing the business of targeting ganglords, he probably thought he was among men who were full of talk but no action.

Jeneker was also incensed because even though he knew several people at the gathering, no one stood up to vouch for him, including a relative of his wife who was present. Why that was so is not clear, but given Pagad's paranoia about police or gang infiltration it is plausible that people were too scared to step forward. Whatever the case, the atmosphere was tense.

The most senior Pagad member in the mosque, Salie Abader, then approached the group, saying they were not allowed to be there. It's not hard to guess the reaction: 'But we are out shooting while all you guys do is sit around and talk.' Jeneker, quick to take offence, was incensed. Things went downhill from there.

'Jeneker basically told them to go and fuck themselves,' a member of the crew said, 'because they had absolutely no courage or understanding of what was happening for the past couple of months. It was us that did all this work, who killed all these gang bosses, and who the fuck are you to tell me anything?'[17]

With that, the intruders stormed out of the mosque. When Boeta Yu and Faizel Waggie finally arrived, they escorted them back inside. Things were partly patched up but not before Jeneker had given the astonished G-Force members a lecture on what his team had been doing. Someone present at the meeting said Jeneker told them he had 'killed all the gang bosses and that they were riding on his coattails'.[18]

The state closes in

That meeting with Pagad was fateful for Jeneker and his team. When they operated autonomously, they were off the grid. When their activities became associated with the wider organisation, they were much more vulnerable to the informer network and they moved further onto the state's radar.

In December 1997, after an extended killing spree, Jeneker was arrested in Mitchells Plain. At that time, the crew's sense was that the authorities did not have a clear profile of them because they operated largely separately from Pagad. This was only partly true. In fact, the police had some idea of the existence of the killing cell but had pinned it down to the wrong area. Jeneker's direct association with Pagad must have been what had led to the police uncovering the cell's existence. It had blown the gaff.

Ironically, it wasn't an assassination but Jeneker's response to an unruly gang that brought him into contact with the law. His arrest followed an incident outside his wife's parents' house in Mitchells Plain. Also present was his brother-in-law, Anees Adams. A group of young gangsters were shooting wildly in the street. It is not clear why, but they were probably flexing their muscles to show the community who was boss. The incident says a lot about the conditions under which people were forced to live.

Jeneker immediately saw red. In the ensuing melee, Adams went into the street and shot one of the gangsters using a licensed gun. Worried about blowing their cover, the two agreed Adams would report the shooting. The police arrived but did not arrest Adams. Instead, he had to go to the police station, and at this point Jeneker called one of the Orrie brothers to assist.

An ambulance took away the severely wounded gangster, Michael Miller, and while Adams was squaring things up with the SAPS news came through that the young man had died in hospital. Angered at the death of one of their own and not knowing who they were taking on, the gangsters got to work shooting into the house of Jeneker's in-laws, smashing the windows. Jeneker, who had weapons and equipment with him at all times, donned a bulletproof vest, grabbed a shotgun and ran into the street. He shot at the gangsters, who retreated while returning fire, but hit an elderly woman who was walking down the street.

Jeneker and Adams were arrested and taken into custody. To Jeneker's surprise, the police already had an inkling of who he was – not detailed information but enough for them to know they had inadvertently hooked a big fish. To some degree this reinforced Jeneker's distaste for Pagad, as he suspected his role had been leaked by a member who had been arrested.

The months following the killing of Michael Miller showed just how ruthless Jeneker could be. Adams was released on bail but before the trial could proceed all the key witnesses were eliminated. In October 1998, Ricardo Miller (Michael's brother), Warren Johnson and Jeremy January were assassinated metres from where Michael had been shot. A white Corolla pulled up and its occupants let fly with a brazen ten-minute hail of bullets.[19] It was a little-reported incident but would have sent a clear message in gangland. The killing of witnesses was, as we shall see, a recurring pattern in cases involving Ebrahim Jeneker.

A taste for killing?

On 15 December 1998, a year after his arrest, Jeneker was granted bail – a sign that the state did not have evidence of the extent of his activities. He had been musing in prison on a key problem facing Pagad: how to obtain weapons? Jeneker apparently confronted Abdus-Salaam

Ebrahim, asking him why Pagad was buying guns when the government had plenty that could be stolen. 'Why don't we just go and fetch the guns?' he is said to have asked. Ebrahim allegedly replied that they could discuss this some other time but Jeneker, impetuous as ever, decided to go ahead on his own.

The location he identified was Claremont police station, a fenced building on a busy thoroughfare. Early on 3 January 1999, three masked men stormed the police station. The officer on duty, Herman Hanekom, reported that the leader of the group wielded an R5 rifle (which had been bought with funds provided by Pagad). Their aim was to supplement it with more of the same. They demanded the keys to the firearms safe before kicking Hanekom twice in the face. 'My mouth and nose were bleeding,' Hanekom reported. 'It was a dramatic experience. It will stay with me for the rest of my life.'[20]

Hanekom's testimony matches what a member of the raiding party told me. But mysteriously, the police station's occurrence book, which contained some of the details about the attack, disappeared two months later, obliterating a key piece of evidence.

Given Jeneker's propensity for violence, his assault on the policeman seemed, uncharacteristically, to have had a haunting effect on him. One reason for this might be that the police station raid was a close call and Jeneker superstitiously believed this was because of his unwarranted violence against the officer. He seemed to operate with a code of honour. Bosses were not to be killed without first receiving a warning; in one case in Sea Point, a kneeling gang boss with a gun to his head was said to have been spared when he promised to get out of the drug business. But others, such as the witnesses to the killing of Michael Miller, were shown no mercy.

Jeneker is believed to have assassinated several of Cape Town's most prominent gang bosses and was unsuccessfully prosecuted for the murder of a veteran police investigator, Bennie Lategan. When he was eventually imprisoned, he acquired a reputation as a tough operator, a proponent of psychological warfare against the gangsters who threatened Pagad members behind bars. While in prison he studied for a BA in history and his reading led to discussions about the motivation for taking action. In the words of his cellmate, Jeneker said that 'if we did not take action in 1997, then the history books would read that the Muslim community in the Western Cape rose up against gangsterism and drugs and that they were utterly humiliated'.[21] This may just be retrospective self-justification, the thoughts of a man who had time to read and reflect. But there is also a ring of honesty about it – that the bloody work of culling the gang bosses was of historical significance in Jeneker's mind. In an August 2013 letter from prison to Boeta Yu, who was key in mobilising the fight against gangs and drug use, Jeneker wrote: 'You represent the people of the Cape and the Muslims at the point of Africa.'[22]

It is impossible to know the exact number of murders Jeneker and his group were involved in. It could be in the seventies or eighties, according to some estimates. Given the sheer volume of incidents, the possibility has been put forward – including by some of those involved – that Jeneker was a kind of serial killer. Serial killing is the 'unlawful killing of two or more victims by the same offender in separate events', with

Ebrahim Jeneker, one of the key violent actors during the Pagad campaign, seen in a rare photo taken while in prison. PICTURE: Author collection

the selection of victims differentiating serial killers from mass murderers (who are less concerned about who their victims are).[23]

He certainly killed a lot of people. However, to my understanding and in contrast to others, he did not seem to experience a high after a killing, with a need to kill again to repeat the rush, like being hooked on a drug or the excitement of the act. Serial killers who express such emotions have been labelled 'hedonistic thrill killers'.[24] One member of the team, a quietly spoken, calm and clever man, was self-aware enough to confess to me that he enjoyed the thrill – it was intense, almost sexual, he said. And for that reason, he wanted to stop.

In Jeneker's case, more complex factors seem to have been at work. His actions displayed a striking set of characteristics that fit the pattern of a certain type of serial killer. These included a history of childhood trauma and fears worked out later in life through violence. Closeness to his mother and the apparent absence of a father figure are other characteristic indicators,[25] as is the targeting of a certain type of person to 'cleanse' society. In some senses Jeneker fits the pattern of 'mission serial killers': 'This murderer is not psychotic,' reads an important study in the field, 'but is impelled to kill people who have been judged by him to be worthy of extermination.'[26] The clinical, unemotional, fearless execution of the act and the almost dismissive referral to the dead person once they have been dispatched is another hallmark of the serial killer's psyche. Then there is the lack of any expressed remorse, just a cold assessment of each killing with no sympathy for the victim.

This lack of sympathy was in direct contrast to Jeneker's self-determined rules about who should die and who should be spared. In Jeneker's case, gang bosses who failed to respond to warnings and continued their activities were killed without mercy. Those who confessed and stopped their illegal activities were apparently spared. Those who were innocent and just associating with a gang boss – such as the man in Bowtie's car – also got a pass. The longer-term guilt that Jeneker had from kicking policeman Herman Hanekom also seems remarkable. But perhaps the issue here is one of ultimate power, and of course revenge against the gangs; Jeneker making the rules based on his reading of the world, deciding who would live and who would die. This mix of power, control and revenge is highlighted in studies of serial and mass murderers and seems to fit the Jeneker case.[27] Even so, Jeneker could be generous: his defence of Miley, his driver, against those who suggested he should also take his turn with the gun, is a case in point.

Police officers and others who have encountered Jeneker often describe him as mild-mannered, approachable and friendly until he is angered or offended; then a different man emerges, one who is precise, cold and intensely dangerous. In that sense, he has a pathological side, working through lists of gangsters as if meeting sales targets for plants. One of the things his team had a reputation for was that they never aborted an operation; once they were under way, they would kill. There was no question, with Jeneker present, that the team would withdraw unblooded.

The conundrum that is Ebrahim Jeneker is not easy to understand. His viciousness, commitment to the campaign, simple guile and generosity in defending some of his fellows were legendary. He became a key focus of state attention.

Jeneker shot his victims, regarding bombing as too dangerous and messy. But it was the bombing campaign that attracted widespread public attention.

7

THE BOMBERS

Bombing gangsters was part of Pagad's strategy from the beginning. It was a technique designed to instil fear. In the early days, simple petrol bombs – classic Molotov cocktails – were the instrument of choice, being easy to make and throw. It was a petrol bomb lobbed by a prominent (and now dead) member of Pagad that set alight Rashaad Staggie, and the rudimentary homemade device retained a certain mythology for members of the organisation. Ironically, in attacks on gangsters the petrol devices were often thrown not by Pagad operatives but by drug users recruited for the task. Hand grenades, presumably from old arms caches or stolen from state armouries, were also often used. But as Pagad's campaign against the gangsters ramped up, pipe bombs – the mythical 'black widows' – became its defining feature. In the end, there were about 400 recorded cases.

It is intriguing, however, that although the bombing campaign was extensive there were remarkably few casualties in the gangster fraternity. Of all the murders of prominent gangsters that I know of, not one was killed by a bomb or grenade. The crime bosses and higher-level merchants who were taken out were all shot, assassination-style, often in their vehicles. Staggie was gunned down before a petrol bomb turned him into a conflagration.

The low casualty rate of the bombing campaign against the gangsters – as opposed to the much higher rate Pagad achieved when it turned to civilian targets – was a function of the devices used. Molotov cocktails and pipe bombs had to be thrown from close range, and unless they trapped the victim in a burning building or landed near the target in a confined space, they tended to cause injury and damage but not necessarily death. The grenades Pagad acquired often seemed not to detonate correctly and caused limited damage. But the purpose of deploying these devices was, at least in the minds of some members of the organisation, to create 'shock and awe': to frighten gangsters and drug dealers into stopping their activities without removing them from the scene. In some cases, this seemed to work. The bombing campaign sowed significant fear in the underworld.

Another reason for the low casualty rate from the bombs was that initially Pagad sent warnings to its targets. Several criminal figures from the period admit they knew they were in Pagad's sights.

In the firing line

Media reports from the time record multiple cases of drug merchants being attacked with bombs, but few were willing to talk about the experience. That reticence stemmed from the fact that they would come across as weak if they expressed how frightening it was. And the older drug merchants and gangsters who are still alive and active in the criminal economy don't want to draw Pagad's ire again. One person who did describe the experience of being firebombed, however, was Junat Adonis, now in her sixties. The reason she was prepared to talk is that the incident was decisive in delinking her family from the criminal economy.[1]

Adonis and her late husband, David, used to run a drug sales business in Parkwood, near gang-afflicted Grassy Park. By mid-1998 the Pagad campaign had gained pace across Cape Town and the Adonises knew what was going on. On 12 June, the same day as Bafana Bafana's opening game in the football world cup in France, Pagad staged a march in Parkwood and shots were fired towards several drug merchants' houses.[2]

The drug trade in any area is often well connected. As the shooting intensified, merchants telephoned one another to compare notes. No one seemed too nervous. The general view was that when Pagad marches were over, the shooting stopped. This is before the days of WhatsApp groups (now commonly used by drug dealers), so you can imagine the SMSes going back and forth in between hushed telephone calls.

Drug houses are not hidden, obscure features of an underground economy – they are visible and often chaotic manifestations of its presence. It is not hard to spot them. At night bonfires outside signal that they are open for business. Other signs are gang symbols sprayed on the walls and people milling around, often playing dice games. Pagad had no trouble identifying where drugs were sold, and as members of the organisation often told me, the visibility of the drug trade and the seeming inability of the police to clamp down on it was central in forging support for Pagad's campaign.

In Parkwood that winter evening, the gunshots were not unusual: they were the normal outcome of a march, perhaps the work of Pagad stragglers. But then a petrol bomb was hurled at the home of a prominent merchant but seemed to be off target and hit an electricity box, which caught fire. No one was hurt or killed but the message seemed to be that the campaign had taken a new turn and more trouble should be expected.

It quickly arrived. One road away from the burning electricity box another petrol bomb was hurled through a window of the second-floor flat of a small-time drug dealer, the front end of a bigger drug organisation in Parkwood. The bottle with the flaming petrol smashed onto the floor, setting the room alight, and the dealer leapt from the window and broke both legs when he landed. He lay screaming in the dust.

The bombers moved to their next target in nearby Gull Road. This was the Adonises' home. It may seem strange to outsiders that a married couple would sell drugs from their house but the entrepreneurial Adonises were among the first drug dealers in Parkwood in the late 1980s. 'They were old-school gang-linked people,' is how an acquaintance described them, 'with the gold and silver teeth, with a ruby'.[3] A jewel-bedecked smile in gangland ('false teeth' in Cape Flats parlance) was a visible sign that you were connected to the gangs and that you had made it. One grin and everyone knew what you were up to.

Inside, the couple, their daughter and her small baby of a few months waited in fear. Junat Adonis heard a crash as a petrol bomb landed in the living room. The curtains immediately burst into flames. The family, shaken by the attack, struggled to put out the fire but the couple's valuable hardwood furniture – another sign of comparative wealth amid otherwise widespread poverty – was now going up in flames.

A quarter of a century later, Junat Adonis is a strong and imposing personality. Yet when she told the story she burst into tears, still traumatised by the event and the thought that her grandchild might have been killed or wounded. It was also the first time she had told the tale in its entirety; previous statements to the police stuck to the basics. The family wound up their drug business shortly after the incident. Adonis is now a born-again Christian and runs a small shop. She ruefully told of how the family knew the attacker: he was one of their regular customers for drugs.

Enter the pipe bomb

By mid-1998, at about the time of the attack on the Adonises, a distinct shift from petrol bombs to pipe bombs mirrored Pagad's growing sophistication and militancy. Petrol bombs were the initial weapon of choice because they were easy to make with simple, accessible components: petrol, a bottle and a piece of rag. They had maximum impact, an experienced Pagad operative reported, if they were used inside a building, as they started fires. 'Sometimes we would just use petrol bombs as a scare tactic,' the man told me.[4] The idea was to sow terror rather than to kill.

There is strong evidence that petrol bombs were often thrown by drug users. 'It was simple,' a then prominent of member of Pagad explained. 'Drug users were always in need of money to maintain their habit and they were easy to manipulate.'[5] Hiring drug users as bomb throwers had advantages: they would get close to the target before hurling the bomb because they were, at least in the eyes of many hardcore Pagad activists, expendable; and, perhaps most importantly, they lent credence to the claim that Pagad was not behind the attacks – the bombings could be explained away as clashes between gangs.

An important point about petrol bombs is that while they caused damage and fear, they were not special or new weapons. They had been used in the struggle against apartheid and by the gangs themselves in internecine conflict over drug markets. What was now needed was something that would brand a new kind of campaign against the druglords.

As mentioned, Pagad also often used grenades. 'We got these in various ways,' a former member said. 'They were often donated by Muslim businessmen.'[6] Whatever the source of the grenades, it transpired that many were duds and did not explode; why this was so will become clearer later. A member of one of Pagad's cells recounted how he swore never to use a grenade again after he threw one at a criminally aligned businessman's house and it failed to detonate. Several armed gangsters then emerged and began shooting at him as he ducked and dived up the road – his getaway car had fled once the shooting started.

While grenades were still mentioned sporadically in press reporting about the campaign, their perceived unreliability was also a factor in providing the push for internal bomb-making capacity. From several accounts, the first pipe bomb was used in late 1997. It was aimed at the house of a drug merchant in Blou Dakke in Strandfontein, a windswept housing settlement strung along the shoreline of False Bay. The details of the incident are now lost but it was followed by other sporadic pipe bombings. The gap between the Blou Dakke bomb and the spate of bombings that followed (the upswing came in mid-1998) signalled an important phase in Pagad's development.

The bomb makers

The strategy of using pipe bombs was by no means a random development – it was introduced in a planned way and reflected a top-down approach by Qibla strategists. An 'explosives expert' was sent to the various cells to provide training. The timing of this development was early 1998, coinciding with the Blou Dakke incident, suggesting the Strandfontein bombing was an experiment with a prototype.

The bomb experts were a handful of men. One in particular, a Qibla member and head of a prominent Pagad cell, was central in spreading expertise.[7] He appears to have learnt his skills from two other Qibla members, who had spent a long time in prison for their involvement in the liberation struggle, during which they were said to have received external training in bomb making.[8] '[This individual] was the guy that was sent to teach everyone initially,' said a member who was involved at the time.[9] In early 1998, the bomb trainer, who has been described as a 'close confidant' of senior Pagad leadership, seems to have been a peripatetic instructor providing bomb-making classes to Pagad disciples.[10]

By the middle of 1998, after a period of experimentation, learning and training, a small group of pipe bomb makers had more or less perfected their techniques. Pipe bombs could be relatively easily mass produced using a piece of pipe, an angle grinder and explosive material. Nails and bolts were added to achieve maximum damage.

Gunpower for the bombs, said several insiders, was often supplied from a source in Johannesburg. It was said to come from wealthy businessmen who also provided guns and grenades. The sourcing of gunpowder also suggested the degree to which the Pagad campaign had wider national support. Gunpowder is highly regulated, and partly because of the threat it posed – most notably at the time from right-wing elements – experts I spoke to suggested that police control over it was strong and remains so.[11] Nevertheless, gun enthusiasts can legally buy gunpowder to make bullets. And although each gun store is permitted to keep only 20 kilograms, if enough buyers with gun licences use different stores it would be feasible to accumulate enough for a sustainable bomb production line.

Some members' bomb-making prowess stood out, and Zaid Abrahams took to it like a duck to water. Abrahams, also known as 'Pang' (a respectful term meaning uncle), taught others how to make bombs. Pang was an older man who lived in Mitchells Plain. He had trained as a welder, an ideal apprenticeship for the skills required to assemble a pipe bomb. But Pang was also reputed to have a secret past: he was said to have trained as a bomb maker in Libya during the liberation struggle. It was perhaps for this reason that he had a good grasp of the chemistry of explosives manufacturing. Under instruction from the Pagad leadership, Pang passed on his skills to other cells.[12]

'It takes about an hour to make a pipe bomb,' explained a former member who was involved. 'But once it's been made you need to use it immediately. A pipe bomb can be dangerous if it gets damp because it has gunpowder in it. If the gunpowder gets wet the device becomes a danger to the person holding it. It's not the type of thing that you want to leave lying around.'[13]

One of the first of a cluster of pipe bomb incidents occurred on 25 January 1998. Significantly, a state target was attacked. Lansdowne police station was bombed just before 4 pm in what was reported as an attempt to free several Pagad members being held there. On 27 April, three pipe bombs were used against gangs after clashes between Pagad

The bombing of Planet Hollywood, a restaurant and bar at the V&A Waterfront, on 25 August 1998, was the most prominent of the campaign. The bomb was fitted with a time-delay fuse. There were two deaths and multiple serious injuries. Planet Hollywood was never to recover and later closed its doors. PICTURE: Reuters

and gangsters. The following month, pipe bombs were hurled at the Lansdowne homes of a wealthy businessman, Zhaun Ahmed, who owned the St Elmo's pizzeria in Walmer Estate. (The St Elmo's in Camps Bay, where Olivia Milner was seriously injured, was bombed in November 1999, presumably because it was an American-style restaurant.) On 10 June, three pipe bombs and a remotely controlled car bomb exploded in Athlone. As an indication of the shifting aims of the bombing campaign, in the Athlone incidents all the targets were leading businessmen in the Muslim and Indian communities. All were reported to have been victims of extortion in the preceding weeks.

By mid-1998, police were using the term 'urban terror' to describe what appeared to be the widening scope of the incidents. The pipe bomb campaign had scaled up, although gangsters and drug merchants were no longer the main targets.

Shortly after the Athlone blast there was an attack on Mowbray police station. In August, the Bellville building housing the police special task force investigating Pagad was bombed, killing a street vendor. The Planet Hollywood blast, in which Bruce Walsh lost his legs, came shortly afterwards, then the Wynberg Synagogue was bombed in December. These bombs were more sophisticated and for the first time they were fitted with time-delay fuses, enabling the bombers to place them then leave. After these incidents, the bombers' targets shifted back to gang and drug merchants, with attacks across the city using black widows.

Bombers with a short fuse

The initial pipe bombs were basic devices with a fuse that had to be lit, usually with a cigarette. What was most frightening about the devices, said people who used them, was the very short delay between igniting the fuse and the bomb detonating. On average, bombers had three seconds to pitch the device, meaning they needed supernatural levels of courage. What made matters even more nerve-racking was that they weighed up to 7.5 kilograms, so it took an effort to throw them. It was difficult to achieve a great deal of distance before they exploded.

'Not everyone was comfortable using a pipe bomb,' a hardcore Pagad operative told me with some degree of understatement. 'Most of the guys continued with their normal business, just shooting the merchants, because we had guns and now and then a hand grenade or two.'[14] 'You would have to be fast,' said another who was involved in several bombings. 'The pipe bomb goes off quickly and sometimes you can be hit by the debris as you turn around and run. Once, a piece of metal from the casing of the bomb hit the car that I was running to get into. The piece of iron was stuck fast in the bonnet. It was lucky for us that no one got hurt that evening.'[15]

As these accounts suggest, the most common technique for Pagad bombers was to approach their target on foot, launch the device and run to a getaway vehicle. 'The best way to be successful with those black widows was just to walk up to the targets and hit them with it and then run away. The thing is that it is fucking risky, and because it is very dangerous many of the drivers were very jumpy because they feared being caught in the blast or any follow-up shooting. It's a very short turnaround window and anything can go wrong, and that's why, I think, they later put timers on them,' a practised Pagad bomber said.[16]

On several occasions bombs were lobbed from the back of bakkies. 'The safest way to throw a pipe bomb,' one experienced operator said, 'was to *gooi* it onto the roof of a house.'[17] If properly delivered, it could cause considerable damage, with high shock value.

Given how unstable the devices were, sometimes the bombers became the bombed. On 30 July 1998, as the pipe bomb campaign was gaining pace, two Pagad members were killed and two injured when a device went off in a bakkie on the way to a target. The vehicle apparently hit a bump in the road and the bomb, resting on someone's lap, went off. Anwar Francis, later a member of Pagad's security council, was injured in the blast and arrested.[18]

For all its dangers, one advantage of the pipe bomb was that it could be delivered quickly: the bomber could approach the target, light the fuse and throw the device. The effect was highly disorientating for the target, and by taking advantage of surprise and confusion the bombing teams could get in and out virtually undetected.

One example of the dangers of throwing a pipe bomb from close range was the Lansdowne police station attack, one of the only cases where bombers were arrested, prosecuted and convicted. Hermanus de Jager, an officer on duty at the station, commandeered a car and chased the two bombers, Ismail Edwards (Ebrahim Jeneker's driver) and Faizel Waggie, both of whom were convicted for the bombing several years later. 'The door was open,' said De Jager, 'and an arm came through and [an orange plastic shopping bag] was thrown over the counter.'[19] There was a small detonation then a flare, reported De Jager. The bomb caused extensive damage. Edwards told me their getaway driver became nervous and fled without them – an irony, as Edwards was regarded as one of the most unshakeable getaway drivers.[20]

As an instrument of terror against the gangs, pipe bombs could be used with devastating effect if correctly delivered and well aimed. Bodies were dismembered or peppered with shrapnel. Even more importantly, the bombs made the news: 'It was always a bigger story in the newspaper if a pipe bomb went off than when we shot a merchant. You can shoot a merchant five times and it won't get as much newspaper coverage as a pipe bomb going off,' a former bomb maker explained.[21]

Former Pagad operatives also revealed another detail worth noting: it was hinted that the state had been turning a blind eye to at least some of the organisation's activities. Drug merchants could be shot, but bombing them with homemade explosive devices was a step too far. The government, they noted, hated the pipe bombs. Ironically, in the Qibla way of thinking, this gave added value to the campaign. It was simultaneously an attack on both the gangs and the state.

The targeting of drug merchants with bombs was not a random affair but planned from above, although as it was described to me there was considerable latitude at street level. The bombings were carried out by Pagad cells and members of the elite G-Force.

A fair amount of intelligence was gathered on targets before the hits. Information would come from community members and, bizarrely, from drug users who gave Pagad details about their dealers. Using this information, the drug merchant's house and movements were mapped. The central aim was to achieve an element of surprise. In most cases, information was gathered and the bombing was carried out the next day. 'We were just like the gangsters would say: *mense van nou* ['now people'], which means we do the job quickly and then it is done,' a former bomber involved in multiple attacks told me.[22]

But the information the bombers gathered was often sketchy. They might have had the basic layout of a home but did not bother to assess how many people would be inside. The bomb teams hyped themselves up, praying and reciting verses from the Quran, then launched their attacks: a Cape version of a jihad.

I was told by Pagad members and police officers that information about which gangsters and drug merchants to target also came from frustrated police officers. It is difficult to ascertain how systematic this was but it is likely that the flow of information slowed when the police and other state institutions came under attack, and internal vigilance within the state also increased.

How people were selected as targets for bomb attacks became a 'distorted' process, said former G-Force members. The result was that bombings were aimed at moderate members of the Muslim community. In July 1998, for example, the Rondebosch East home of a UCT religious studies academic, Ebrahim Moosa, was attacked with a pipe bomb. Fearing for his life, Moosa left South Africa.

There were also, reportedly, 'false flag' bombings of religious leaders and mosques to give the impression that the entire Muslim community was under attack. In December 1997, in one of the first pipe bomb attacks, a device was thrown at the home of Samarodene Stemmet, imam of the Kalksteenfontein mosque, allegedly by a member of the Hard Livings gang.[23] It is difficult to believe at this early stage of the campaign that the Hard Livings were manufacturing pipe bombs, and there is no evidence to suggest they ever did so.[24]

The hardcore

Against the backdrop of the bombing campaign, Pagad's popular support began to drain away. Ordinary people in gang-afflicted neighbourhoods, many of whom knew or had family connected to gangsters, saw the bombs as just another source of violence. The support of middle-class Muslims remained stronger but later all but collapsed when the campaign shifted decisively to state and civilian targets. Attacking gangsters was one thing but targeting the institutions of the democratic state was a step too far. 'It was not what we signed up for,' a Muslim business leader told me.[25] That part of the wider killing campaign was masterminded and orchestrated by the more radical wing that now presided over Pagad.

The core group of bombers and bomb makers who began to experiment with more sophisticated devices was very small – no more than six individuals at any one time. The group were ideologically hardened and operated in great secrecy.

An affidavit provided by a prospective witness, Yusuf Enous, provides remarkable insight into the bomb makers' methods and secrecy, in this case detailing the activities of Faizel Waggie.[26] As the affidavit makes clear, Waggie's strategy was to manufacture and hide bombs in properties that could not be easily connected to him. Enous was to have been a witness in the trial of Waggie, regarded as one of the key bombers,[27] but he and his wife – both of whom were by then in witness protection – were assassinated on 26 December 2000 (see Chapter 14).

At the end of September 2000, in the weeks after two failed car bombs in central Cape Town –in Heerengracht and outside Bronx – Enous advertised motor spares for sale. He was contacted by Waggie, who looked at the parts and bought some. The two became friendly and Waggie asked to leave a package in Enous's garage and to take the keys so he could do further work there. When Enous looked at the contents of the package he found a length of piping welded on both ends, pieces of wire, putty and loose components. (Enous, who had never seen a pipe bomb, said he suspected Waggie may have been manufacturing drugs with the equipment.)

A short while later, Waggie and another man contacted Enous and they met at the Blue Route Mall in Tokai. At the Hyperama supermarket, Enous said in his affidavit, Waggie 'asked a shop assistant for directions to the gardening section and on arrival he went to the fertilisers that were for sale'. He bought some fertiliser but (the term the 'banality of evil' comes to mind here) not before commenting on how expensive the pot plants were. Waggie continued to use Enous's garage for a while before phoning to say he was done and arranging to return the key. The bomb manufactured in the garage went on to play a crucial role in the campaign aimed at civilian targets.[28]

By the second half of 2000, it was clear the bombers' techniques had reached a higher level of sophistication and the state was getting jittery: a campaign that had started with random attacks on drug merchants was noticeably morphing into broader, deadlier violence against civilian targets. The bombers had graduated from black widows to devices set off by timers or cellphones, and car bombs that used ammonium nitrate. The bomb-making group were an exceptionally dangerous crowd and the state struggled to bring them to book.

8

MEN IN BLACK

The government response to the bombings and the shootings creaked and almost broke in 1998 and early 1999, though not for want of trying: the state had launched a series of operations to curb the escalating violence since 1997. Operation Recoil was followed by Saladin in January 1998 and Good Hope and Crackdown in 1999 after the violence took on the dimensions of urban terror.

But the state seemed to work clumsily and at cross-purposes. Internal frictions and personality clashes, inevitably fuelled by distrust between old political and ideological enemies, continued to undermine its efforts. The bomb at Planet Hollywood in August 1998 was a shock to the system, reversing any support Pagad might have enjoyed among police officers. Nevertheless, it did not immediately lead to a collective or coordinated security apparatus that could respond effectively.

A component of the state's response that was continually at the sharp end of the crisis was the police bomb disposal unit. In miniature, the story of the bomb squad shows how a transforming security agency, strained by the burdens of South Africa's past and its own position in the police, had to face up to the unexpected challenge posed by a small group of increasingly skilful bomb makers. It was a small division, crammed with technical expertise and comparatively isolated from the rest of the police, and as a result it was one of the first response structures that was able to reorganise itself and reach out to others.[1]

The bomb disposal experts were housed in a nondescript and ramshackle collection of unmarked prefab huts next to the police station in Pinelands, on the edge of the city's affluent southern suburbs. The buildings were packed with decommissioned and deactivated explosive devices, grenades and various other weird and makeshift constructs of death; they were like macabre exhibits in a private collection showcasing South Africa's violent military and civil history. Some dated back to the South African War while others were from the two world wars, the Korean conflict, the Rhodesian war and of course the South African liberation struggle. Kept there too were samples of commercial explosives used by the mining industry, a prodigious consumer of dynamite and a sector that has long played an important social and economic role in South Africa.[2]

After 1994, bomb threats declined. Although devices planted by the white right wing were still on the radar after a series of attacks around the time of the elections, fewer state resources were allocated to the bomb squad and to some extent it withered on the vine. '[We were] misunderstood, underfunded, and the red-haired stepchild of the police,' one former member told me.[3] The rundown buildings in Pinelands seemed to symbolise this demise.

If the officers at the bomb disposal unit by the time the Pagad campaign started were a depleted bunch, they had an enormous reservoir of experience from the old regime. That was a function of the years of the liberation struggle, when the apartheid state ensured the security establishment had the capability to locate and defuse devices placed by those intent on attacking white rule. Those former opponents now made up the state apparatus that oversaw the activities of the bomb experts, all of whom came from the old SAP. It must have seemed ironic in retrospect, but when Pagad emerged the unit was a much weaker version of its former self under apartheid, having lost men – police specialist functions were still a male-dominated world[4] – and resources. Under democracy, the bomb squad was treated as an anachronistic outcast.

Even so, its members were a professional, skilled and tight-knit group, and they were sorely tested as explosions multiplied across the city. There were some close calls, particularly when unexploded devices were found, and several of the team told me they felt lucky to have emerged physically unscathed.

At whose disposal?

It was perhaps no surprise that the bomb squad was viewed with scepticism by the incoming ANC executive. Not only had the explosives capacity of the old SAP been part of the notorious Security Branch, but the units were put to work for nefarious purposes. The bomb expertise of the old police was as much an offensive as a defensive weapon in the toolbox of the white state. It was a highly respected if somewhat maverick outfit at the core of the old security establishment, but the perspective changed in the democratic era as heroes turned to villains. Just as Pagad struck, the unit's role in planting rather than defusing bombs was being interrogated by the TRC, attracting wide media coverage. It is little wonder that the often conspiratorially minded ANC securocrats remained uneasy about how the police's bomb expertise might be deployed. Even after live devices were deactivated, applications for commendations by the unit's leadership were flatly turned down, the standard response being 'it's part of your job'.[5]

Bomb squad insiders from the 1980s explained that its standing then was due to the efforts of one policeman in particular. George Hammond was 'Mr Bomb Disposal in South Africa', a former member of the squad told me. A walking encyclopaedia of bomb making and disposal, Hammond was said to have 'built and trained the capacity that would be essential to respond to the Pagad bombings'.[6] True to the unorthodox style of the unit, he also enjoyed notoriety for conducting training using live explosives.

Hammond received numerous awards for bravery during his SAP bomb disposal career. In July 1990, just as the transition began, he faced what has been described as a massive 110 kilogram bomb in the 25-storey Hallmark Building in central Pretoria. With only five minutes remaining before detonation, Hammond defused the timing device. It was the heart-stopping stuff you see in action movies and Hammond was awarded a police cross 'for outstanding bravery while in extreme danger'.[7]

In another incident, in March 1988, Hammond defused a limpet mine outside Krugersdorp Magistrates' Court. It was reported that if the mine had exploded, 'dozens of lives would have been lost'.[8] The man evidently had nerves of steel.

Shockingly, however, Hammond also placed mines to blow up soft targets, attacks which could be blamed on the liberation movements, and this signifies the distinctly Janus-faced nature of bomb disposal in South Africa. Besides limpet mines and improvised explosive devices, he and other officers from the bomb disposal unit helped to prepare and place explosive devices that targeted the offices of the Congress of South African Trade Unions in May 1987 and the headquarters of the South African Council of Churches in August 1988. Both buildings were badly damaged and several people were injured. Cinemas showing *Cry Freedom*, a film about Black Consciousness leader Steve Biko and newspaper editor Donald Woods, were also bombed. The same police officers who placed the explosives were then appointed to investigate the blasts.[9]

For apartheid-order members of the bomb disposal unit, the period in which the Pagad campaign began to scale up was also tense for other reasons. TRC hearings were under way, revealing that the bomb disposal function had been more than it seemed in the chaotic days of the 1980s. Many in the police felt middle-level commanders such as Hammond were being left to carry the can as political leaders effectively slithered away from their responsibilities.

In July 1998, a few weeks before the V&A Waterfront bombing, Hammond was before the TRC. He was asked: 'During that period of time is it correct to say that you supported the ideology of the National Party? And you were a supporter of apartheid? You also believed that you were fighting against the liberation movements and the dangers of communism?' 'That is correct,' said Hammond in all three cases.[10] He received amnesty for his role in placing the bombs.[11]

The Security Branch explosives unit was a creation of the burgeoning security state in the 1960s and had accumulated decades of know-how by the time the Pagad urban terror campaign began. The course used to select those wishing to work for the unit was rigorous. With a minimum mark of 80 per cent required to pass each module and only one reassessment allowed, it was not uncommon to lose a trainee in the last days of the course despite months of effort. Participants were continually scrutinised and evaluated, and if there was any doubt about a man's mental or social skills he was summarily ejected. Security Branch members trained in the sensitive area of explosives were also thoroughly vetted. The unit was a brotherhood within a brotherhood.

The post-1994 political changes had major implications for the unit and there were two key changes: The first was that the Security Branch was broken up and the bomb squad emerged blinking into the light. The second was that many older security police personnel, uncertain of their prospects or not supportive of the new regime, left.[12]

That meant a new intake joined the unit in the first years of democracy – predominantly white and drawn by the squad's reputation. The fact that they no longer needed to come through the Security Branch eased their entry. Many seemed to come from SAP riot units and were presumably looking for a new start. The training course for this new stream was still of the strictest standard, taught by a small cadre of Security Branch veterans who stayed on. Without that training, there would have been little expertise to counter Pagad's urban terror campaign. 'You can say what you like about the old Security Branch guys but they passed on their knowledge,' one man who benefited from their teaching told me.[13] Several officers who played a role in combating the Pagad campaign 'graduated', describing themselves proudly as 'bomb techs'.[14]

The bomb squad seems to have been a rough-and-tumble kind of place, out of step with what would now be regarded as acceptable. Colleagues booby-trapped each other's offices with small devices which in several cases blew out the windows (admittedly not too difficult a task in the rickety huts). Ashtrays were 'treated' with flash powder and tear gas was let off in the offices as a joke. Many squad members were said to have PTSD but in the 'cowboys don't cry' culture of the police it was hidden behind backslapping macho humour and heavy drinking and smoking. Despite the bomb school motto – 'it only hurts if you survive' – former members said they faced crushing levels of fear, including the possibility of being horribly disabled or disfigured.[15]

When sporadic Pagad bomb attacks began in 1996 it was not clear what direction the campaign would take, one grizzled member of the bomb unit told me. There was certainly no inkling of widespread attacks on civilian urban targets and the police themselves. In fact, he emphasised, there was sympathy for Pagad's cause at the start, even among the bomb technicians. The view was that gangs were out of hand and the bombings were seen by many as part of the solution to a societal crisis.

There was also an argument among conspiracy-minded types in the new security establishment that a high-profile bombing campaign against criminal elements would show that the new government could not control crime or manage an Islamic-style insurgency – something Western governments would be particularly sensitive to. In retrospect, that theory now seems far-fetched but it was a more widely held view than many would today admit. Throughout the 1990s there was apprehension about a right-wing kickback against the new regime and a major intelligence operation was mounted to root out the remaining radicals.[16] Some anti-government groups had bomb-making know-how, often acquired by servicemen within the apartheid military; they included the so-called Boeremag, the Afrikaner Weerstandsbeweging (AWB) and the New Israelites, a motley collection of white right-wing and neo-Nazi-style groups with separatist aims; the Suidlanders, a group whose ideology centred on an imagined white genocide that would come with black majority rule; and some black (notably from the Border War 32 Battalion) and Coloured soldiers who had served in the South African Defence Force.[17]

Given the trajectory of history, with its clashing political interests, it is inevitable that the bomb squad itself came under a pall of suspicion: who else was better placed to teach Pagad how to make bombs than those from the old order with bomb expertise? That there had been sympathy for Pagad in the beginning can only have heightened these concerns. Officers in the bomb squad believed their buildings were bugged by national intelligence. 'The line of thinking was that there must be members of the Boeremag in the bomb squad,' an ex-member said. It was a period of heightened uncertainty and suspicion. 'We were starting to go out day after day to scenes of explosions and they honestly thought that it could have been us,' another told me, shaking his head.[18]

The exploding city

Case files recording the details of explosions that rocked Cape Town from 1996 to 2001 are still stored in the huts that were used as the bomb squad's base, piled high in cabinets and cupboards among the decommissioned explosive relics.[19] By the squad's estimate, there were thousands of incidents and call-outs, and at the height of the campaign there were bomb scenes to examine every day. 'We were called from early in the morning to late at night,' said one of the experts.[20] At the same time, the unit had dwindled to just half a dozen bomb techs. As the number of explosions picked up, things soon became unmanageable for the small team.

The unit had always been busy, responding to emergencies such as suspicious packages and cases of arson-linked extortion (a common gang tactic), but as the fear and insecurity sown by Pagad grew in intensity it became near impossible to keep on top of the work, particularly when attacks on civilian targets meant every unattended bag or parcel triggered a call-out. On some days, more than a hundred incidents were referred to the unit. 'We dealt with every item as a bomb,' said a senior bomb tech.[21] So jumpy were city residents that the noonday cannon shot from Signal Hill, which emits a hefty thump, resulted in a call to the unit that a bomb may have gone off.

An experienced bomb tech who attended many of the Pagad incidents explained that, technically speaking, a pipe bomb is not actually a bomb. It is an improvised explosive device, widely known as an IED. It creates a confined explosion catalysed by a chemical reaction. But that makes it no less effective or lethal. Pressure builds in the device due to a chemical reaction until the container 'can no longer maintain its integrity' and it blows apart, spraying shattered pieces of the body of the device and any shrapnel inside it.[22] Over time, the designs became more sophisticated, and bigger. 'The more complicated you make [the device], the more complicated it is for the bomber,' said the tech.[23] 'What difference does it actually make if a piece of shrapnel is travelling at 200 metres per second or 1000? It will still kill you.'[24] By far the greatest number of injuries the disposal unit witnessed were not caused by the blast itself: 80 per cent of the wounds were the result of 'primary shrapnel', including nails or ball bearings placed inside or packed around the device, as well as 'secondary shrapnel' in the form of flying shards of glass from shattered windows.

In a confined space, the blast waves from a pipe bomb cause even more devastating injury and damage. That was the case in the August 1998 Planet Hollywood bombing, where the device was placed inside the restaurant. 'It was terrible,' said the unit men who attended. 'The place was covered with body parts, blood and glass.'[25]

This site took an inordinate amount of time to investigate. Bomb techs had to crawl around among the gore and debris looking for minuscule bomb fragments that might provide vital clues to identify the device used, how it is was made, and ultimately who made it. 'We left the body parts to the forensic guys, although flesh often contained shrapnel that we wanted to take a look at,' said an experienced bomb tech.[26] A lot of people had already been on the scene – first paramedics, then politicians, police officers and detectives – which meant it had been progressively contaminated before the bomb techs could get to work.

Even in the Planet Hollywood case, the bomb techs felt people suspected them. Bomb disposal experts were brought in from the US to supervise. After three days of shadowing the local team, the FBI advisers reported that the South Africans were doing a good job. It was an important reprieve and a vote of confidence. But things were only getting tougher for the unit.

They feared attacks on their homes and there was increasing evidence that they were being followed. In late 1998, some of their cars were damaged: tyres were slashed, windscreen wipers broken off and graffiti etched on the paintwork. 'People had got to know who we were. It was not very difficult: we drove the same old vehicles, we were at every scene, and there were only a few of us,' said one.[27]

'The intelligence people told us there was a real threat to our lives,' said an old salt from the unit.[28] Team members were sometimes followed back to the office from bomb scenes, so security was stepped up. The group began to drive in convoys or request protection from other police units, and they took precautions when they left home or arrived back after work. This was the time when one police investigator, Bennie Lategan, was killed in an assassination and another, Schalk Visagie, badly wounded, so there can be little doubt their fears were justified. In June 2000, a device placed in a bin near a Sea Point restaurant exploded after a false bomb threat was called in. Police intelligence believed the device was aimed specifically at the bomb squad.

At one point, unit members began to sleep under the parade room table on inflatable mattresses, not returning home for days. Ironically, said a bitter ex-member, requests for their homes to be upgraded against attacks were turned down while senior police officers not involved in the investigations had their homes secured at taxpayers' expense.[29] An additional room was eventually constructed in Pinelands to serve as accommodation so squad members would be immediately ready for any call-out.

The psychological strain on core members of the unit became immense. Their rundown base contained a small recreational room and it was there that inevitable tensions surfaced. 'We would leave ranks and titles at the door then get shitfaced,' said one.[30] The informal debriefings and interactions would occasionally be resolved physically. A few minutes later, the men would walk out of the room having forgiven each other, ready to respond to another call. 'We would basically laugh and then we would cry,' reported another.[31] The makeshift bar was also the scene of bleak humour. One of the team remembered how, over a beer, they decided to nickname a gang member and bomber 'Flipper'. That individual had been severely injured when a fire extinguisher filled with explosives blew up prematurely, and he was found alive and waggling what remained of his arms. Humour was a coping mechanism and one of the ways to survive. During a compulsory group psychological debriefing, the psychologist left in tears after being told about 'Flipper', and screamed at the members that they were sick and beyond help.

Getting into gear

There were a lot of quiet heroes in the bomb squad. The techies tended to avoid the eye of the media, unlike their sometimes publicity-hungry colleagues in the detective service, many of whom cultivated images as hard-bitten case-solving policemen.[32] Two colonels, Bernie Posthumus (now deceased) and Robbie Reijnders, led and improved the effectiveness of the unit in the teeth of the bombing campaign. If you look at the grainy police photos taken at bomb scenes you can often make out the same individuals with heads down searching for fragments of evidence. In the beginning they dressed in civilian clothes, often in the police civvies 'uniform' of leather jacket and jeans, a handgun bulging under the belt.

Lieutenant Colonel Robert Reijnders, head of the Cape Town bomb disposal unit, collecting evidence at the bombing of Rashied Staggie's home in Sea Point on New Year's Day 1998. The bomb squad would shortly change their civilian clothes for their own distinctive uniform. PICTURE: Benny Gool

One figure present in many of the photos is a stalwart of the Cape Town bomb squad, Frank Gentle. While only a warrant officer, he stands out as a key individual in the unit's response.[33] A tall, dark-haired chain-smoker, Gentle closely monitored the unfolding bombing campaign. Although there had been previous attacks on police stations, the January 1999 explosion outside Caledon Square in the city centre seems to have jolted the unit. It was partly because the city's central police station was targeted but also because 11 bystanders were wounded – most of them Muslim. Gentle, 'puffing like a steam engine' on box after box of Chesterfields according to someone at the scene, was enraged. He was described by former colleagues as having an ability to say the most inappropriate things but always with a smile on his face. 'He could tell you to bugger off and make it feel as if he was doing you a favour,' recalled one hard-bitten ex-member.[34] It was an important skill in a unit where rank counted less than elsewhere in the police.

Gentle seems to have been the person almost all bureaucracies produce, a behind-the-scenes operator who works hard and has expertise.[35]

He was described to me by a former colleague as a '110 per cent bomb technician' and a true gentleman. Gentle brought enthusiasm and drive to the bomb disposal business and was always the first to volunteer for risky assignments. A former member of the riot unit, he transitioned into bomb disposal as democracy dawned. 'He always taught you the right way to do things. He had also been a direct product of George Hammond's unique teaching methods at the bomb school.'[36] In the bomb squad, as Gentle knew, the right way could be the difference between going home in one piece or being picked up in pieces.

Gentle, who died in 2021 at the age of 51, has never been publicly recognised for his role.[37] He and the other squad members were not promoted and did not receive any form of acknowledgement for their actions. After the Pagad campaign, during which they accumulated hundreds of hours of overtime, they were informed that the 'time registers were simply going to be zeroed, as the police weren't going to pay their accumulated overtime and couldn't very well give everyone a few months off'.[38] Gentle was later recognised by a different unit and was promoted to lead the president's explosives team.[39]

From 1996 the bomb squad started honing their response. 'As the bombers were progressing, we were progressing too,' said a member. That simple phrase captures a lot of effort. A contemporary of Gentle, Warrant Officer Jacques Britz – a hardcore cop who also came up through the riot squad, where he was part of a door-kicking reaction unit – was instrumental in changing the way blast scenes were investigated and devices reconstructed. Blonde and blue-eyed Britz, whom other members likened jokingly to the Swedish actor Dolph Lundgren, was technically orientated and methodical. Under his watchful eye, members bought mechanical timers, phones, batteries and other components out of their own pockets to compare them with remnants found at bombing scenes. They brought in chemists and metallurgists from police forensic science laboratories to analyse chemicals and shrapnel. When a new type of electronic remote firing switch appeared, the bomb squad asked their global counterparts for advice and input.

One of the biggest challenges for the team was the contamination of evidence at scenes. For purposes of evidence collection, the area that needed to be cordoned off was also generally much larger than the area the first police responders ran the yellow tape around. The norm was that the first responders' cordon should be extended by 50 per cent beyond the furthest point at which shrapnel was found.

Another challenge was that shrapnel and bomb debris could often not be collected at the scene; instead it went to mortuaries and hospitals embedded in the bodies of the dead and wounded. Bomb squad members toured hospitals, alerting surgeons not to discard shrapnel they removed from survivors but to hand it over so a better picture could be formed of the devices used in attacks. They also asked for clothing and other items belonging to the injured and dead. The members attended post-mortem examinations of bombing victims to guide pathologists in their evidence collection.

In 1998, the disposal unit began to reach out to other police divisions, notably the K-9 units that were often first at the scene. Training was provided to police colleagues and emergency fire and medical teams on how to seal off scenes and on the importance of marking and preserving possible evidence. Instructions were provided on creating access corridors in and out of explosion sites so the bomb techs could get in faster.

A standing instruction was introduced to create an inner and outer cordon and to prevent non-essential people entering the area. VIPs such as mayors and police commissioners were to be politely escorted away. The secondary cordon also kept any prospective bombers, who might be waiting to remotely detonate a device where the responders were gathering, at a distance.[40] Role division became clearer too: the bomb techs scoured scenes for evidence and visited hospitals while police investigators took statements from victims off site.

One case illustrates much about the changing response at the scene. A bomb had exploded outside a police station and the area had been cordoned off. The bomb disposal technicians were at work when Leonard Knipe, the mercurial commander of the Serious & Violent Crime unit in Cape Town, marched in. Knipe made a beeline for the bomb crater and stood there, looking around. In the view of the bomb techs he did this purely so press photographers on the other side of the cordon could get a picture of the famous detective at work. The lead bomb tech at the scene, who is also the source for this story, ordered Knipe to leave – in his socks. He had walked over ground zero of the explosion, said the expert, and his shoes would be needed for evidence. Knipe left the scene grumbling, gingerly picking his way through the rubble.

Knipe was not the only one. Several dignitaries' shoes were confiscated, including the high heels of the then mayor of Cape Town. The message began to get through: leave the scene to bomb disposal for everyone's good. Later, politicians such as the DA's Hennie Bester told me they did not visit scenes because it would disturb the technicians' work, and in any event it just attracted more attention, which favoured the bombers.[41]

At least part of the problem for the bomb disposal unit was that they lacked clear identification: their Security Branch background had always meant they wore civilian clothes and operated incognito. Indeed, in the early days, one of the first challenges the unit faced was that when they arrived at a scene the police at the cordon turned them away. Gentle was having none of that. He believed the unit needed visibility to do its job and that this outweighed the threat posed by what seemed to be ever-present Pagad watchers following them. Black cotton overalls were introduced, funded by a public donation, and the men were now clearly branded as a bomb disposal team. The outfits were later replaced with navy blue flashproof and fireproof garments which were adopted by the SAPS and are still used to this day. Attending scene after scene in this garb, the unit became known as 'the men in black'. Their vehicles were also marked and they attracted public hostility: Why were the bombs still exploding, people wanted to know. What were they doing about it? It ratcheted up the pressure. Keep calm and do your jobs, Gentle advised in the Pinelands recreation room.

There was competition between members of the unit to get to a bomb scene first. The first to arrive was responsible for the scene, for writing up the necessary paperwork and for directing the post-blast investigation, regardless of rank. Under his direction, the scene was combed for evidence and the cordon maintained. The first task was to find the seat of the explosion, then radiate outwards. It could take days of methodical work which proceeded even if new bomb scenes were being created.

Posthumus and Reijnders ordered that each scene be given the attention it deserved. In the case of the major urban terror incidents, elaborate reconstructions were made of each scene under the watchful supervision of the Lundgren lookalike, Britz, bringing together as much evidence as could be extracted.[42]

In Pretoria, too, the system was being shaken. Because the Cape Town bomb techs could not keep up with the work, officers from elsewhere were summoned. One of these was Willem Els, now a researcher at the Institute for Security Studies. He recalls the overall commander of bomb disposal units countrywide, an old policeman called Manie Schoeman, ordering him to the Cape, saying simply: 'Enough is enough.' Els asked whether he could go home to pack and travel the next day. 'No, go now,' replied Schoeman.[43] He drove through the night to reach Cape Town the next morning, reporting almost immediately to a bomb site. Resources and personnel were poured into the bomb disposal unit in Cape Town, and Posthumus and Reijnders absorbed and directed them with an eye to improving the response.

When I asked a member of the unit what it was like, he referred me to a book that he said captured perfectly what he felt. It was a mid-1990s piece of fiction by Terence Strong, *The Tick Tock Man*. The cover tag line seemed particularly pertinent to our discussion: 'In bomb disposal every decision could be your last ...'[44] I ordered a copy. It was the story of a British army officer turned policeman whose job was to defuse bombs during the IRA terror campaign while pitted against a cunning bomb maker.[45]

There was something like this in Cape Town during the Pagad attacks. 'All the bombs had a similar signature,' a bomb tech told me. 'We were not finding a great degree of variance in the designs.' Metallurgical analysis of the pipes that contained the bombs also revealed they were from a relatively limited number of sources. The conclusion was that just a handful of people were making the bombs: a few cutting the pipes and one or two welding. As the bomb makers changed designs, the bomb techs adjusted their response. A perverse game of cat and mouse played out. It was six bomb techs against six bomb makers.

While they were at the front end of the explosives response, the men in black could not solve the problem of the bombs nor of Pagad itself. And their work was painstakingly slow, causing tensions with the detectives. 'We struggled with the investigators,' said a leading bomb tech. 'They were under huge pressure. They would want answers now – especially the Serious & Violent Crime unit and Crime Intelligence. But we could not give answers immediately. We needed time to do our investigations at the scenes and lab reports to confirm what we already suspected.'[46]

The men in black could collect evidence and testify in court. They could outmatch their bomb-making adversaries in knowledge and expertise. But solving the cases and arresting and convicting the perpetrators relied on investigators, prosecutors and intelligence operatives. Progress was slow and often seemed to lack strategy and focus. A series of developments in late 1998, however, marked a crucial step forward.

9

TOUGH TIMES, TOUGH MEASURES

If the bomb squad was a small, tight-knit group that by necessity kept a low profile, the city's detectives were a prominent bunch and their work was devoured by the media news machine. Leonard Knipe was particularly well known as the head of the city's special investigative units, under which the Murder & Robbery squad fell. Before Pagad, he was involved in several high-profile investigations, including the 1993 Apla attack on St James Church in Kenilworth, in which 11 members of the congregation were killed and 58 wounded. Investigating cases like that put you on the front pages. Knipe was a hardworking but sometimes hard-to-like detective with a good track record, but as a senior manager he struggled to build cohesive teams and was leery of cooperating with others.

In the early stages of Pagad's campaign, Knipe's detectives did not distinguish themselves. It was not for want of trying, but their efforts were hamstrung by internal competition and poor coordination. It was also true that the democratic-order police faced new obstacles that many from the apartheid detective service had not had to deal with; for a start, suspects could no longer be tortured into providing confessions, as had been relatively common in the past, with Murder & Robbery particularly guilty.

Handling the handlers

The other key challenge, one of the only senior black officers with an SAP background who worked in Cape Town told me, was that 'there was precious little intelligence for the detectives on Pagad'.[1] Murder & Robbery detectives, one senior investigator confirmed, 'developed their informants in the city's criminal underworld'.[2] Security Branch officers who had moved into the detective branch often also lacked contacts for intelligence in Cape Town's Muslim community, given their largely political focus in the past. Many Pagad members had not had contact with state law enforcement agents in the way other established criminals had. They simply fell outside the intelligence net that the elite detective units maintained.

As the next chapter will show, intelligence on Islamic organisations such as Qibla, when it even existed, was tightly guarded by a small clique within the police and unlikely to be shared with those investigating cases on the streets. In any event, detectives were dismissive of the new Crime Intelligence units; purists such as Knipe saw them as the stepchild of the Security Branch, which he despised, or, even worse, the ANC's Department of Intelligence and Security. Hard-bitten investigators believed Crime Intelligence was unlikely to deliver information that could be used as evidence, a gripe that grew in volume as the pressure from Pagad's attacks mounted.

The links between Murder & Robbery detectives and the underworld were a source of tension for another reason: Pagad insiders believed the police were colluding with gangsters. A senior police officer explained that one problem with the system was that informants in the gang world were seen to advance up the gang hierarchy in line with their handlers – a kind of 'parallel system of promotion', as he put it.[3] A controversial meeting between Knipe and Rashied Staggie at the V&A Waterfront in July 1996 added fuel to that fire.[4] In his defence, Knipe had been eager to find a way to reduce gang violence and negotiate the disarming of gangsters. But the publicising of that meeting added to a perception in Pagad that the police were communicating with ganglords but not arresting them, and that communities were left to face the consequences.

Incidents such as Knipe's meeting with a senior Cape gang boss undoubtedly reinforced the Pagad narrative of an indifferent and compromised state, and hence the agents of the state would be a justifiable target if the problem of drugs and gangsterism was to be solved. A prominent Pagad G-Force member who served a long jail sentence said: 'In the [initial] bombing campaign, we at first targeted gangsters and druglords, but afterwards we discovered that these drug merchants all had their handlers within the police. The gangsters were being helped by the police. Pagad's target range then widened because the scope was now no longer only gangsters and drug merchants.'[5]

The small group of detectives were soon to find themselves in the eye of the storm. One of the first to investigate Pagad was an intriguing man called Schalk Visagie. He was the son-in-law of apartheid former president PW Botha, having married his daughter Rozanne. A former Security Branch officer, Visagie subsequently published a colourful account of his experiences, including his involvement in the Pagad investigations.[6] Despite his connection to Botha, to whom he remained loyal in his writings, he also developed a close link with Nelson Mandela, who genuinely seemed to like him.

In June 1997, Visagie was appointed by Knipe to run the Pagad investigation unit.[7] In his frank, often acid memoir, he explains how this was a collection of Murder & Robbery, firearms, gang and hijacking detectives. 'They were purely investigators. They were not trained to address urban terror on this scale. There was no time to train them. It was literally all hands on deck.'[8]

Visagie records the mounting frustrations they faced by the second half of 1998 as the Pagad campaign ramped up. 'We had seen police stations, courts, synagogues and homes bombed,' he says. 'Police stations were raided by criminals and weapons were taken to attack gangsters and gang leaders at will. There were more murders than I care to remember and more hatred than I have ever seen. More than seven witnesses were killed to prevent successful prosecutions.'[9]

After the offices of the Pagad investigation unit in Bellville were attacked in August 1998, days before the Planet Hollywood bombing, he reflects: 'There wasn't much progress in the investigation and no easy leads to follow. These acts are always faceless and very difficult to investigate.'[10] Visagie was in shock after the Bellville attack as he had been outside talking with a street vendor just minutes earlier. Tragically, she died in the explosion moments after Visagie asked her to set aside a pair of shoes for his daughter. He came within a whisker of losing his life again a few months later.

Visagie's feelings of despair were widespread. Things looked out of control, and in many ways they were. The period from August 1998 to February 1999 saw a sequence of events that seemed to show state efforts to respond to Pagad were at their worst. Tempers frayed and the detectives felt under-appreciated and increasingly under threat.

As a member of the National Safety and Security Secretariat, I was dispatched from Pretoria to Cape Town by the Minister of Safety and Security, Sydney Mufamadi, to ascertain what could be done to support the hard-pressed investigators. The detectives proved difficult to pin down, despite the order from the new minister (or perhaps because of it). I eventually persuaded a veteran member of the Murder & Robbery unit, Mike Barkhuizen, to talk to me. Further consultations with the detectives revealed that they felt the constitutional changes were hindering their work. Their constant refrain was that the law favoured criminals.

At the time it was hard to fathom why the detectives took the line they did. They liked to style themselves as some of the world's best detectives (and some of them were indeed very good), but they were quick to criticise what they saw as the shackles of the democratic order's policing regime. (In fact, world-class detective agencies they likened themselves to – Scotland Yard or the FBI, for example – worked under the same conditions as a matter of routine.) Whatever the burdens and challenges – even perhaps the psychological damage – they bore, the specialised detectives seemed to relish the idea that they were a band of brothers that the world was determined to persecute. Arguably, they had a form of victim complex. The verbal attacks on Murder & Robbery units by ANC politicians only encouraged these behavioural tendencies. Perhaps it was a 'we'll show them' attitude as they waited for a breakthrough against Pagad that would show their true credentials – and turn the tide of opinion.

The three years between Pagad's formation in 1995 and late 1998 were frustrating for detectives working the cases. Professional rivalries and the need to defend institutional turf made them difficult to work with, but as one very senior police officer told me, 'Pagad was running rings around them.' They were also remarkably few in number given the scale of the threat. In Western democracies, several hundred detectives might be mobilised to deal with a serious threat to the state of this ilk; in Cape Town there were seldom more than several dozen. It was also hard to complete one case before overworked detectives were racing to the next grisly scene. Pagad's campaign put the tightly wound spring that was the city's specialised detective service under intense and unrelenting pressure. It is little surprise that the men seemed to go into a defensive shell.

Just how much they retreated on the Pagad issue is illustrated by how hard it was to secure interviews with ex-detectives for this book. Citing security threats or a standard refrain that 'these things are in the past', they dodged my requests to contribute information. In the end, enough were willing to speak and one senior ex-officer was particularly helpful, but it was hard work. My theory, which might explain why most were reluctant to share their experience, is that they know they failed and are disappointed in themselves.

Behind the scenes, however, there were developments that shaped the later response from the state. While muted in the news at the time, they had significant long-term consequences for criminal justice and politics in South Africa.

'Things are serious'

Arno Lamoer's appointments diary during the Pagad campaign makes interesting reading.[11] He was a senior police officer and his diary shows the changing focus of the state's security apparatus at senior levels. On 29 August 1996, President Mandela, Safety and Security minister Sydney Mufamadi and church leaders held a press conference at the office of the attorney-general in Cape Town, which Lamoer attended. Mandela and Mufamadi vowed to crack down on violence stemming from Pagad and the gangs.[12]

Lamoer's entries for 1997, however, reveal a shift to attempts to negotiate with Pagad. These conflicting signals caused confusion in the overall security system, in my opinion: who should be investigated and arrested if negotiations were under way? There was also internal disagreement in the state over this strategy. By late 1997, Lamoer mentions discussions with the Pagad investigation unit (where Visagie and others were working), but by the second half of 1998 the detectives were still struggling on alone and under threat, as Visagie records in frustration.

The tempo of meetings about Pagad began to scale up dramatically in September 1998 after the bombings of the Bellville SAPS office and Planet Hollywood. On 17 September, Lamoer received a call from his boss telling him to attend a meeting the next day with advocate Percy Sonn, then deputy attorney-general for the Western Cape. Lamoer declined, as national commissioner George Fivaz had summoned him to the SAPS soccer championship.

That day, in a discussion with Fivaz and other senior officers as players scampered around the football fields, Lamoer was startled to be told he would lead the police contingent that was about to be integrated into a special investigative and prosecutorial unit under the direction of Sonn. Officers would no longer fall within police command structures for the purposes of the investigation against Pagad and organised crime. Instead, a new animal was being brought forth, explained Fivaz. It was to bear the uninspiring acronym Idoc, the Investigating Directorate for Organised Crime, and its reporting line was to the new prosecution service.

In the institutional confines of the police, the creation of Idoc was nothing short of an earth-shattering development, and while it was not advertised as such, it was born of an assessment that the detectives were not succeeding: most cases did not reach court, and even when they did they were often poorly investigated. It also broke the mould of police-led investigations, with prosecutors now taking the lead. The formation of Idoc followed a critical moment within the criminal justice system: the appointment of the first National Director of Public Prosecutions (NDPP) in the shape of the charismatic Bulelani Ngcuka in July 1998.

Ngcuka was appointed under a new law, the National Prosecuting Authority (NPA) Act, which had wide implications for criminal justice.[13] The act established the NPA and provided for the appointment of specialised investigative bodies, or directorates, outside the police.[14] It was controversial for a variety of reasons but the issue of specialised directorates attracted comparatively little comment.[15] The directorates were to be established in critical areas 'to enable prosecution-driven investigations,

Bulelani Ngcuka, appointed as the country's first black chief prosecutor in July 1998, quickly identified Pagad and its campaign of violence as a threat to the new democracy. PICTURE: Juda Ngwenya, Reuters

where investigations are conducted under the close guidance and assistance of a senior prosecutor to ensure that evidence collected can be effectively used in court'.[16] It was a fundamentally different approach from the prevailing system in which detectives provided prosecutors with their completed investigations and guidance from prosecutors was limited.

Sonn was the main instigator behind Idoc, including the idea that it should be run from the Western Cape. He was born and raised in Athlone and continued to live there, well attuned to the impact of the violence Pagad was generating. He was a man of great energy and action and well networked across the communities of the Western Cape, in particular among liberation struggle comrades. A cricket devotee, he was a highly social character who was not averse to a drink.[17]

By-mid 1998, Sonn had become vocal about how the attacks could not go on – the investigative system was broken and a change was needed.[18] He was widely known for his direct manner and salty language, his conversation liberally sprinkled with expletives. He was determined, he said, 'to shift the fucking system'. That opportunity came with the appointment of Ngcuka, who was looking for new ideas at a point when the wheels seemed to be coming off. Sonn was also conscious of the issue of race: he was later seen as a controversial figure among whites for supporting racial quotas in the national cricket team when he was president of the United Cricket Board. That the investigators were all white and linked to the old police would not have escaped his notice. In his view, the new government needed to shake things up. New challenges demanded new thinking.

Sonn visited Ngcuka as soon as the former ANC MP was appointed NDPP. He was predictably blunt in his approach. 'Your priority must be to deal with Pagad. Things are serious,' Sonn told him. 'We need to take this away from the police as they are not coping. The police need to work for *us* if we are to succeed.'[19] Sonn was also not one to duck a challenge. 'He told me also,' Ngcuka later recalled, '[that] he wanted to lead the Investigating Directorate for Organised Crime. He had prepared the terms of reference and had a list of the names of people he wanted to work with him. He was well prepared.'[20] Ngcuka promised to see what he could do and consulted Mufamadi and Intelligence minister Joe Nhlanhla.

Mufamadi introduced Ngcuka to Fivaz, who unhesitatingly promised the new NDPP his support: 'I will give you all the people you need.'[21] It was perhaps a sign of the seriousness of the times but it was also the mark of the man Fivaz is. He was a career policeman and well understood what he was doing. It is true that there was a distinct political imbalance between the two: Ngcuka, the newly appointed ANC-aligned man with ties to the incoming president, Thabo Mbeki, promising an era of action; Fivaz, the old white holdover nearing the end of his term and recognising that he was a temporary bridge to a new order.

In the discussion between the two about which senior police members might be seconded to Idoc, Knipe's name came up. 'I am from the Eastern Cape, he is from the Eastern Cape,' reflected Ngcuka, 'so I thought I perhaps could understand him. But I had also not heard good things.'[22] Fivaz nixed other names on the list, telling Ngcuka: 'These guys are a disaster. In the interests of the country, leave them.'[23] Arno Lamoer, presumably having been put on the list by Sonn and a favourite of Fivaz, made the grade.

The establishment of Idoc caused friction between those who were transferred out of the police and those who stayed. It was also a compromise: the specialised units remained within the police and were responsible for handling the caseload not picked up by Idoc investigators. Inevitably, this seeded a wider discussion about cherry-picking of cases by the better-resourced Idoc. For the time being, Knipe remained in charge of specialised investigations in the province, although he was later 'kicked upstairs' to headquarters as frustration with him grew. Barkhuizen, who had been at the front line of the Pagad investigations in Murder & Robbery, elected to stay in the police, maintaining his loyalty to Knipe. Kerrie Heyliger, who had taken over from Visagie at the Pagad unit, went to Idoc.

Tensions were accentuated by the fact that Idoc was created because police investigators were failing to crack Pagad-related cases. In the eyes of those who stayed behind in the SAPS elite investigative units, it seemed they were being further marginalised and regarded as second class. But Sonn was a determined man and got his way.

Idoc on its own could not solve all the cases and the challenge the Pagad phenomenon posed. It would take wider cooperation led by the new directorate to achieve that and, as in all bureaucracies, the shift took time. In the immediate period after its formation, however, Idoc was a distinct shock to the Western Cape security system. Sonn had been particularly enraged by the Pagad protest outside Justice minister Dullah Omar's house after the V&A Waterfront bombing, during which protesters claimed the police were involved in a witch-hunt against Muslims. He saw danger signs and believed the police were too inept to respond. Sonn had sharp bureaucratic elbows and he used them. That power had been diverted away from the police was clear, but so too was the sense that the new initiative might fail. Lamoer was so concerned that he sought assurance that his move would not affect his promotional prospects within the SAPS should he return.

At a political level, Idoc also symbolised the new democratic order taking over from the old: not only were police to be subordinate to prosecutors (and by implication the rule of law), but the leaders of Idoc were not white, including Sonn, Lamoer and an ex-ANC intelligence man, Mzwandile Petros, who led SAPS undercover operations that fed into the new outfit's work.

It couldn't have been easy for the likes of Knipe and other old-order senior detectives. The dual pressures of resolving an escalating number of urban terror cases with extremely limited resources and the sense of being irrelevant in a changing political-institutional order must have felt like an enemy pincer movement. Perhaps they felt unappreciated by a new regime they still to some extent mistrusted. But they probably knew they did not have the means to beat Pagad, and the state had decided a new solution had to be found. With Idoc, it began sowing the seeds.

An inadvertent murder?

The transition to Idoc placed a massive administrative burden on Lamoer. Police officers were eager to understand where they stood as the changes were implemented. On 13 November 1998, as a tumultuous year was drawing to a close, Lamoer met Captain Bennie Lategan, a well-regarded Murder & Robbery detective who had been selected for Idoc and was keen to make the move. Lategan wanted to inquire about his salary and conditions of employment in the new directorate. Three months previously, Ebrahim Jeneker had threatened Lategan when he had been in charge of taking specimens of blood and hair for DNA analysis. Shaken by this experience, Lategan asked for a transfer but was refused. He seemed to have settled down and was now keen to join Idoc. Within two months he would be dead.

Lategan, an ex-Security Branch cop who had developed unusually good working relations with former ANC types in Crime Intelligence, had been investigating many of the explosions around Cape Town. Visagie, never one to hide his views, says he was 'a pleasant guy', although it is perhaps telling that he makes no comment on his investigative abilities.[24] Visagie was working with Barkhuizen, one of the longest-serving men on the Pagad investigations. After Lategan's murder, however, rumours circulated that Lategan had been about to expose wrongdoing at Murder & Robbery, Barkhuizen's unit. It is hard to know whether there is any substance to this, but the fact that such talk was circulating was confirmed to me by three senior police officers. In the febrile atmosphere of the Pagad police campaign, a conspiracy theory after his death said Lategan had either been dispatched by his own colleagues or they had not acted on information that he was to be targeted.

On 14 January 1999, Lategan and his colleague Kobus Roelofse went to Philippi, a Cape Flats community where much of the fresh produce consumed in the city is grown on semi-urban holdings. The purpose of the trip, for which a search warrant had been obtained, was to follow up a tipoff that a Pagad arms cache was hidden on a farm called South Fork and that a training facility was operating there. The information must have come through the informer network. The high Cape summer temperature of the previous day had dropped and it was pleasant to be outside. After searching the dry, sandy area where they had been directed, they found what appeared to be a makeshift shooting range with spent cartridges lying around. The detectives had coordinated the search with the bomb disposal unit, so the 'men in black' were working alongside them.

After the initial discoveries, Lategan left the group to return to his office in Bellville. This involved driving through Mitchells Plain, then taking Vanguard Drive (now Jakes Gerwel Drive) before turning right onto the R300, or Cape Flats Freeway. It's an extremely busy intersection, with two lanes of traffic feeding into one of the main spinal routes traversing the Cape Peninsula. The vegetation is sparse, the road lined with a few scattered bluegums.

Just before 7 pm, Lategan was waiting at the traffic lights to turn right. The outline of the Table Mountain chain extended in the distance out on his left. A broken-down Mercedes-Benz was being pushed across the road by several young men, holding him up as he waited to get onto the R300. Lategan, in a last kindly act, gave some small change to one of the street kids who had pushed the Mercedes Benz. While he waited, a Toyota Corolla approached from behind and drew up alongside. Fifteen shots were estimated to have been fired at Lategan's car and 13 hit him. The detective was taken to hospital but died shortly afterwards.[25]

One of the witnesses was courageous enough to follow the Corolla (which had been stolen a few days earlier) from the scene and counted three people in the car. Boeta Yu, in his horse-whispering voice, told me just before his death that he was one of them. While the police assumed Lategan's car had been followed for a while and that the killing was well planned, Boeta Yu said the shooting group stumbled on the detective by accident. They were on Vanguard Drive and happened to pass Lategan waiting to turn off, recognising him as a Pagad investigator. 'Hey, isn't that the cop,' Boeta Yu reported one of the group saying.[26]

The men decided there and then to try to kill Lategan. They executed a U-turn and drove up next to the policeman. It is difficult to know whether Boeta Yu was telling the truth in this case, but he proved to be a reliable source for my research in other areas. There is no doubt in my mind, though, that Pagad killed Lategan. I don't give any credence to the notion that his colleagues either arranged for him to be killed or did nothing to prevent it because he was about to expose illegal activity.

Lategan's death sent a shockwave through the police's senior leadership. Investigators who previously felt unprotected henceforth had highly trained members of the SAPS Task Force riding shotgun with them as they did their work. Nevertheless, the sense of unease deepened considerably; they realised how brazen, ruthless and practised the Pagad killers were. Lategan's death seemed symbolic of the failing state response. Sonn immediately contacted Ngcuka, urging him to provide more support to set up Idoc. As outlined in Lamoer's diary, a flurry of internal meetings shortly followed.

Given how the case rocked the South African security establishment, it is reasonable to assume the police would have gone all out to present a watertight case against the Pagad operatives they identified as Lategan's killers, or held off until they had one. As it turned out, the investigation could only be described as amateurish, underscoring Sonn's assertion that something different was needed.

Two accused, both of whom we have already encountered, were brought to trial for the murder: Ismail Edwards, the chunky driver of Ebrahim Jeneker's getaway car, and Jeneker himself. The elusive Boeta Yu, if indeed he was present during the murder, seems to have escaped notice; while the man who followed the fleeing Corolla suggested a third person was present. The state maintained there were only two accused at the scene (in fact detectives believed, wrongly in my opinion, that Zain Cornelsen, the muscular and practised operative, was also there.) Judgment in the case was delivered in April 2003, four years after Lategan's murder, and it shows a deeply concerning failure of the investigative process.

What seems clear from documents I have been able to access from the court file, corroborated by the judgment, is that far from expending a great deal of effort to bring the killers of their former colleague to justice, the investigation had a strong whiff of massaged witnesses and manufactured testimony. Perhaps the pressure to arrest Lategan's killers – Jeneker in particular – drove this, but it leaves the strong impression of an investigative process in disarray. Police and prosecutors disputed this, however, and muttered darkly about the judge and her apparent sympathy for the defence.

A statement was not taken from a key witness, even though the police spoke to him the day after the incident when he acted as an interpreter for another witness at the scene. It was only in May 1999, four months after a murder which created a national outcry, that a new investigating officer, Captain Heinrich Cooper, turned up at the intersection to take a statement.

The judge was particularly scathing about the way police managed a photo identification parade. This was conducted by a Sergeant Swartz and runs to the comical; less funny is the implication that the police were trying hard to find a way to set up the evidence. The process was conducted on two separate days in which the police ran through a photo album of possible suspects with a key witness (a street child who had been on the corner). Based on the photos, the boy identified the driver (Edwards) and the passenger (Jeneker) and pointed them out from the witness stand.

What was strange about Swartz's actions was that he initially claimed to have shown the young witness the book in which one suspect was identified, then discovered he had not shown the full album to him. He then said he returned, whereupon the witness pointed out the car's passenger, Ebrahim Jeneker, from photos he had missed the first time around. In the court's opinion, this smacked of the police creating evidence to suit their case. Swartz 'did not impress as a witness' and 'his explanation does not rub', said the judge.[27] She was also critical of the police for not holding an identification parade, although she did not mention that Jeneker refused to stand in one.

Another important witness for the state was similarly compromised. Nico Uys claimed to have been the prison cellmate of Anees Adams, Jeneker's brother-in-law. It should be noted here that Uys had appeared as a witness in a murder case where Adams was the accused and it seems likely he was a police plant. Uys testified that Adams informed him he was a member of Pagad and that the prison contained another member (Edwards). Edwards was said to fraternise with Adams in his cell, where Uys was also present. According to Uys, Edwards said Adams contacted Lategan to tell him he had information and that he would meet the detective on a farm in Philippi. Edwards then added that he, Adams and some others waited for Lategan to turn up in order to murder him.

Uys testified that 'he had become tired' of Edwards and Adams bragging about the crime they committed, so he informed the prison authorities on 7 October 2000.[28] The police were apparently much speedier in their response this time and an officer turned up the next day. Since Uys had also testified in a separate murder case against Adams, these court records were produced during cross-examination. In the Adams trial, Uys attributed comments about the murder to Adams, while in the Edwards trial he attributed the same comments to Edwards. As for Uys's statement that he had grown tired of Edwards's boasting and reported it to the authorities, whereupon a police officer swiftly arrived, it was shown that Edwards had been transferred from the prison on 2 October, five days before.

It was little wonder that the judge concluded, 'it is clear that he tailored his evidence in order to incriminate the specific accused against whom he was testifying'.[29] Uys, the judge said, agreed to testify solely so he could buy drugs at the court (presumably because security was lax in and around the holding cells) and later sell them in prison. 'His head,' said the judge with an unusual legal turn of phrase and a bit too much benefit of the doubt being provided to the police, 'just pointed in one direction and that was to obtain weed and Mandrax.'[30] Another prison witness also testified that Jeneker told him he wanted to kill Lategan in 1998, but there were several contradictions in this statement too. Unsurprisingly, the case against Edwards and Jeneker collapsed and they were found not guilty.

A state under attack

For the struggling police officers in Cape Town in early 1999, more bad news was to follow. On 19 February, a month after Lategan's assassination, the Pagad hit squad struck again. This time the target was Schalk Visagie. Although he had recently moved from his position as head of the Pagad investigation unit to focus, ironically, on the city's gangs, this was not something Pagad would have necessarily known. He was still a high-profile target. The attack took place on one of the busiest highways in Cape Town, the M5, next to Valkenberg psychiatric hospital and not far from the bomb squad's prefabs in Pinelands.

A VW Kombi pulled up alongside Visagie's car and those inside fired multiple shots at the detective. He stopped the vehicle and the assassination squad also screeched to a halt, exited the Kombi and continued to fire into the car from a few metres away. Presumably believing Visagie was as good as dead, they then departed. Miraculously, the detective survived, although suffering terrible injuries. On hearing the news, Mandela, who was about to land in Pretoria after a trip to Cape Town, asked for the plane to be turned around. Back in Cape Town, he went straight to the hospital where Visagie was receiving emergency treatment.[31]

The attack on the Pagad investigation unit in Bellville in August 1998, in which Visagie narrowly escaped death, the killing of Lategan, yet another bomb at the V&A Waterfront and Visagie's attempted assassination all occurred within seven months. These events seem to snap the state to attention. Sonn, as we have seen, had been highlighting the emerging dangers since at least the middle of the year and had begun the process of getting Idoc established. The rest of 1999 was punctuated by further attacks, including the Blah Bar bombing in November. Thabo Mbeki, newly installed as president, summoned Ngcuka and other senior officials and read them the riot act at the end of the year. But it was clear that by early 1999 the wind had already changed and a wider recognition had dawned that more needed to be done. Important seeds were being planted which were to have long-term consequences for South Africa.

Behind the scenes, a furious battle was already being fought in the shadowy world of intelligence. For the spies, internal competition and distrust – already deeply ingrained only a short period into democracy – continued to mar their engagement. This was shockingly clear in an incident involving the betrayal of the state's senior informants in Pagad in early 1999, which we will examine in detail next. But the reverberations of that incident at senior level and wider changes that were already under way had a transformative effect on intelligence activities against Pagad.

10

STATE V STATE AND ANOTHER

The relationships between intelligence agencies and spies have provided material for some of the world's most intriguing political scandals, not to mention best-selling literature and movies since the Cold War era, when the world of espionage and counterespionage came of age. Stories of good agents and double agents still enthral millions of readers and provide glamorous action material for Hollywood blockbusters.

The function of intelligence is to gather information on risks to national security from a firmament of sources that are largely unreachable by the orthodox tools available to law enforcement. The role of the handler is to manage, cajole and coerce the spy to get that information so it can be presented as evidence. But what if the secret agent cannot be trusted? What if the intelligence agency has ulterior motives? What if both parties are conflicted? The spy game is murky and complex. Paranoia goes with the territory.

By late 1998, the pressures were mounting enormously on the state security services to bring Pagad's bombing and shooting campaign to an end. The public messaging was crafted to reassure South Africans and the world that they were doing the job and that the violence would be halted. But despite an anti-terror operation named Good Hope set up in January 1999, the response remained disjointed. The spate of violence meant Pagad was now a target for intelligence penetration. The state needed a secret agent, an informant on the inside, and it found one.

A remarkable set of events in early 1999 shine a light on the intense competition between South Africa's state intelligence agencies, which were fighting not only Pagad but each other. Interviews I conducted for this book more than 20 years later indicate the scale of the competition – and the blunder, largely hushed up at the time. The case centred on Ayob Mungalee, Pagad's chief coordinator in Gauteng.[1]

Mungalee was central to how Pagad took off in the Johannesburg area. The Gauteng organisation was a different animal from its Western Cape counterpart, which was captured by radical interests and defined by an escalating shooting and bombing campaign. The Johannesburg outpost was regarded as a tamer version of the Cape mother ship and was thought by some more radical members to be too closely aligned to the ANC. Religious fundamentalism played less of a role in the Gauteng campaign. In Mungalee's words, the 'primary concern was to help communities get rid of gangsterism'.[2] The focus was not on a targeted killing campaign of the sort Jeneker and his team pursued, but that did not mean it was not violent: 'We beat the shit out of gangsters and we closed up the drug houses,' he said proudly.[3] But a line was drawn at murder.

In one incident in June 1997, four Pagad members led by Mungalee turned up at a venue in the Rosebank area where drugs were sold. With them was a Radio 702 reporter. Bouncers confronted the group, and Mungalee and another Pagad member suffered minor injuries.[4] A few weeks later, a bouncer was shot but not killed, a message clearly designed to convey that drug dealing must stop and that Pagad could calibrate the level of violence it employed.

In chasing down the gangsters, Pagad in Johannesburg also seemed to win support from elements within the state apparatus. While at a butchery one day, Mungalee was introduced to another customer as one of the leaders of Pagad in Gauteng. 'This guy, who the butcher said was from the army, told me to come to a certain location that Friday evening. I asked him what he meant. He said that I should just trust him because they were there to help our case. I took some of my guys along and they handed us R4 rifles with ammunition and trained us to use them.'[5] In this case it may have been unclear where the guns came from, but in other instances there was no doubt. Mungalee said he and his men were given R5s and AK-47s by South African National Defence Force (SANDF) soldiers. Favours in return were expected: Mungalee and his men were asked by the gun suppliers to sort out drug dealers in the Krugersdorp area. There were hundreds of similar cases where gangsters were chased from their homes and drugs destroyed.

In late 1997 Mungalee received a call from Abdus-Salaam Ebrahim who was concerned that outside the Western Cape, Pagad was too aligned with the ANC. Mungalee was not cosy with the ANC either so he did not need much persuading that the organisation needed a new strategy. Ebrahim flew to Johannesburg and Mungalee was subsequently elected the leader of Pagad in Gauteng. From the beginning, Mungalee was convinced that the level of violence generated by their counterparts in the Cape meant lower-level threats were enough to intimidate and scare off the Joburg gangsters. 'We did drive-by shootings and we threw petrol bombs, but we never killed anyone,' he told me.[6]

One reason Mungalee was so important to Ebrahim was that he could access funds from wealthy Muslim businessmen in Johannesburg. The Gauteng chapter of Pagad became an important cash cow for Western Cape operations, although Mungalee grew suspicious of what became of the money, believing it was not all used for organisational purposes.

Today, Mungalee has few kind words for Ebrahim, describing him as a highly manipulative leader: 'Abdus sees everyone as a tool and he is the user ... but he is one of the weakest people I've ever met.'

Mungalee had a high profile and a loyal following in Gauteng, having gained credibility as a community activist opposing gangsterism and drugs. He was quoted in the press and spoke at public meetings. He had extensive insider knowledge about the group's operations. He was also a paid informer for the National Intelligence Agency (NIA).

At the end of the millennium, the NIA was the fledgling outcome of a merger between the former apartheid intelligence structure (the National Intelligence Service, or NIS) and the ANC Department of Intelligence and Security. The agency's role was to provide strategic analysis based on information its officials collected. Unlike the police, the intelligence agency does not have powers of arrest. The NIA was riven with internal challenges stemming from the fact that former operatives who only a few years before had been spying on each other were now colleagues in the same building.[7] The ANC also apparently inflated the numbers of its intelligence personnel and many inexperienced people joined. It was a messy business. Many in the old guard resented the arrival of new officials with ANC credentials and few skills, some of whom were fast-tracked to senior positions.

The NIA and police intelligence structures were also falling over each other to demonstrate their relevance – and by implication justify their budgets. That set the stage for fierce rivalry; if one agency could show that the other was blundering in the fight against Pagad or, even worse, supporting it, the newly minted political masters would decide which would lead the state's operation.

The old NIS and police Security Branch competed in the dark and troubled days of apartheid.[8] Old habits died hard, it seems. And the Mungalee case did not cover either intelligence agency in glory.

From journalist to spy

Mungalee was not recruited by the NIA to provide intelligence on Pagad. In his telling, an NIA official who introduced himself as Andre van Staden asked him in 1994 to collect information for Nelson Mandela's office, and Mungalee soon established a financial relationship with the spooks. The way he was recruited followed an NIS playbook that was used to monitor people under apartheid. He was at the time a journalist able and willing to engage with communities and edited a local newspaper, *The People's Voice*. His NIA handler, Van Staden, first asked him to cover the issue of illegal land invasions by squatters in Nancefield, Soweto.

In terms of access, Mungalee was a choice recruit. As a community leader, he was widely known and sought after. He told me: 'My home at the time was like a civic centre as everyone was coming for help or financial relief. I was involved with churches, with pensioners, with people that wanted grants from the state.'[9] For an intelligence agency reporting on local developments, he was a prime information node in a wider network.

Mungalee had had a difficult relationship with the ANC. Before moving to Johannesburg in the late 1980s he was a member of the UDF in Nelspruit and an anti-apartheid activist. In the early 1990s, as the country staggered through the turmoil of the transition to democracy, he and others formed the Concerned Residents' Association. He was approached by the ANC, which was courting him to be a local councillor or member of parliament. The relationship soured, however, partly because he lambasted the party in his stories in *The People's Voice*.

The enmity seems to have resulted in the paper's closure, and with his income now compromised, Mungalee was even more reliant on the largesse of the NIA.

Mungalee and his handler seemed to get on like a house on fire. Van Staden trained him in surveillance and counter-surveillance and intervened when Mungalee found himself in tight spots. Van Staden told him his superiors greatly valued his reports and that he submitted them verbatim. 'I had to report on things like taxi violence, wildcat strikes, gang violence and the like. This was the same type of thing that I had been doing for my newspaper, so it was money for nothing and I had all the resources to provide him with anything he needed.'

The informant took his tasks seriously and worked hard. A surprising friendship blossomed between the Muslim community activist and the Afrikaner old-order spy, and they even met off duty at Mungalee's home. But their affable relationship deteriorated rapidly. Sometime in 1996, Mungalee had problems with his car and the ever-helpful Van Staden stepped in to assist. He gave Mungalee his own Honda and the two made a gentlemen's arrangement that Mungalee would take over the monthly loan payments. The vehicle had a service contract and the two of them decided not to change the ownership details so Mungalee would be able to service the car at no extra cost. When he eventually took the car in for a service, however, he found it was not registered to Andre van Staden but to someone called Frans Richards.

For a spy, this was incompetence at the highest level. Perhaps Richards, aka 'Van Staden', had developed such a level of trust in Mungalee that he no longer worried about exposure, or no longer cared about such details because he was about to call it a day at the NIA, as he had told Mungalee. In retrospect, it seems like an almost laughable breach of security.

Richards, one of the old-order spies in an agency undergoing a painful transition, may have read the writing on the wall and simply given up following protocol.[10] Their trust now irreparably damaged, Mungalee suspended communication with his handler.

Closing in on the centre

According to sources, the spy agency was given the go-ahead in 1997 to run intelligence operations against Pagad to determine if it constituted a threat to the fledgling constitutional democracy. After the spate of bombings, the pressure was on the NIA to get intel about who was behind the killings.

Mungalee, always in step with community sentiment, joined Pagad's Johannesburg chapter in its early days. Greta Bezuidenhout, a slender and careful NIS field operative who was the NIA's new Gauteng operational chief (and one of the few senior woman managers in the organisation), had been thumbing through files looking for recruits to penetrate the group, and Mungalee was an obvious answer. He was skilled and connected, had risen fast through the Pagad ranks in Gauteng and had shown his mettle under Richards.

The ambitious Abdus-Salaam Ebrahim also set his sights on Mungalee. Always well informed, Ebrahim would have known of Mungalee's early falling out with the ANC and his popularity as an activist in the Muslim community of Johannesburg south. When Mungalee faced internal political opposition, Ebrahim, in the process of solidifying his power, was quick to intervene.

The NIA had already got there. In early 1997, the newly exposed Frans Richards acting under instructions patched up relations with Mungalee and introduced him to his superior, Bezuidenhout. Senior as she was, Bezuidenhout ran Mungalee, an indication of his importance to the agency. But the dynamic of the relationship was different. If Richards had been a jovial and ever-present friend, things with Bezuidenhout were altogether more formal. Perhaps that was a result of the new handler being a woman, but it was also because she kept the relationship at arm's length while, in Mungalee's own words, still showing 'a degree of caring'. The relationship also seemed more directly contractual: 'I didn't give her anything outside of what she asked me,' he said.[11]

As Mungalee's involvement in Pagad activities ramped up and he became increasingly active in operations, he became too busy to file reports for the intelligence agency. Meanwhile, his public image was growing. He was sought after by the media. He was also about to cross swords with his old nemesis, the ANC.

As his profile rose, Mungalee was not afraid to challenge the new political elite. He gatecrashed a meeting being addressed by then Gauteng premier Tokyo Sexwale and handed him a memorandum. The document detailed allegations that ANC members were involved in drug trafficking. Mungalee's Pagad team had tracked a vehicle whose number plates matched those of an ANC official involved in moving drugs from Lanseria airport to Vosloorus. The memorandum also listed names of other ANC officials reputed to be involved in drug trafficking. Not long after that meeting, Mungalee said he faced an assassination attempt.

After the publicity generated by the encounter with Sexwale, Jessie Duarte, the ANC MEC for public safety in Gauteng at the time, summoned Mungalee to her office. They already knew each other from the world of provincial politics. Duarte, a pint-sized firebrand of a woman, was on the up in South African politics. Outspoken and willing to confront the police when she felt their performance was poor, she was eager to be seen to reduce crime in the province.[12]

Mungalee claims Duarte sent her bodyguards to fetch him and that a stand-off ensued between Pagad and the heavies while everyone worked out what was going on. In the end he was taken to Duarte's house in Observatory, where the MEC was waiting. She motioned to a pile of police case files next to her and told him: 'You are accountable for all these operations where these druglords' houses are being shot up and petrol bombed.' Then the sting: 'The police can arrest you for these crimes.' But then she smiled and said she would have 120 files destroyed and that Mungalee was doing a 'stellar job'. 'Don't be an idiot,' Mungalee said she told him. 'Don't do things overtly, do them covertly.'[13]

If the story is true, and I have no reason to doubt it, it was an astonishing intervention in police operations by a senior politician. Not only a monumental breach of protocol, it also effectively sanctioned vigilantism as a proxy enforcement tool.

Until his meeting with Duarte, Mungalee had not reported on Pagad activities to the NIA. He was feeding the spy agency information about taxi violence, protest actions and the like. No one in Pagad had any inkling that he was a government informant with a handler in the NIA. For his part, Mungalee appeared to compartmentalise his Pagad activities from his NIA work; there was no conflict between them, he reasoned, as both were justifiable in supporting his community. The Duarte meeting, which was presumably relayed to the NIA, seemed to raise Mungalee's profile in the eyes of the spooks.

Yet they remained nervous about Mungalee as a source, and for good reason: he was outspoken, prone to exaggeration and in the public eye – not ideal credentials for a spy. In particular, the worry at NIA regional headquarters was that Mungalee might be drawn into illegal activities himself. In the new democratic framework, spying had become much more regulated. While the business of intelligence is often considered to be a wild affair (and in some places that is indeed the case), in democracies it can and should be highly regulated. As a result, it is more subject to oversight than outsiders may suspect. Following protocol, the NIA obtained a taped agreement in which it was explained to the recruit that he should stick to the straight and narrow and avoid unconstitutional and illegal activities. The tape was apparently made in May 1997 and it is unclear if Mungalee knew he was being recorded. The outcome was that if Mungalee broke the unwritten agreement he would effectively face the full force of the law on his own.

It is unclear to me how Mungalee internalised this agreement. In his mind, being part of Pagad's mission made him an ideal informer on the organisation's activities. He wasn't telling his masters at the agency the whole story about what he was up to, yet he kept it no secret that he had been involved in violence, and he even publicly threatened drug dealers. In June 1997, after the incident in Rosebank, Mungalee was quoted in the media as saying: 'We feel we have a right to kill these people because they are killing many other people with their drugs.'[14]

The newly minted NIA was determined to stick to the letter of the law. In October 1997, one of its sources reported that Mungalee had an illegal firearm. On that basis, Bezuidenhout was ordered by her superiors to break off contact with her informant. It may seem surprising that a well-placed source should be dropped because he has a gun, especially given the immense pressure the state was under to respond to Pagad, but this was before the bombing campaign against civilian targets had started. When it did, some of the rules of democratic spying were bent.

The NIA nevertheless decided to maintain ad hoc contact with Mungalee, perhaps to determine the extent to which he was involved in illegal activities and reactivate him if he was clean. In March 1998, a decision was taken to reinstate him for intelligence on gangs and corrupt members of the police service. But it was clearly a prelude to requesting intel on Pagad. From mid-1998, when Pagad's activities shifted to attacks on state and civilian targets, Mungalee again began to report to the agency on the vigilantes. He had taken a step back from Pagad but returned after a close acquaintance was attacked by gangsters.

By the end of 1998, after several bombings of civilian targets and attacks against state institutions, the NIA urgently needed to find a fix. The assertive Mungalee was increasingly well placed to help. His access to the group was now extensive, largely thanks to his relationship with Ebrahim. The intelligence agency received a stream of reports from him. As Ebrahim confided closely in Mungalee, there is little doubt the agency must have been fully aware by now of all the key actors in the violent campaign.

Smoke and mirrors

To embed himself in Pagad, Mungalee played a complex game – one he assumed handler Greta Bezuidenhout understood. As noted, Bezuidenhout did not at first ask him – surprisingly, he felt – for information about Pagad. In his mind that may have justified his NIA activities, since he wasn't being asked to betray his comrades.

At the same time, Mungalee felt Bezuidenhout was building his confidence – and she seemed to deliberately drop titbits of information about Pagad's internal workings. He listened carefully to her and relayed the information to Ebrahim, without revealing the source. 'I didn't tell him everything Greta told me but the limited amount that I told him enthralled him because I could tell him he was infiltrated. I was privy to information of a meeting that had just happened between Abdus and his executive members.'[15]

In this game of mirrors, Mungalee used the information provided by Bezuidenhout to strengthen his relationship with Ebrahim. 'I had the capacity to tell Abdus who his opponents were in Pagad.' Ebrahim seemed fixated on those plotting against him. 'He was definitely paranoid about the frailty of his leadership as he was easily threatened by any charismatic person around him.'[16]

Ebrahim did not ask where the intelligence came from but it fed his paranoia, and with good reason: the person conveying it was about to considerably deepen his relations with the secret state.

As Mungalee embedded himself deeper into the Pagad fold, positioning himself close to its most critical and violent figure, the NIA must have felt like the cat that had got the cream. By the end of 1998, Mungalee was back on the NIA payroll, and source and handler began to speak every day – a sign, if one was needed, that Mungalee was seen as a valuable recruit. The agency put R10 000 into Mungalee's account every two weeks, a considerable amount of money at the time, but his closeness to Ebrahim was like gold.

I am told the relationship with Mungalee became known by too many people at the NIA. Perhaps it was to demonstrate to senior managers that the agency was doing its work, but the information may also have reached the ears of police intelligence. The poor spy trade craft with Richards's car may also have raised suspicions.

For participants such as Mungalee, the spy game is a never-ending shifting set of interlinked paranoias. One of Mungalee's fears was that he was being watched by the agency he was spying for – or another. His instincts were correct.

A few days before he was summoned by Duarte, Mungalee was at the home of a member of his Pagad team. He needed to write down a phone number and asked the team member's wife for a scrap of paper. Noticing that something was printed on the reverse side, he looked more closely and recognised it as a petrol claim form of the sort he had filled in many times to account for fuel usage for his paid NIA work.

In the hands of his Pagad comrade, the form confirmed what Mungalee had already intuitively sensed: that Pagad, at least in Gauteng, had been

Yusuf Jacobs moments after being hit by a police rubber bullet during a demonstration against British Prime Minister Tony Blair on 8 January 1999. A set of events in the wake of Jacobs's death drew Ayob Mungalee more closely into Pagad's Cape Town network. PICTURE: Reuters

comprehensively penetrated by the state.[17]

As we have seen, the end of 1998 was a crucial turning point in the Pagad campaign. In the second week of 1999 during a visit to Cape Town by British Prime Minister Tony Blair, Pagad medic Yusuf Jacobs was hit in the head by a police rubber bullet and died a few days later. Pagad members were incensed by the killing, framing it as another attack on the organisation by a state more interested in protecting drug dealers than law-abiding citizens.

Mungalee drove from Johannesburg to attend the funeral of the young man. As it turned out, he missed the funeral but was in Cape Town when police investigator Bennie Lategan was assassinated. Jacobs had a

twin brother, Jacob, who was deeply traumatised by the shooting of his sibling, and Ebrahim asked Mungalee to take the young man back to Johannesburg to get him away from the increasing tensions in the Cape.

These incidents meant Mungalee got drawn into Pagad's Cape Town network, helping with the information that he could provide to the NIA. But besides exposing him to a new cadre of vigilantes, it also increasingly convinced him (not least through comments from his handler) that Pagad was comprehensively penetrated, and that his own movements were being reported on. He became increasingly paranoid. There was also clearly considerable competition between state agents engaged in spying on the organisation.

Then things took an even stranger turn, feeding his paranoia even further. Bezuidenhout told Mungalee the NIA had information that when he had driven to Cape Town for the funeral he had transported gunpowder to make a bomb. The intelligence report, as it was recounted to him, provided details of where Mungalee had met Abdus-Salaam Ebrahim and where the gunpowder was said to have been passed on to the bomb makers.

In a memorandum to the police, Bezuidenhout recounted a different story: she said it was Mungalee himself who told her about the gunpowder transfer and she was shocked that he had been involved. The memorandum notes that Mungalee never touched the gunpowder.[18] Whatever the truth of the matter, this may have been the point when the NIA began to get nervous about Mungalee. But in its eagerness to guard a key source and keep up with police intelligence, it retained him.

The infamous five

Mungalee said he was under a lot of pressure to find out who the bombers were. The state had now turned its guns on the individual (see Chapter 7) who was suspected of being key to training other Pagad members in bomb making, and who spent some time in Mungalee's home. There were a series of other house guests too, including an energetic, plainspoken activist from the Cape, who was also a reputed Pagad hitman, although whether the state knew the extent of his activities at the time is unclear.

Mungalee claimed the NIA provided him with a 'terrorist handbook' so he would understand bomb-making technology. That would allow him to draw more information from his house guests. In a later affidavit submitted to the court, Bezuidenhout said Mungalee told her he had obtained the handbook from a student at Wits University at the request of Jacob Jacobs. He gave it to his handler in January 1999 to be copied and she then returned it.[19]

Mungalee was surrounded by hardcore Pagad activists, at least one of whom he suspected was spying for an opposing state intelligence outfit. Wealthy and influential people in the wider community offered support to Pagad's efforts. 'People wanted to give AK-47s and bombs and various things to take down to Cape Town and I was getting nervous because they were all in my house and I refused to receive any of these things.'[20] Mungalee conceded that given all the activity, the group must have been under police surveillance and being reported on by informers.[21]

At some point it was decided the group had attracted too much attention and would slip away to Cape Town. Mungalee said he encouraged the move, and in early February 1999 the five Pagad members – Ayob Mungalee, Nizaam Shaik, Yassiem Adjouhaart (also referred to as Adams), Afzal Karriem and Jacob Jacobs – headed south in two cars. (They had a busy period before their departure, sourcing firearms and detonators, fighting with gang members and even taking the time to beat up a local druglord.) Bezuidenhout, desperate to understand what was going on and having had little contact from Mungalee, called him as they were getting under way. Mungalee spoke cryptically, saying he had 'two dets'.[22] Bezuidenhout could not work out what he meant and they were cut off.

Meanwhile the police, eager to make a breakthrough and presumably acting on intelligence from their own informer network, were ready to act. On a clear February day, between Laingsburg and Beaufort West, they swooped on the two cars. It was a major operation in which a truck was used to create a roadblock while the cars were assailed from helicopters by police special task force members. The five Pagad members were forced out of their cars and made to lie on the road for hours. In the vehicles, police said they found firearms, substances to make explosives, detonators and a bulletproof vest. They also found a copy of the 'terrorist handbook'. The arrests and seizures made national news. Arrests were made in Johannesburg at about the same time, during which arms and ammunition were seized. The Karoo swoop was clearly part of a wider operation.

For Mungalee, things went from bad to worse. During questioning he revealed he was a source for the NIA. In fact, it is highly likely the police already knew this – Bezuidenhout herself had probably been under police surveillance. But the police were in no hurry to get in touch with the NIA for several days after the arrest. Mungalee faced conflicting demands. The police and the court wanted a full statement while the NIA asked that elements of the statement referring to his work with the agency and any role in the delivery of explosives be deleted. A lawyer for Pagad also arrived, presumably advising Mungalee to keep mum. He was in a tight spot, especially as it became increasingly clear that the NIA would not or could not spring him from prison. The statement Mungalee had written was torn up and flushed down the holding cell toilet.

Sensing an opportunity in the ever-changing game of inter-agency competition, a tough-talking police general called Suiker Britz intervened and Mungalee was flown to Pretoria for a meeting. Britz was hardcore: he had come up through the Murder & Robbery units of the old SAP and had a reputation as one of the country's premier detectives. During a long career, he was also not averse to applying a little pressure. He wanted two things: a statement from Mungalee that implicated the NIA in wrongdoing, and a commitment from Mungalee to transfer his allegiances to police intelligence and make a statement implicating Pagad members in the V&A Waterfront bombing the year before. Charges would then be dropped, the police said, and Mungalee would receive a R1 million reward and resettlement. The request was made several times. If that was the carrot, the police were not opposed to using a bit of stick: he was placed in a cell with gang members. He wasn't taking the bait.

Having failed to 'turn' Mungalee, the police – without warning – revealed to the Oudtshoorn court where the case was being heard that he was an NIA source. There can be little doubt that this was authorised by Britz. Predictably, a media furore ensued, with questions asked about whether the NIA was assisting Pagad in its bombing campaign. The two organisations slugged it out in the press. 'We don't know why the police did it,' an exasperated NIA official was quoted as saying.[23] Henry Beukes, a former Crime Intelligence man turned detective and the police officer charged with the case, was even more direct: 'The police and the NIA need to talk together, otherwise we will murder each other at a crime scene.'[24]

The NIA was in a tight spot. Its agent had been burned by the police and was potentially in grave danger. Public accusations that the NIA could not protect those who worked for it would make recruiting agents harder still. The agency was also being accused in the media of supporting a bombing campaign in which innocent civilians had been killed. The NIA seemed unable, or increasingly unwilling, to extract Mungalee. 'They could only manage it,' said a police intelligence official, 'but it always had a fishy smell to it.'[25]

Tensions between the two state agencies were at fever pitch. The police and prosecutors accused the NIA of knowing that Mungalee and his co-conspirators were transporting weapons and explosives. The head of Idoc, Percy Sonn, never one to mince his words, stormed up to Bezuidenhout and accused the NIA of 'knowing all along what they were doing'.[26] (Reporting from Mungalee had been going to Arthur Fraser, the NIA head in the Western Cape, who seems to have chosen not to pass the intelligence along. Several people told me Fraser did not trust anyone and played his cards close to his chest. Fraser was a controversial figure long after the threat of Pagad subsided, but he did play an important role in responding to it.[27])

In an unprecedented step, NIA senior managers authorised a selection of Mungalee's reports to be handed over to the prosecutor so she could determine the degree to which he had provided assistance and insight to the state. The prosecutor was reported to have been impressed by the reports, suggesting they would not have proceeded with the prosecution if this had been known at the outset. The reports also presumably contained evidence that the NIA was not aware of what was in the vehicles. But it was too late, and the trial proceeded. In an unprecedented development for the spy agency, Mungalee's handler, the diminutive Greta

Bezuidenhout, was summoned to appear in open court to testify. In defending itself, the NIA effectively relinquished responsibility for Ayob Mungalee.

The February 1999 arrest of the Pagad Five was not the breakthrough the police hoped for. It was a huge missed opportunity for the state. In the end, Mungalee was sentenced to eight years in prison for possession of illegal firearms and served just over three and a half years. He was found not guilty on the charge of possessing the detonators, as the police's video evidence was disputed. (Mungalee maintains the detonators were planted by the police.) Shockingly, Mungalee was the only member of the five who served a prison sentence: the cases of the others quietly disappeared on appeal and they were released.[28] Mungalee later had several other run-ins with the police, including being accused of being a hitman. He said the police were setting him up and planting evidence, and he was not convicted in any of the cases.[29]

In the view of NIA insiders, a more cooperative approach would almost certainly have led to intelligence from their network of informants triggering arrests and trials of the senior ringleaders behind the Pagad bombing campaign. But the incident led to only one man's arrest once his cover had been blown. The whole episode reflected poorly on the state, which had failed its citizens. There was an urgent meeting between Sydney Mufamadi, the Minister of Safety and Security, and the wizened veteran ANC spy Joe Nhlanhla, the Minister of Intelligence. The plan was to focus on 'cooperation and communication' between the police and the NIA.[30] Dodging a wider inquiry, the ministers agreed more needed to be done to coordinate between the various security players. They also shut down any talk of an independent investigation – for good reason, given what had transpired.

When Bezuidenhout attended a training session of security officials after the incident, a police undercover agent in the same room boasted of how the police had managed to 'outwit NIA agents time after time' – referring in particular to the Mungalee case.[31] That is hardly something to be proud of, given that the agencies were meant to be on the same side. It only goes to show how much competition existed between the different security players and the degree to which they were spying on each other. Bezuidenhout left the NIA in 2007.

It has been suggested to me that Mungalee was to some extent captured by the objectives of Pagad – in effect, that he was a double agent with divided loyalties. When I put this to him, he prevaricated and did not deny he had some loyalty to Pagad. But he emphasised that he was totally opposed to the bombing of civilian targets. This could explain why, for example, he chose not to submit a statement after the intervention of the Pagad lawyer. It may also plausibly explain why he was able to live as long as he did: if Pagad had learnt that he was an NIA informer, especially one so close to Abdus-Salaam Ebrahim, his life would have been in mortal danger.

My reading on Mungalee, then, is that he was always a committed

Ayob Mungalee continued to maintain a profile as a dogged community activist in the years after his release from prison. Seen here in May 2022, nine months before his assassination, in Cape Town engaging with Western Cape Premier Alan Winde. PICTURE: Mungalee family

member of Pagad (something he never denied and which arguably was essential to his role as a state informer) but was also genuine in his attempts to limit the violence of the organisation. I have little doubt that he would have reported to intelligence on the bomb-making campaign in more detail as he uncovered information. Perhaps it was because he never in the end ratted out his colleagues that he was spared. Like so much involving Mungalee, it remains something of a mystery. Whatever the case, and knowing how brutally efficient the Pagad assassination squads were, he was a brave and a lucky man.

The Mungalee debacle unfolded at the same time as the intelligence system faced sustained pressure to respond more effectively to Pagad. In the Western Cape, significant steps were taken from mid-1997 to achieve this. If anything, Mungalee's case added urgency in the shape of orders from the top to cut the internal competition and do a better job. While today it has become *de rigueur* to eviscerate Crime Intelligence, some of the greatest victories against Pagad were the result of patient and risky intelligence work.

Sadly, Ayob Mungalee is no more: as I was completing this chapter in February 2023 he was assassinated. True to character, he had been publicly challenging the activities of two gangs and corrupt police in Eldorado Park. It is likely that he was killed by the hardcore Varados gang (members of which drove past immediately afterwards to check he was dead, so they are the prime suspects). It was a clean hit: someone held him from the front and he was shot from behind with a single bullet. The gun jammed before a witness who was standing close by could be killed too. Thousands of people paid their respects to him.

11

FLAWED HEROES

The Pagad phenomenon was novel compared to other challenges facing the secret state. These were damping down violence in volatile KwaZulu-Natal and suppressing right-wing opponents of the majority government, although in these cases intelligence sources were better developed. The significance of Pagad went unrecognised by state intelligence for some time, and because the organisation was driven by religious fervour it made recruitment of informers more challenging. Pagad operatives, for the most part, were also not on the state's radar, so the intelligence networks had little information to go on. Mungalee, one of the few sources who provided intelligence to the state at a senior level, was originally recruited to pass on information about political and social incidents and was only later recognised for his ability to provide briefings on Pagad. The movement also worked in tightly knit cells of people with close ties to one another, making it harder for intelligence agencies to get under its skin.

The Crime Intelligence response to Pagad is a story that has remained largely untold and provides fascinating insight into how the movement was eventually tapped. A very small group of intelligence officers, many with an ANC background but involving several key players from the old SAP, began to drive the response to Pagad just as Percy Sonn's investigating directorate, Idoc, was being conceived. For these former ANC spies, recently integrated as Crime Intelligence agents in the SAPS, Pagad was one of the first real challenges.

'The detectives were failing,' as one former senior policeman summed it up, and intelligence filled the vacuum.[1] In the absence of a credible police detective response, the covert intelligence work was ultimately one of the most crucial interventions in crushing urban terror. The role of intelligence did not come to fruition until late 1999 but earlier work by several officers was central in laying a foundation. To tell their story requires an understanding of how the threat was originally conceived among the country's spies.

'The challenge was convincing people this was a problem'

Intelligence activities, while providing exciting content for movies and Netflix dramas, are also often highly bureaucratic. Assessments are written based on information from undercover and overt sources, and these are subjected to internal scrutiny. When the assessments point to a security threat, a panoply of measures and resources can be deployed. Sometimes a vicious cycle develops: if too few intelligence resources are focused on an emerging problem, it does not make its way up the chain so no new resources are allocated, and the threat grows.[2]

Something like this occurred in the Pagad case. Between 1995 and late 1996, only a handful of people in the secret state worked on Islamic extremism. To some degree that made sense: it had never been a major threat and resources were needed to address other issues. Determining the threat is a crucial step to agreeing on the response and the state was slow to read the writing on the wall about Pagad.

Based in premises in Loop Street, Cape Town, two police officers formed part of the 'internal security' function of the fledging Crime Intelligence operation of the new SAPS. One was David Africa, who was recruited into police intelligence after working underground for the ANC. Africa, who grew up in that crucible of conflict and community cooperation, Manenberg, was central to identifying and acting against the Pagad threat.[3] It is interesting to juxtapose him and Ebrahim Jeneker, who grew up nearby at the same time. Both were products of South Africa's contested transition, both highly intelligent, and they were key in shaping the war between Pagad and the state from opposite sides of the front lines. Jeneker developed his delusional ideas of community and action from his personal experiences and lonely, self-reflective world view. Africa, in contrast, emerged from the underground fight against apartheid, with all its shadows and secrets. Bookish, he consumed all the available texts in his Manenberg school library and with the help of underground reading groups graduated to parsing Marx, Lenin and Gramsci. Without a matric certificate to show for his studiousness (he was expelled from school for political activity), Africa graduated to student politics and the fledgling structures of the UDF.

By 1990, as politics began to shift into the transition, Africa worked for the UCT Student Representative Council by day and trained liberation fighters in the use of weapons by night. In 1992, the ANC sent him for military training in Uganda, and on his return the liberation movement asked him to join the police.

Africa's soft-spoken style belied a strong-willed and highly independent personality. He was assigned to the 'extremism desk' in Loop Street. Two officers worked the file: Africa, initially appointed as a lieutenant, and a former sergeant from the SAP Security Branch.

The Loop Street facility was not known to the public, yet it was an 'open' office in that its staff, while careful not to attract attention to themselves, did not work covertly. An undercover unit, one of only four in the country, operated from separate premises under Gordon Brookbanks, the innovative, energetic and hard-drinking Jeremy Vearey ally who played a key role in the intelligence integration process.[4] At the time, Brookbanks's unit did not cover Pagad.

In November 1995, the head of the small unit where Africa worked, Captain Johan Marais, handed him a newspaper clipping. The item covered a march in Bo-Kaap organised by an Islamic group protesting against gangsterism and drugs. 'Look into this,' instructed Marais.[5] That march, brought to the attention of the state by astute reporting, was the first blip of Pagad on the intelligence radar. The two officers went digging around and recruited their first source, someone close to them told me. It was a good choice – a person not on the inside but operating on the fringes of Pagad who could ask questions and who was in contact with Muslim leaders. The source met their short-term requirement of understanding what was happening. Over at the NIA's regional office in Cape Town, there was little focus on Pagad either, so the Loop Street unit effectively took the lead. When they scratched around a bit, what they found was concerning.

Talking to their source and poring over reports they received, something seemed amiss to the Loop Street duo. 'It became clear to David early on,' a former police intelligence analyst said, 'that something unusual was going on – that Qibla was laundering itself. Qibla were never able to grow on their own, so their modus operandi was to do it through other organisations.'[6] Once you applied this formula, many of the happenings around Pagad seemed clearer and it was difficult to read the situation in any other way, even when the daily details threatened to obscure the bigger picture. But the idea that Pagad was some sort of front was hard to stomach for most, including some academic analysts at the time. What was the point of Qibla doing this when democracy had just been achieved? And why did Pagad have so much popular support? Within the police, too, newly attuned to the concept of community policing, the idea that the emerging anti-crime entity was to be cooperated with, not crushed, was understandably all the rage.

'The biggest challenge in 1996 in particular was convincing people that this was actually a problem,' an experienced police intelligence operative told me.[7] Africa, intellectual and self-willed, and his sergeant colleague wrote reports and gave briefings, pushing the line that what was happening was a real concern: Pagad was the state's foe, not its friend. For this he faced internal criticism that he was anti-Islamic, ironically from a member of the old apartheid intelligence service.[8] While the events of 9/11 were still some way off, there was already a sensitivity that the notion of Islamic terrorism was a narrative driven by external forces (for which read the US and UK).

The first threat assessment of Islamic extremism was written in 1996 and incorporated into the National Intelligence Assessment, a high-level review of security threats against the country. Significantly, and because of the Loop Street team's work, the assessment put the case that an anti-state movement driven by Qibla was emerging and was beginning to amass firearms. The report also noted that people were being trained to engage in violence. It was a prescient articulation of what was to come. Yet, among the many priorities facing the state at the time, it was 'difficult to get us to understand the seriousness of this', according to a senior government official.[9] In the fight to attract attention, several confidential police reports found their way into the media.[10]

The papers were being processed and the reports read in the offices of the secret state in Pretoria, but the need for an information flow from the ground was becoming more urgent. Loop Street wrote a warning in late July 1996 that a series of violent activities was imminent. It called for substantial resources to be deployed, most notably in respect of the march on Rashaad Staggie's home in Salt River planned for 4 August. Arno Lamoer's diary entries from the time show a sharp uptick in activities as the police moved to respond to the march. Remarkably, Africa and the ex-Security Branch sergeant with whom he shared the extremism desk were among the mob who marched to Staggie's house, their faces concealed. Another former ANC operative, Peter Jacobs, who became head of Crime Intelligence and then lost his job in controversial circumstances, was also in the crowd.

Staggie's death was the tripwire that first alerted the state to focus on the problem. It coincided with the reports that were now on the desks of those working within the secret state. Nevertheless, as a Pretoria-based insider told me, 'it was not taken seriously enough and the capability that was deployed was minimal. Sydney [Mufamadi, the Safety and Security minister] came down to Cape Town in a huff and a puff – what's going on here, he wanted to know, even though the reports had been written for him too.'[11] Another Crime Intelligence person told me: 'There were about 2000 people on that march, yet [police] undercover operators in the march saw only one or two policemen present.'[12] After Staggie's death, the state's response and rhetoric were characterised by confusion. On one hand, they sought to talk down the significance of Pagad; on the other, they tried to show they were cracking down on vigilante violence. Meanwhile, there was incredulity that so many gang bosses were dying: surely they were being killed by other gangsters, as usual? In any event, are dead gangsters not a good thing? It takes a long time to shift a prevailing view in a large security institution. But what the Staggie killing did do was unlock resources needed for the secret state to develop a network of informants and agents within Pagad.

In late 1996, David Africa was transferred to head office in Pretoria where he worked in a small unit investigating extremism under the direction of former Security Branch officer Willie Els. Els is a calm and considerate man with good people skills and an ability to get people to work together. By mid-1997, Els and Africa – another pairing of the old and new orders – were convinced a more strategic orientation was needed and that the case-by-case investigative approach would yield little in the long run. The intelligence system runs on documents and position papers, so Africa, with Els's support, wrote another one. Someone who received a copy summarised its contents as follows: 'Basically, it said that we were dealing with a phenomenon that was independent and home-grown. But it was connected, not organisationally but ideologically, to a larger global movement. We were talking about a very fundamental fact – this was driven by Qibla, and because Qibla refused to recognise the negotiated settlement of 1994 this had crucial consequences for the new political and constitutional order.'[13] Els and another police officer who later rose in the system, Mark Hankel, went on to play a crucial behind-the-scenes role in the response to Pagad from headquarters.

Africa's paper was widely read within the secret state and influenced decision-making that eventually reached the National Intelligence Coordinating Committee, known in the security community by its inelegant acronym, Nicoc. His thinking was torn apart in some debates but the key conclusions stuck and the paper was eventually approved by a cabinet meeting chaired by Nelson Mandela.

Greater political acceptance that Pagad posed a threat was accompanied by a series of activities in the Western Cape. First came Operation Saladin, an intelligence-driven counterinsurgency campaign which tailed off by mid-1997. This was quickly followed by Operation Recoil and in January 1999 by Operation Good Hope. But these operations were generally about providing a visible presence of police and military personnel and did not properly target key perpetrators. Vearey, who played a role in the intelligence side of Saladin, recounted later that each of the operations lost their focus and 'could not be sustained at consistent levels'.[14] And, he argued, although more visible policing might be helpful in displacing the threat, a longer-term covert focus on key individuals would be required to dismantle it.

There was also an initiative involving detectives and intelligence officers who were brought together to work on the problem. But things broke down almost immediately in the SAPS, the conflict only accentuated by Knipe's abrasive management style. I was told that at one memorable internal meeting there was a stand-up argument between Knipe and Africa, who had returned to Cape Town. The Crime Intelligence officer was junior to Brigadier Knipe in the rank-obsessed police and at this meeting Knipe instructed him to take statements from witnesses. It was an undeniably crass move, compromising not only an intelligence officer's identity but also his time. There was a fierce exchange as Africa protested that this was not the work of a Crime Intelligence officer. He stormed out. The police telephone lines ran hot as Knipe complained up the chain of command, but to little avail. The much-vaunted experiment in cooperation fell apart before getting off the ground.

'Where have you been all this time?'

Recruiting intelligence sources is tough, messy work and takes time. By 1998 and into 1999, the position was better but by no means perfect. Some Pagad cells had been penetrated by Crime Intelligence but the core groups of bombers and members of the most violent outfits (Jeneker's group, for example, which appears to have become active in late 1997), as well as the organisation's security council, were too hardcore to be lured as informants for the state. From late 1996, Africa and a small number of Crime Intelligence colleagues mounted an all-out effort to get a better picture of what was going on.

After successfully recruiting a source able to engage with the ideological principles of Pagad, the Loop Street team turned to finding someone closer to the organisation's operational core. Their first catch was Rushdien Abrahams, a G-Force member who had been arrested during a Pagad march that turned violent. Officers on the scene took him to Bellville police station and beat him up. One of the officers involved told me: 'He was cold and hungry, and they'd roughed him up a bit, so we organised him a halaal meal.' Meanwhile, the Crime Intelligence team had learnt of the arrest. 'We took him to the beach to chill out. He was almost relieved to be recruited.'[15]

Abrahams was a long-standing member of Apla and was reputed to have fought against the Soviets in Afghanistan. Given his liberation background, it was not surprising Africa might have found some affinity with him, especially as Abrahams had begun to be concerned about the scope and scale of Pagad's violence. His words to one of the Crime Intelligence officers when they asked him to be an informer were reportedly: 'Where have you been all this time?'[16] It was early days, but Crime Intelligence now had its real first window into what was happening operationally in Pagad. It was an opening that was shortly to be slammed shut.

After he was recruited, Abrahams led police intelligence to a deeply disturbing finding: Pagad was acquiring arms from government sources. Grenades had been stolen from arms-manufacturing parastatal Denel's facility on Swartklip Road, not far from Mitchells Plain.[17] What to do with such information? In the mind of the intelligence operatives, it provided an ideal opportunity to dig deeper and follow the breadcrumbs. Parts of this story are shrouded in mystery but it seems the essential elements are that police intelligence took the grenades to the bomb squad – with whom they were developing a good working relationship – and had them neutralised. A small amount of explosive material was left in the detonators but the grenades were essentially rendered harmless. The idea behind this ruse was for the Crime Intelligence team to determine where the grenades were ending up. By following the duds, they would find Pagad's targets and the sinews of its operations.[18]

Later, while he was operating as an undercover source for the intelligence men in Loop Street, Abrahams was arrested at a crime scene for possession of a grenade. He had apparently used a neutralised grenade in an attack on a suspected drug dealer but it failed to explode. To put up a defence, he told the detectives he worked for Crime Intelligence but they were not convinced; another grenade from the same batch, they maintained, had reportedly killed a pregnant woman.[19]

This incident 'caused a rift in the Western Cape police', reported journalist Marianne Merten at the time.[20] When Knipe learnt that Abrahams had been recruited as a source for Crime Intelligence he went ballistic, dismissing the operation as 'stupid'.[21] Knipe said there had been no attempt to trace the source of the confiscated grenade and argued that Crime Intelligence was therefore implicitly 'involved in terrorism'.[22] Crime Intelligence lashed back, accusing the police of 'scuppering a long-standing infiltration' that could have provided crucial information about how Pagad operated, leading to arrests of ringleaders.[23]

The grievance went to the core of what the police perceived as the unchecked powers of the intelligence services and the highly unorthodox, if not unethical, ways in which they used criminal actors to elicit information. It turned out that Knipe had arrested Abrahams many years before after he had been involved in an attack on a drinking establishment as a member of Apla. He said he knew Abrahams for what he was. But the hostility was undoubtedly aggravated by the narrative that the detectives thought the ANC intelligence operatives were somehow involved with Pagad.

Knipe subsequently had two police officers charged for arming Pagad and the case went to Frank Kahn, then attorney-general of the Western Cape, for a decision.[24] The case was quietly dropped but Abrahams was convicted. To save him from prison, the detectives and his former Crime Intelligence handlers urged him to give evidence. But the veteran fighter was a hard nut, unafraid of prison: 'I will sit and after some time I will get parole,' he was reported to have told his handler.[25] 'I met him afterwards and he wasn't even angry,' someone who worked on the case said.[26] Sit he did: he was sentenced to ten years, serving seven.

It's largely conjecture, but it may have been that Knipe, who considered himself an old-school, do-it-by-the-book senior officer, expected Crime Intelligence to bend the knee. Perhaps, as a self-described progressively minded servant of the state, and evidently disaffected by the ways of the old Security Branch, he was disappointed that the new ANC-aligned intelligence officers (of whom he was probably immediately mistrustful) were operating no differently from their rogue apartheid-era forebears in gathering covert intelligence. Some would argue, however, that given the emerging nature of the Pagad threat to the state, a completely new approach was needed – however ethically abhorrent and flawed it may have been – to obtain the intelligence the state needed to win this war. We know that Knipe's men were not getting results through their investigative work. Making intelligence subordinate to investigators made zero sense in a struggle where processing hundreds of cases and clues was leading nowhere and took up valuable time.

Protestations from Crime Intelligence that, despite his criminal past, Abrahams could have been a useful source of evidence against Pagad when there was little else to go on fell on deaf ears in the SAPS.

Sex, spies and police videotape

By 1997, there was a slump in the recruitment of intelligence sources in Pagad. Operation Saladin was being wound down and David Africa was summoned to Pretoria, leading to the disintegration of the Loop Street office's efforts. Fragmented, and with competing interests, the system was no longer working as it should, said insiders, partly because there was no dedicated covert intelligence-gathering capacity on Pagad in the police.

It is difficult to establish with certainty what occurred next, but several interesting and ultimately decisive developments were getting under way, the most critical of which was the establishment of a small, highly secret unit tasked with finding sources in Pagad. In mid-1997, Mzwandile Petros was appointed to run this team, known as the undercover operations unit, which worked on several issues (including taxi violence) but had not previously focused on Pagad. I met Petros around this time in a rainswept Greenmarket Square in the city centre, where he outlined in stark terms the challenge he felt needed to be addressed. Dressed in leather jacket and jeans, he disappeared as quickly as he had arrived into the gathering gloom of a damp Cape winter evening.

Petros decided a different approach was needed to tackle Pagad and he drew on his old ANC police networks: the quietly effective Anwar Dramat, then working for Leonard Knipe, was summoned to the new unit; and David Africa, hoping for a transfer home from Pretoria, was also ordered to report to Cape Town. They were joined by a handful of other officers, several with Security Branch backgrounds (including a former actress), but the number of undercover operators focusing on Islamic extremism remained very small until 2000.

While Petros's covert unit was coming together, the lease for its premises was inexplicably not renewed. Inevitably, the ANC insiders viewed this as a malicious act by an old-guard police bureaucrat. Displaced, the small group worked from a Crime Intelligence safe house in the southern suburbs. To complete the package, Africa also assumed the role of point person for Pagad on the Provincial Intelligence Coordinating Committee, which was run by Vearey. All the key posts in the Western Cape working on collecting intelligence on Pagad were now filled by ex-ANC operatives.

With only a handful of sources on the books by late 1997, the need for more information hardened the resolve of the group to find alternatives. Recruiting sources is a highly creative process but also time-consuming. The small team began to work 16- to 20-hour days. Drawing on their intelligence training, they profiled members of Pagad, meticulously combing through the files in the search for vulnerabilities that might make them inclined to turn. Even a small detail could be helpful: disillusionment with Pagad and its objectives (as had been the case with Abrahams), evidence of a drug habit, money problems, a sexual vulnerability or an extramarital or gay affair.

Police surveillance on possible targets was upped in the search for compromising titbits. It was dirty work in more ways than one. Rubbish bags from Pagad members' homes were examined by police officers who wore latex gloves as they sifted through the detritus of people's lives for a detail that might provide an opening. One surprising discovery was how many Pagad G-Force members were having affairs with each other's wives.

Despite uncovering a potentially fruitful seamier side to Pagad, the police spies received many rejections to their approaches for assistance. And although many original members who supported Pagad because of their belief that gangs and drugs needed to be confronted were willing to talk, they did not have the information needed to break into the circle of hardened operatives, including the bomb makers, the shooters and the bombers themselves.

Pagad also ran a system of counterintelligence and approaches from the state were reported. Its ideological core group held their beliefs too strongly to be easily swayed from their mission. And the price for exposure was high: Pagad had little compunction about murdering members who were thought to be acting for the state. As we have seen, it also regularly killed witnesses planning to testify against its members. A mix of ideological commitment and fear kept the organisation's most committed supporters beyond the reach of police intelligence. (As noted in

Chapter 10, this was one reason why Ayob Mungalee seemed to live a charmed life after his exposure as an NIA agent.)

In one case, shrewd police surveillance showed that a prominent Pagad member from Heideveld was making regular trips to Camps Bay. It was an interesting detail, more so because he was meeting a woman there, also a member of Pagad. The two were conducting an affair and presumably chose Camps Bay as a venue for their trysts because they were unlikely to bump into Pagad compatriots in the predominantly white suburb better known for its Atlantic views and foreign tourists than vigilante killers. The individual 'had a very good sense of security', reported a police surveillance expert who was involved in the case, making tracking his movements more difficult than for most.[27] When it was believed that the time was right, police intelligence made their move: a meeting was arranged and he was shown a video of his indiscretions. The result was not what the intelligence team were expecting. 'He told us straight away to fuck off,' a member of the team said.[28] Others were made of weaker stuff. In a repressed society, sex was a useful tool for Crime Intelligence operatives eager to blackmail Pagad members into cooperation, as we will see.

In cases where no indiscretions could be found or appeals to the newfound spirit of South African patriotism and unity would not do the trick, more sophisticated methods were used. The ANC Department of Intelligence and Security operatives and their Security Branch colleagues were well acquainted with the ins and outs of espionage. Qibla's Iranian alignment provided a vulnerability, and in one intelligence operation a young, ideologically committed G-Force member found himself being propositioned by a member of Iranian intelligence eager to understand the operational workings of Pagad. It was in fact a member of police intelligence in a 'false flag' operation. The man believed he was feeding information about Pagad's activities to Iran (which was an inspiration to Qibla), but it was being sifted and analysed by police spooks.

Network of change?

It became clear to the police spies that a more strategic approach was required. From an intelligence perspective, Pagad needed to be mapped and its soft points attacked – including by strategic investigations. Under the stress of the Pagad bombings and in a situation of general mistrust bred by the past regime, the ANC spies drew closer together in their network. They also developed bonds with other useful or sympathetic 'outsiders' – detectives such as Bennie Lategan (he was 'different and understood the role of intelligence', said one intelligence official[29]) and other like-minded colleagues from the old spy service such as Els and Brookbanks. They also found an affinity with the bomb squad, who, explained a former police spy, 'helped us to properly understand what we were dealing with when it came to Pagad'.[30] And, like Percy Sonn, the intelligence officials believed Pagad's violence was a test of the new ANC government. Convinced the system was failing, they were eager to play their part in responding.

Another ex-ANC intelligence man enters the picture around late 1998: Arthur Fraser, appointed as the new head of the NIA in the Western Cape just as the Mungalee case came to its climax. The intelligence agency was well staffed with former ANC people but relations with police intelligence were generally distant and often mistrusting, as the Mungalee case illustrated. Fraser, given his later association with Jacob Zuma, has something of a hard man reputation, ruthless and uncompromising, and not undeservedly. On his arrival in the province he was determined to make a difference. Except for Petros, whom he had never met, he also knew the former ANC men of the police undercover unit well. They updated each other and Mungalee, languishing in prison, was not mentioned. They were to be a formidable group. Over a drink in a southern suburbs pub, they resolved to 'crush Pagad'.

In theory, the moment for detectives and prosecutors working in close collaboration should have arrived with the establishment of Idoc, except the relationship didn't seem to have changed. If anything, it had deteriorated after the new ANC arrivals, with their wider political influence and legitimacy, went into intelligence. Schalk Visagie, then head of the Pagad investigation unit and reporting to Knipe, recounted a story from early 1998 when he obtained a search warrant for the house of Pagad national secretary Abida Roberts (known as the 'iron lady' on account of her tough talk and hardline views). During the search, Visagie and his colleagues found a government document marked 'top secret' and Roberts remained silent when asked where it came from. Back in his office at 3 am, Visagie was surprised to be introduced to two men from the NIA who said they had heard that Roberts had been arrested and that the police had a document from her house. They asked for the document to be handed over to them. 'I asked them politely to leave my office,' recounts Visagie. The case file, with the document inside it, then disappeared from the desk of the investigating officer and Roberts was released.[31] The detectives were never told what had happened or why. It was understandably infuriating.

Probably around late 1998, Pagad decided that David Africa and Anwar Dramat should be killed. Even though he worked behind the scenes, Africa came to the attention of Pagad's intelligence network as the result of a police intelligence slip-up and his cover was blown. He had been working to recruit someone under a 'false flag' operation, telling the Pagad target he represented business interests. In the desperation to recruit sources, it was decided someone else in the unit would make a direct approach, basically threatening the source and telling him he needed to work for the police. It was a careless choice, partly because the potential source already knew where Africa lived. The target was placed in a police vehicle and threatened: 'We will fuck you up if you don't work for us.' It backfired. I am told the man replied: 'Fuck you – I will never sell out my people.' It was not hard for Pagad to piece together that Africa's original approach must have come from the police.[32]

A fatwa was issued, and as the man police intelligence had targeted was from the Grassy Park Pagad cell, the same cell was ordered to eliminate Africa. The cell, which had been active in bombings and shootings across Cape Town, had about six members led by Moegsien Barendse, a striking, tall man with a full beard and a deep ideological commitment to the Pagad cause. He talks slowly, chooses his words carefully, and at the time he was on Pagad's security council, giving him strong influence in the organisation. Barendse was also an imam, meaning Grassy Park had one of only a few cells led by a religious man. But it had been penetrated by the state. The agent in the cell was Martin Manuel, a courageous former soldier who converted to Islam to penetrate Pagad and changed his named to Mansoor.

Almost immediately after the fatwa was issued in October 1998, the cell set out to attack Africa's house. Why they adopted such an immediately confrontational approach is not clear, but one explanation may have been that once the command to kill was given they were beholden to act immediately. I am told Africa received a call at about 9 pm while at home in Wynberg where his pregnant wife and daughter were getting ready for bed: 'They just left Grassy Park four minutes ago.' Wynberg is no more than a ten-minute drive from Grassy Park in quiet, late-evening traffic. (In the shadowy world of intelligence operations, one detail is worth mentioning here: the source of the warning was travelling with the hit squad and must have taken an opportunity to warn his handler. He knew Africa personally and would have had to shoot at him with his Pagad compatriots.)

Africa apparently rushed his wife and daughter into the back room and piled mattresses over them as protection against a possible bomb blast. He then went to the front of the house and waited, his Vektor Z88 service pistol drawn and ready, for the men of the Grassy Park cell to arrive. He was convinced he would have to face them on his own. Even though he pressed the orange button on his police radio – an emergency feature for when officers needed help – and reported that he expected an attack, he was not confident the police would respond in time. They did: the request was broadcast immediately on all police channels and dozens of officers were at his house within minutes, blue lights flashing and sirens blaring. Eager to arrest the would-be killers, Africa begged the phalanx of officers to lie low but the uniformed men – with a job to do and no regard for the niceties of intelligence operations – were having none of this. They stayed put, blue lights advertising their presence.

The agent in the Grassy Park car contacted his handler later that night and told him that as the cell approached the house they were confronted by a mass of sirens and blue lights and decided to turn back. The irony is that the cell immediately suspected there had been a tipoff and that they had an infiltrator in their midst. They didn't suspect the state agent but turned their attention to the unfortunate young man whom the police had unsuccessfully tried to forcibly recruit. Pleading innocence, the man drifted away from the cell.

It was a small victory in an otherwise bleak year, and a reminder of just how dangerous the underground war had become. The families of David Africa and Anwar Dramat were moved for their safety and the small group of undercover police officers resolved that the Grassy Park cell would be taken down, whatever it took.

12

TOPPLING THE RINGLEADER

During 1999, the Pagad bomb squads continued to unleash a wave of violence. After the V&A Waterfront car bombing there were numerous other attacks, including the bombing of a Kentucky Fried Chicken outlet in Athlone in January and the attack on Caledon Square police station that so enraged Frank Gentle. In late January there was a bomb attack on another police station, this time Woodstock, and in May a blast outside Athlone police station.

The end of the year saw a string of horrific bombings targeting popular civilian venues. On 5 November, the summer evening on which this book opens, the Blah Bar in Green Point was bombed, and a few weeks later Pagad targeted the St Elmo's pizza restaurant in Camps Bay, leaving young waitress Olivia Milner in a wheelchair.

Another device, also detonated remotely, exploded on Christmas Eve in Green Point, injuring seven police officers. That attack was carefully planned for maximum impact in a teeming part of the city a stone's throw from the Waterfront. It was preceded by a bomb threat on Mano's restaurant and it appears the plan was that the device, placed in a rubbish bin nearby, would be detonated once a number of police officers had arrived to secure the scene. Some speculated that the blast was designed to target the bomb squad, the ubiquitous 'men in black'. The planning was sophisticated and one of the seven injured police officers, Natasha Pillay, lost a leg. So ended the bleakest year in the state's inept attempts to mount a viable response to the vigilantes.

Almost everyone involved on the state side agrees the Christmas Eve incident was a decisive turning point, not only in the battle against Pagad but in how it ultimately shaped a more confident approach to organised crime.[1] The period from the formation of Idoc in 1998 to a successful, if controversial, Crime Intelligence operation in November 2000, marked a key chapter in the development of criminal justice. Arguably, it was also the most important period for the formative democracy in terms of how it found its way through a morass of security challenges, including serious and organised crime.

The Mano's explosion made a mockery of earlier government pledges to end the bombings. In his inaugural speech as president, Thabo Mbeki had announced the creation of a special unit to fight serious crime: the Scorpions. It evolved from Idoc both conceptually in terms of the prosecutor, police and intelligence mix, and in terms of the personnel already involved. The unit, its name coined by the new Safety and Security minister, Steve Tshwete, was launched to some fanfare on 1 September 1999, but by the end of the year that's all there was: a name. It did not become operational until January 2001, and Frank Dutton, its head, was not even in South Africa at the time of the launch.[2] With seven police officers injured in the latest attack, Mbeki's announcement of a fancy new unit would have rung like hollow propaganda.

And the timing couldn't have been worse. The Mano's bombing occurred just a week before large crowds were expected to see in the new millennium with a party at the V&A Waterfront. Furthermore, there was to be a symbolic handover from Mandela to Mbeki on Robben Island. The prospect of another bombing must have been unthinkable to the government and security agencies.

The scruff of the neck

At the end of 1999, Mbeki administered a shock to the system that significantly altered the course of events. He needed concrete responses to the mounting challenges the country faced, and after being told of the Green Point bombing he read the riot act to his security officials. I have heard the story from several sources and it has acquired a kind of mythical status. Events seem to have unfolded as follows: early on Christmas Day, Mbeki phoned Tshwete, the tough-talking new Minister of Safety and Security, who had replaced Sydney Mufamadi. The president said something along the lines of, 'This is enough. Stop it now!' Tshwete called Ngcuka, who was in Cape Town. 'It was 7 am on Christmas morning,' Ngcuka told me. 'I was at home and about to go for a walk. Steve called. He said the president wanted us to go to the scene and visit the victims. Mbeki put fire in our bellies. The message was, "We can't afford to have bombs exploding. Get your act together."'[3] The expectation was that arrests needed to follow.[4]

Ngcuka left home immediately and called Percy Sonn and others to meet him at Idoc's offices. Ngcuka, Tshwete and the bluff Justice minister, Penuell Maduna, then visited the scene of the bombing. As he walked carefully around the debris, Ngcuka recalled, he had an exchange with Leonard Knipe. The detective had been at dozens of explosions, and exhaustion and frustration must have been setting in. 'Please take this case,' he pleaded. 'There is lots of proof lying around here. It can't be done within the SAPS. It should come to you.'[5] That Christmas morning there seemed to be an understanding that the time for petty, factional institutional politics was over. Ngcuka left the crime scene with a new respect for Knipe.

Tshwete, squinting through his Coke-bottle glasses at the media, flatly told a group of assembled reporters: 'This is an organised terror campaign.'[6] Although he would not be drawn on who might be responsible, in private he let it be known that he believed it was the work of the Pagad G-Force, and within a few weeks, as explosions continued to rock Cape Town, he directly pointed the finger at Pagad. When the press conference ended, the team at the centre of the struggle against Pagad – police, prosecutors, spooks – returned to Idoc's offices in the deserted city centre. The atmosphere was pregnant with the sense that this Christmas Day call-out and the president's orders were about to change things. There was also considerable anger in the room, partly because of the deliberate targeting of the police but also because of a sense that enough was enough.

It was significant that the meeting was held at Idoc's premises, a confirmation that the directorate had taken the reins in the struggle against Pagad. A police general would normally have chaired a security meeting like this. Now it was the country's lead prosecutor, the energetic, driven and politically sussed Ngcuka. Hermione Cronje, then Ngcuka's assistant, told me in reference to the bombing: 'He can grab a situation by the scruff of the neck and take it somewhere.'[7] With his close ally Percy Sonn, Ngcuka had something to prove – and he had significant political backing.

Ngcuka's appointment as NDPP was accompanied by controversy. There was a feeling that the new director, with his ANC connections, might ride roughshod over the independence of provincial attorneys-general and impose a political flavour on what should be a neutral prosecutorial body bound by the prescripts of the law. A few years later, Ngcuka told an academic interviewer the attorneys-general were left alone but insisted he had to act decisively to stop the bombings in the Western Cape. They were not being dealt with, he said, and he saw 'an opportunity to do something different without interfering with anybody'.[8]

I have often wondered why that Christmas meeting and Mbeki's message to Tshwete were so significant. After all, other ministers – and Mandela – had promised action. Why was this time different? The answer is that things had fundamentally changed. There was now a clear chain of command and an identified person in the form of Ngcuka who was not only clearly in charge but willing to take risks. That individual was also personally and politically close to the president in a way old-order white police officers could not be. So, when Ngcuka spoke, what he said carried significant weight. Urged on by Sonn's belief that the threat must be confronted, he was eager to move into the vacuum that he felt existed in the response to the bombings. Ngcuka was also politically astute and unlikely to have missed the significance of the moment. At the time, he was arguing for the expansion of the Scorpions, so he had much to prove.

Around the conference table were Sonn's newly minted investigators: SAPS men now incorporated into the Idoc fold; a scattering of prosecutors and other NPA people, including Dawood Adam, a former human rights lawyer; and Crime Intelligence's undercover unit of Mzwandile Petros, Anwar Dramat and David Africa, who were determined to make things work. Once everyone was seated, Ngcuka gave a briefing on what he had gleaned from discussions at the Mano's bomb scene, including his exchange with Knipe. He also spoke about the condition of the injured officers.

There was silence as people processed the information, then Ngcuka underscored that he had instructions from the president to arrest those responsible for this attack and others. He intended, he said, to honour those instructions. No one at the table had attended a Pagad meeting quite like this one.

The team picked on the food Ngcuka had ordered, and he produced a bottle of whisky to lubricate the discussions. I am told by several people close to the process that the state still did not know which individuals were responsible for the bombings. The Pagad bomb squad remained cyphers. The intelligence people did not have a list of perpetrators who could simply be rounded up. How then should the state respond? The debate interrogated this, exploring the structure of Pagad and various members known to be active in violent operations. Some current cases and suspects were reviewed. But there was no easy way forward, no clear target where evidence was available to make an arrest and prosecute.

Then an idea emerged, and like a wave it swelled until it broke over the meeting, breaking what felt like a stalemate. Was it not clear who was responsible, someone asked. Why was the group discussing a wide net of targets? Who else should they nail other than the leader of Pagad, Abdus-Salaam Ebrahim himself? It's not clear who had the initial idea but the tenor of the argument was along these lines: 'Why are we beating about the bush? It is not necessary to catch him red-handed. We have evidence of Pagad killing Rashaad Staggie in full view of the cameras. We need to go for Abdus.'[9]

Everyone around the table knew Ebrahim had been caught on film among the group that marched in 1996 to London Road and killed Staggie. It was widely agreed that, given the seriousness of the situation, this evidence should be used to bring down the leader. The argument was that if the Pagad mob had killed Staggie, was not Ebrahim, their leader, the instigator of the crime? It may seem an obvious solution in retrospect, but Pagad had constantly denied its involvement in the bombings and there had been no usable evidence against Ebrahim.

It was a hugely significant decision. Going for Ebrahim identified the key player at the head of Pagad's campaign of violence. But it also focused on a crime which, among the Pagad faithful, was emblematic of their response to gangs and drugs. Staggie's flaming body was the symbol of Pagad's crusade against the underworld heathens. There was another advantage: Pagad had never claimed responsibility for the bombs directly, so arresting Ebrahim after political pronouncements about responding to the terror attacks built a direct bridge between the bombs and the organisation. For the authorities, this was a highly audacious way of connecting Pagad directly to the bombing campaign.

Idoc did not, however, hold the dockets. In the Staggie case, investigative work had not moved on for years and the docket was buried somewhere in Leonard Knipe's detective section. Phone calls were made, a sharp word from Ngcuka overcame the detectives' resistance, and the dockets were delivered to Idoc.

Willie Viljoen, who started work as a prosecutor straight out of Stellenbosch University in 1976 and handled several ANC and Apla cases, was Cape Town's senior prosecutor before being integrated into Idoc. As he explained the contents of the dockets to some of the people he had sought to imprison in his younger years, it became apparent that the investigations had basically gone nowhere. Ngcuka was too polite to tell me this, but others confirmed that Viljoen took the brunt of the participants' frustration as they listened to him. It was a sign, if any more were needed, that things had to change.

The Staggie case presented serious obstacles for the prosecution. Ebrahim had indeed been caught on film at the scene but there was some important background to the matter. An inquest into Staggie's murder had been held earlier in 1999. Several members of the media who witnessed the lynching were served with subpoenas and argued that journalists 'are gatherers and disseminators of news for public consumption' and that 'it is not their function to assist any government ... in criminal proceedings'. Media representatives emphasised that several witnesses to the murder had already lost their lives, as had others in related cases. Viljoen, meanwhile, accused the media of 'not doing their civic duty by refusing to make evidence available'.[10]

In that Christmas Day meeting, however, there was the feeling that perhaps the media would now capitulate, given the seriousness of the situation. Benny Gool, a *Cape Times* photographer, apparently had pictures of the events of that night, and Sonn contacted him. While Gool was sympathetic, he refused to provide evidence.[11] Several editors were phoned, but they were 'nervous' or 'played for time'.[12] Taking on the press would be a tough fight, with no guarantee of victory. Ngcuka heard out the arguments of his team and decided to proceed with Ebrahim's arrest anyway. 'Let's cross that bridge when we get to it. I can't in all conscience allow this to continue,' he concluded.[13] It was a decisive and courageous move. The unconscionable prospect of another bombing – perhaps one targeting new year revellers – had to be avoided at all costs.

Ebrahim was apprehended in an early-morning raid on his Lansdowne home on 29 December. The military secured a wide perimeter and the police Special Task Force made the arrest. Pagad members mobilised but soldiers stopped them converging on the house. Ebrahim was surprised to be arrested, even more so to be taken in for Staggie's murder. Roused from his bed, he submitted quietly, although at his bail hearing a few days later he held forth from the witness stand for over three hours. Unexpectedly, his wife, Zanie, was also arrested for the illegal possession of a firearm. In a police raid earlier that day in Rylands, incriminating evidence – cellphones apparently being modified in a similar way to those used in other attacks, as well as bomb-making guides – was also found. This action was a belated follow-up to a three-year-old investigation which was also tabled at the Christmas Day meeting.

The arrest met with criticism from some. Why, new SAPS commissioner Jackie Selebi wanted to know, were Ebrahim and others arrested for three-year-old cases? Why had these cases not been followed through? It was a pertinent question that caused internal ructions in the SAPS, now ever more sensitive to the idea that the NPA-based Scorpions might steal their thunder (and resources).

'This is our town and our country'

Questions about the role of detectives after the Mano's bombing and Ngcuka's decisive action to nail Pagad's kingpin led to some soul-searching for Selebi, newly installed at Wachthuis, the increasingly rundown police headquarters in Pretoria. Selebi was an old ANC cadre close to Mbeki, and after Fivaz's more consensual approach he was like a blowtorch applied to the police: he demanded action and was decisive.

Although later convicted of corruption and jailed, he shook up the police, and many officers felt he was a breath of fresh air.[14] His untouchable sense of political legitimacy meant few would have crossed his path and emerged unscathed.

With Selebi now in charge, a political balance between the police and the NPA was struck. Selebi, who never saw eye to eye with Ngcuka (although they tried to avoid direct conflict), looked askance at the establishment of the Scorpions, hoping, like Tshwete, that the specialised unit would be in the SAPS portfolio. But for the moment everyone agreed the focus had to remain on the problem.

In his last months in office, Fivaz had grasped one nettle: he promoted Knipe to Pretoria with the intention of easing the relationship between the police and Idoc in the Western Cape. Knipe led a new unit tasked with investigating crimes against the state (effectively replacing Suiker Britz, whom we encountered in the Ayob Mungalee case). This appointment was made despite criticism that 'Knipe had failed to effectively deal with violence in the Western Cape'.[15] Fivaz's thinking, it appears, was less about promotion and more about getting him out of the way, and there was some speculation as to what the Pretoria unit would do. 'He was promoted upwards, as the general feeling was that no progress was being made,' a former senior detective told me.[16] Unlikely to find a comfortable place under Selebi, Knipe took early retirement within a year, three and a half decades of service under his belt.

Knipe's move left a vacancy for a new face on the front line of the SAPS investigative efforts against Pagad. Riaan Booysen, an old station-level detective from Philippi who had worked exclusively in and around Cape Town, was installed in the post. Before joining the police in 1983 he served in the military and worked in several government departments, and because he was an outsider to the tight Murder & Robbery fraternity he was warned not to take the job. Some Murder & Robbery detectives went as far as meeting the provincial commissioner to try to block the appointment, to no avail.

Booysen struggled to find his feet. Someone who worked with him at the time explained the disrespect he experienced: 'Riaan was treated extremely badly by the old cohort of detectives. When he arrived at the first meeting, nobody stood up.'[17] It was a show of disrespect unheard of in the rank-conscious police. Taken aback, Booysen nevertheless addressed his command. He began emotionally by saying, 'This is our town and our country,' and told the detectives they had a responsibility to get it right.[18] Booysen was much more dogged and street-smart than his detractors expected. He felt strongly that the detectives had to align their efforts with others if the state's strategy to counter Pagad was to succeed, and he arranged for a cohort of station level detectives from across the Cape to immediately join the specialised units.[19]

Booysen also believed a new institutional approach to problems within the SAPS was needed. At headquarters, Tim Williams was pushing for a triumvirate approach – in part a reflection of his engagement with his former ANC intelligence colleagues, who itched for greater independence. Booysen embraced the concept, which constituted intelligence, investigative and operational pillars led by Petros (Crime Intelligence), Booysen (special SAPS detectives) and Arno Lamoer, who chaired the structure and ensured smooth police relations with Idoc. Lamoer was soon promoted to cover a large area of the city where Pagad was active, and he and Booysen developed a close working relationship. Lamoer also had excellent relations with André Pruis, who ran SAPS operational efforts to deliver police resources, rapidly scaling up numbers where they were needed.[20]

The policing approach spearheaded by Booysen, Lamoer and Petros, with teams that cooperated and interacted with the Scorpions, heralded arguably the most innovative spell of policing serious and organised crime that South Africa had seen since the start of the democratic era. Their methods stood in stark contrast to the fragmented and tension-filled system Knipe had overseen. To his credit, Knipe later told Booysen: 'I was wrong about you.'[21]

In September 2000, magistrate Piet Theron was assassinated in his car outside his home in Plumstead. Theron, a wiry marathon runner and a conscientious and well-prepared judicial official, was presiding over the case of two Pagad members, Faizel Waggie and Ismail Edwards, who stood accused of bombing Lansdowne police station in January 1998.

It was a critical case in the expanding number being brought before court thanks to improvements in the system. In several other Pagad cases that made it to court, witnesses had been killed; seven had been murdered by April 2001,[22] and the judiciary were well aware of threat.

Waggie and Edwards (the driver in Jeneker's killing operation) were key members of Pagad and responsible, according to several knowledgeable sources, for multiple acts of violence. The gun that killed Theron had been used in several other Pagad killings and the licence number of the assassin's car was later shown to be linked to the engine number of a car that exploded outside the popular Obz Cafe in Lower Main Road, Observatory. Waggie and Edwards's case continued under another magistrate and they were convicted and jailed for 25 years.

No one has ever been arrested for Theron's murder and Pagad predictably denied involvement, but there was little doubt in anyone's mind that it was lying and Tshwete, whose tone had become increasingly angry, said bluntly that if Pagad wanted to deny involvement it should dissociate itself from the attack. It never did so. 'We in the government are at war with Pagad. We are at war with people who use instruments of terror,' Tshwete declared a few days later after another bomb explosion near a rally Western Cape premier Gerald Morkel was about to address.[23] More ominously, and in a sign of how serious the state was becoming, Justice minister Penuell Maduna suggested two days after Theron's murder that Pagad could be banned, and so prevented from operating, while the cabinet considered the reintroduction of detention without trial.[24]

In St George's Cathedral a week after the assassination, more than a hundred black-robed members of the judiciary stood in solidarity. The main message of the service was defiance. By 2001, several plots to murder other magistrates and judges had been discovered. Theron's murder, like Lategan's, seemed to jolt the system. At police headquarters there was a grim set of exchanges. Behind the scenes, Selebi was thumping his fists on the table, demanding action.

The undercover unit unleashed

The ex-ANC network within the police were instructed by Selebi to understand what was going on. Selebi did not entirely trust the Western Cape Crime Intelligence hierarchy and reached out directly to Petros's undercover unit. The group argued that things could be improved in Cape Town if they had greater independence and a line directly to Selebi. In what was now clearly an emergency, they said, the state needed a more coherent approach to using its intelligence resources against Pagad.

So, with the triumvirate falling into place, police headquarters moved to clear interference around Petros's unit. Tim Williams intervened, with Selebi's backing, and the unit was given the sole mandate within the police to run intelligence operations against Pagad; the relevant resources were to be provided; external interference, namely from provincial Crime Intelligence and the provincial commissioner's office, was to stop. André Pruis, now one of Selebi's deputies in charge of operational responses, was delegated to deliver the word to the politically fractious Western Cape police.

During a meeting at the Bishop Lavis police base in September 2000, Pruis explained that the decision on the undercover unit came from the national commissioner and that he was there to ensure it was enforced. Pruis was a formidable operator and few, if any, challenged the new diktat from Pretoria. Members of the covert unit were told: 'Go and tell your families you won't see them until all of this is over.'[25] One of the first things they did was buy camping mattresses so they could sleep in the office.

The new orders reinvigorated a discussion among unit members about how they should structure their work. Petros had a list of more than a hundred suspects, too many to bring any focus on even if resources and personnel were about to be increased. The question the undercover men asked themselves was how to strategically tackle Pagad in light of the organisation's 'strategic patience' – a term that denoted high resilience and a willingness to wait out attacks on it by the state.

The suspect list was whittled down to a core group. The idea was to 'attack the centre of gravity of the network', including those who

Mzwandile Petros, a former teacher and ANC underground operative from Paarl, was head of an undercover unit that played a key, if controversial, role in the response to the bombings. Pictured here in April 2011 serving as Gauteng Police Commissioner, Petros would rise up the ranks. PICTURE: Gallo Images / Foto24 / Theana Breugem

conveyed information from the Pagad security council to the cells (Boeta Yu was a target here), so the organisation would eventually disintegrate. It was essential to target bomb makers, bombers and shooters to decimate Pagad's capacity for violence. Ray Lalla, widely respected in the team for his strategic abilities, was summoned from Durban for a series of brainstorming sessions. The plan that was hatched took concrete form as Operation Lancer, with a critical focus on gathering information that could be used to obtain indictments. The cooperative interaction between intelligence and investigations was formally emphasised, thanks to the work of the triumvirate and with Selebi's blessing.[26] Lancer also provided 24-hour protection to all investigators, prosecutors, magistrates and judges involved in Pagad investigations. Lalla subsequently became the head of Crime Intelligence nationally.

Now operating with a reporting line straight to the top, the undercover unit set out to recruit a score of intelligence operators they regarded as the best 'collectors' in the police. Three hundred new SAPS recruits were on a SWAT course at the police training facility in Groblersdal. Selebi told Williams to tell the team they could have their pick of the best: 'You can have all 300 if you like.'[27]

For a while, the unit had tracked and profiled an accomplished Pagad killer. Like several other recruits, he was a drug user who had been through a rehabilitation programme supported by Pagad. Such young men were often vulnerable to being psychologically strong-armed into the organisation's clutches. A former Crime Intelligence officer described the equation to me as follows: 'The drug dealers turned you into an addict so now you must kill them.'[28] The man appeared to have had a relapse and was using again, and after the 1999 holiday season bombings the unit wanted to 'turn' him to spy for the state. The method chosen to trap him was blackmail because it was believed his drug use made him vulnerable.

The unsuspecting hitman received a phone call in January 2000 from a friendly woman. More calls followed and the two flirted, the hardcore killing machine melting at the sultry tones of the telephone temptress. When the women suggested they meet at a southern suburbs hotel, the hitman was quick to agree.

Now that killer had been hooked, the undercover officers scrambled to reel him in. A sex worker from Manenberg was procured. She was not told she was about to have sex with a violent killer, only that the man had committed adultery and a video was needed for his wife's divorce case. I have no doubt she was well compensated for her services. A hidden camera was rigged up, focused on the bed, and a package of drugs was placed in the hotel room. The original seductress, in reality a police officer, sent the man the room number and agents waited as their target made his way to the hotel.

He knocked on the door, and before the sex worker could say much he blurted out, 'Are you from intelligence?' The woman knew nothing of an intelligence link or that he was from Pagad and seemed genuinely surprised by the question. Satisfied, the killer entered the room and the act of passion ensued. The target was nicknamed 'Curly Toes', as that is what the camera recorded in his moment of ecstasy.[29] I don't think I need to repeat here that gathering intelligence is a dirty business – even more so when conducted under pressure.

The operation went entirely to plan, remarkably given its riskiness. When the two had done the deed, a group of uniformed police (actually Crime Intelligence operatives) stormed in, demanding to know the man's identity. Naked in the corner and overcome by shock, he told them. The police told him they were 'running his name' – an element of police procedure added purely for verisimilitude – then an officer returned wearing a serious expression: 'You are wanted and somebody else is coming to speak to you.' The target was kept waiting until another intelligence officer from the unit arrived. He had been in the room next door but allowed a realistic 45 minutes to pass as Curly Toes stewed. At this point, the sex worker was 'arrested' and taken away, only to be released.

Now the police vice began to tighten. 'You are in big trouble. Prostitution and drugs – it will not be pretty for you.' The emphasis on *you*, then a clearing of the throat: 'And by the way, we have checked the car you arrived in and it is stolen.' The target, now confused and in shock, was not thinking clearly. The intelligence man chose his moment: 'I can make this all go away'. Curly Toes hastily acquiesced; an out, even if it meant working with the police, would be better than the shame of being arrested for prostitution and drugs.

Two detectives from Riaan Booysen's outfit took a statement and almost unbelievably the man admitted 30 murders. This confession, and his recruitment as a source, meant a sword hung over his head from the moment he returned to the Pagad fold.

It is in the little details of this sordid tale that we can see how state enforcement efforts finally began to work together, intelligence paving the way for solid evidence. As distasteful as his recruitment was, Curly Toes soon delivered on the bargain: his information saved lives, including those of several detectives in Booysen's group.

The undercover unit had been working on plans to place agents inside Pagad so they could testify. As a senior prosecutor explained, 'witnesses in Pagad cases were mainly accomplices and had been involved in Pagad criminal activities, undermining their credibility. The worry was that they would change their story in the witness box, particularly under cross-examination, and indeed they often did.'[30] The answer was to infiltrate the organisation with undercover officers who would then have credibility as witnesses. But even this was not foolproof, as the case of state agent Mansoor Manuel (who warned of the attack on David Africa's house) showed. He was infiltrated into Pagad's Grassy Park cell but had to take part in attacks to sustain his cover.[31] The undercover unit went in search of appropriate candidates in the SAPS. It is hard to overstate how courageous these people were. Some volunteered and uprooted their lives to serve the new democratic order, knowing they would not be able to live openly under their old identities again, nor hope to receive any public recognition. While agents' identities could be hidden from the media and the wider public in court, it was still a requirement that they be made known to the defence, meaning that after such an assignment a new identity was needed.

There was also an equally secret side to operations that developed in line with new technologies. At the beginning of the Pagad phenomenon, it was not possible for police to intercept cellphones, only landlines. What seem like simple steps today could not be contemplated then. But over time, and led by innovative officers, Crime Intelligence developed the capacity to provide linkage analysis of Pagad members' phones (although a warrant was required to obtain billing information from mobile phone operators[32]). The unit that developed this capacity was rushed to Cape Town in late 1999. (They were caught for speeding en route.) Software tools such as Analyst's Notebook, now commonplace in law enforcement, were introduced, and Pagad connections were mapped. The technology painted a much clearer picture of the organisation.

Meanwhile, Abdus-Salaam Ebrahim's bail application was successfully opposed by the state, and during his months in detention awaiting trial the undercover unit mounted its most daring and decisive operation.

13

THE LAST BOMB

Early on 3 November 2000, the 'men in black' were summoned to Durban Road in Bellville, as there were strong indications a live device would need to be defused. Inevitably, it was Frank Gentle who stepped up and disarmed the bomb. He was his usual calm self as he worked on the unstable explosive device that could have exploded at any time. 'He was never recognised for this,' said a former colleague.[1] For Gentle, it was all in a day's work.

Once deactivated, the components of the bomb were carefully separated for later examination. That could wait: for the moment there was a sense of huge relief. It would have been unconscionable if the device had exploded, maiming and killing the numerous passers-by and police officers who had now gathered on the busy road.

If the killing of Rashaad Staggie triggered a violent acceleration in Pagad's activities, a police intervention to prevent the Durban Road bomb exploding effectively marked their end. After this there were no further bombs targeting the public or police;[2] the state's response, while still imperfect, was finally showing signs of paying off.

Efforts to prevent the Bellville attack came within a whisker of failure, as we shall see, but the law enforcement agencies who got so much wrong during the Pagad campaign were finally 'getting ahead of the game', said Hennie Bester, the Western Cape MEC for Safety and Security.[3] In the words of a police officer who was involved that day in Bellville, foiling the bomb attack was 'seminal and controversial. Although it was a mess, it gave us confidence.'[4] The attempted attack also left several important questions hanging, not all of which have been resolved. It is a story that has never been told in full.

The flowerpot bomb

By November 2000, undercover unit officers had been working night and day for weeks to recruit sources and exploit more effectively those they had already.[5] Then a major opportunity presented itself. Curly Toes, blackmailed into turning after his dalliance with the sex worker, was being run as a source and through him the unit had penetrated the obscure workings of Pagad's violent core. The officers met their man furtively, carefully checking for counter-surveillance. After the failed car bomb outside Bronx three months previously, the unit could not relax.

On 2 November the informant had compelling news: he had been asked to visit imprisoned Pagad members in Malmesbury and would be driving there in Faizel Waggie's car, a blue Ford Sapphire. Waggie, an intelligent and uncompromising man, was a key target of the intelligence unit but they knew he was security-conscious and adept at detecting physical surveillance. The opportunity to have access to his car, which the informant would be driving, was too good to pass up. The few hours in which Curly Toes was inside the prison provided a perfect opportunity for police technical experts to fit a tracking and listening device in the vehicle.[6]

When Curly Toes returned from the prison to Cape Town, Waggie's car now bugged, he met other members of the core bombing group. They told him of a plan to plant a bomb in a flowerpot somewhere on Durban Road in Bellville. He couldn't report much more detail but it was enough, and the intelligence proved surprisingly accurate.

Whatever you might think of his violent past, it is to the informant's credit that he told his Crime Intelligence handlers about an urgent threat to innocent people. It was the kind of breakthrough the unit had waited months for – information about an impending threat which would give them the chance to prevent it and an opportunity to catch members of the elusive bombing group red-handed.

A snatch of conversation transmitted by the bug in the car also let the Crime Intelligence operatives know that the Sapphire would be used to deliver the bomb. And the attack was planned for the next day. Two of the team immediately drove to the location of the planned bombing.

Durban Road is near the University of Stellenbosch Business School and runs in a north-westerly direction from the N1 freeway towards Tyger Valley shopping centre. It's lined with fuel stations, restaurants, car showrooms and offices. As the intelligence men arrived in the early-summer evening light they were startled. Hoping to find an easily identifiable place that matched the intel, they saw instead, in the words of one, that 'the whole fucking road was full of flowerpots'.[7] They were stumped; where to begin to know where the device might be located?

Back at the safe house in the southern suburbs, the team tried to work out what time the bomb would be placed. It wasn't clear but the assumption was mid-morning. It was decided that Special Task Force officers would be on the route to Durban Road, and on the word of the team monitoring information from the Sapphire, they could intercept and arrest the bombers. Mzwandile Petros, who was exhausted, said he wanted to go home to sleep and volunteered to stop at the task force base to ask them to deploy in the morning.

The men tried to get a few hours of rest, readying themselves for a tough but hopefully successful day when the bombers would finally be arrested with a device in their possession. The night passed uneventfully, save for the snoring from prone bodies on Cape Union Mart mattresses. By early morning, the technical operator monitoring the tracking equipment had also drifted off. Then by chance, in need of the toilet at 5 am, an officer looked at the computer tracking the car. Shocked and immediately shaken from his sleep, he saw that the Ford Sapphire was already on the move.

In a matter of seconds, everyone was up and ready to go. The team called Petros. It quickly emerged that he had forgotten the night before to alert the Special Task Force to be ready to make an arrest. It was a significant oversight: after all this work, no experienced armed team was in place. What had felt like a certain breakthrough a day earlier now looked like an imminent catastrophe. For a start, a live bomb was being delivered to one of many flowerpots along a lengthy road. And if the bombers were not intercepted by the police, all chance of a clean arrest would instantly evaporate.

Wiping the sleep from his eyes, Petros raced towards Durban Road.

He phoned Riaan Booysen just after 5 am, rousing him from bed. Petros told the senior detective he was searching for the bomber's Ford and Booysen headed to the scene. A public order police reaction unit was also mobilised.

With the seconds ticking away and the possibility of arresting the bombers rapidly slipping out of their grasp, the undercover team threw caution to the wind. They phoned the 10111 public emergency line to report that a car with a bomb in it was heading towards Bellville. The operator – despite the sustained bombing campaign in the city, or perhaps because of the number of hoax calls that had been made – did not believe the exasperated caller. Eventually he identified himself as a Crime Intelligence officer and the operator got the message: all units across Cape Town were instructed to look out for the blue Sapphire.

Harsh words were exchanged: after all this work, it looked like things were about to fall apart. The undercover unit had been granted the autonomy and resources they had asked for and now success was slipping from their grasp. Their golden opportunity was looking like 'an absolute fuck-up', as a senior police officer put it.[8] It's little wonder there was panic in the air.

The all-units alert came too late and the bombers made it to Durban Road. Just before dawn, they placed the bomb under the flowerpot they had chosen during reconnaissance trips and drove away. Frustratingly, the opportunity to arrest them red-handed had now passed.

A short while later, a VIP unit responded to the all-units alert and flagged down the Sapphire in Vanguard Drive near Acacia Park, about 15 kilometres from where the bomb had been planted. The occupants were taken into custody. Faizel Waggie and Naziem Davids were already known to the police: they had been under surveillance and had been arrested for the abduction of a state witness.[9] But it was just too late. As a senior law enforcement officer said, 'what they have is just two suspicious guys in a car without much else: it would be hard to use in court.'[10]

On Durban Road, meanwhile, a substantial police operation was under way with officers examining flowerpots up and down the road. 'I almost died as I walked past that bomb several times,' said an officer who was part of the search team.[11] Eventually the pipe bomb was located under a pot next to the outside seating area of a pub, the Keg and Swan, and deactivated. It was designed to cause maximum injury and loss of life.

For the relieved but perplexed authorities, the choice of the Keg and Swan (which no longer exists) for a bomb attack could not possibly have been random: the pub was just 200 metres from the offices of Riaan Booysen's Serious & Violent Crime unit, and the detectives often went there for lunch or a drink after work. In fact, a lunch had been planned for later that day. The bomb squad found that the device was set to go off at midday, just as the pub would have been filling up. A member of the bomb squad at the time told me it was particularly suspicious that the bombers knew the date, time and location of the Pagad investigators' team lunch. 'Where did they get that information?'[12]

On Durban Road, Mzwandile Petros must have been feeling the pressure. Two Pagad operatives were in custody, but without evidence linking them directly to the planting of the bomb, he had lost his quarry. They were desperate for anything now, said a member of the undercover unit.[13] There was a fierce exchange between unit members and anger at Petros, who subsequently wrote an affidavit about the incident. In it, he said he received information about the planned attack at about 5 am from a 'reliable informant' and immediately headed to the area.[14] He described how the prospective bomber 'placed the container on the pavement next to the restaurant called Keg and Swan', and that he communicated this to Booysen.[15] Later he observed a police vehicle stopping the Ford Sapphire opposite Epping fire station, he said.

In his affidavit, Petros painstakingly attempted to make an unequivocal link between the bomb and the bombers but he could not reveal the source of the information.[16] It was the classic challenge of converting intelligence into evidence. The day's happenings became bogged down in controversy and conflicting versions of events. A senior detective told me that almost immediately Eunice Gray, a leading prosecutor in Pagad cases, raised concerns about Petros's version. 'The prosecution suggested,' the detective told me, 'that the police planted the bomb themselves because they weren't having much luck cracking down on Pagad.'[17] That was a serious allegation and untrue, but it was clear that some of the details about the discovery of the bomb could easily be challenged in court. Although carefully worded, Petros's affidavit raised too many questions.

To complicate matters, Johannes Badenhorst, the police officer from the reaction unit who found the bomb, retracted his sworn statement just before the trial was due to start in 2003. In the statement he had said he 'started searching at the Keg and Swan after his superior told him to look there on the basis of information received'.[18] Now he said that statement was untrue; instead, 'reaction unit members were told to search along a 500-metre stretch of road without a clear indication of where to look'.[19] As it was, the bomb was found 80 or 90 minutes after police in the area were first alerted, supporting the idea that officers did not have exact information about its location, contrary to Petros's affidavit. Adding to the web of inconsistencies, a police press release said the bomb was found by a police sniffer dog. If that was true, and not just cover for the police intelligence work, it suggested a wide search rather than a targeted find.[20] Petros had also alerted Booysen to the bomb, as we have seen, but the senior detective looked in the wrong place. Booysen's own affidavit says he 'started searching in rubbish bins' in an area where Petros had stopped at a set of traffic lights, not 200 metres down the road where the bomb had been planted.[21] Did Petros really have eyewitness evidence linking Davids and Waggie to the planting of the bomb?

Validity of evidence aside, a horrendous disaster had been averted. Zelda Holtzman, the acting Western Cape police commissioner, released a statement congratulating the team: 'The discovery [of the bomb] was the direct result of concerted and coordinated police operations during the past month. ... It is indeed largely due to the outstanding cooperation between the various roleplayers involved in the implementation of the strategy that this success has been achieved.'[22]

The tenor of the statement rang true and members of the undercover unit received awards from Jackie Selebi for their work that day. But it was a bittersweet honour for most of them and attracted criticism from others in the SAPS. In their hearts, they knew they had failed. The state had good reason to be disappointed too. A prosecutor had raised the alarm about the veracity of Petros's statement, saying she had issues with the credibility of witnesses given the conflicting sequence of events recounted by Crime Intelligence, detectives and the reaction unit, and it was even suggested the police may have planted the flowerpot bomb in order to be seen to have a win against Pagad.[23] That suggestion was a fallacy but it was true that Petros's affidavit did not stand up to scrutiny. The NPA also reported that no judicial authority had been obtained to use the bugging device in Waggie's car. Without it, the evidence acquired was not usable in court.

14

THE LAST DEAD WITNESS

Bombings ceased after the Keg and Swan episode but Pagad's potential for violence was not quite neutralised. The incident led to the murder of two witnesses who were in protection.

Other arrests linked to the bomb were made. Based on police surveillance, Shahied Davids (Naziem Davids's brother) and Haroon Orrie, a slim and articulate man long believed by the state to be associated with the bombings, were taken into custody charged with assisting in the plot. Yusuf and Fahiema Enous were also arrested after their Grassy Park home, where the Keg and Swan pipe bomb was said to have been made, was raided. The Enouses turned state witness and were moved into protection. Another piece of detective work provided a useful link to the bombers. This was the discovery of Orrie's fingerprints on a tube of glue used to make the bomb in the garage of Yusuf Enous's property. Despite the failure to arrest the bombers in the act, this, combined with witnesses placing Naziem Davids and Faizel Waggie together at the bomb-building site, could have been compelling evidence in court. It was not to be.

Enous recounted how Waggie and a partner used his garage to do some work, presumably to sort the bomb's components and construct the device. This testimony was clearly important for the state and detectives persuaded the couple to testify, pointing out that they were implicated because the bomb had been made on their property. They were subsequently placed in the witness protection programme and relocated to Gouda, an isolated village just over 100 kilometres north of Cape Town by a tributary of the Berg River.

After only a few weeks in the safe house, the couple began to feel bored, isolated and lonely. They longed to see their family. This was a common complaint of witnesses under state protection and should have been read as a danger sign.[1] The Enouses had few contacts in Gouda and as the only Muslims in the village must have 'stood out like a sore thumb', an NPA official told me.[2] The couple phoned their relatives in Cape Town and begged them to visit during the end-of-year holiday. Pagad learnt of the visit, followed the family and located the safe house. It was criminal neglect in the extreme, given the ruthlessness and desperation of the men the state was up against.

On 26 December 2000, just after the family visit, the couple's bodies were found in the safe house. The trial judge later described the murders as executions. 'Both of the victims were shot numerous times with fatal bullet wounds to the head. Clearly [the] intent was that under no circumstances could either victim be left to ever speak again.'[3]

After the killers broke in, the couple appeared to have fled into their bedroom. Tragically, Fahiema Enous died trying to protect her four-month-old daughter, who was found lying beside her mother with a cracked skull.[4] The killing of the young mother was particularly callous, as the judge noted, because although it was unclear whether she would be a state witness, she would have been able to identify the killers and so had to die alongside her husband.[5]

In another incident, the state tightened the noose earlier in the year when legendary Pagad pipe bomb maker Zaid 'Pang' Abrahams turned prosecution witness. This was potentially a crucial moment for the state, with a key insider ready to give evidence. But it also ended badly. Why Abrahams changed allegiance is not clear – perhaps his former colleagues in the liberation struggle prevailed on him. But he was betrayed by another informant, arrested and subsequently made a statement. There are claims that he was tortured. Pagad's response was ruthless. Pang was declared *munafiq* and a hit was put out on his life. Those who worked for him recall this ruefully: 'Pang had done so much for Pagad's cause, sacrificing family and teaching us how to make bombs and to be tactical, and still the leadership wanted him dead.'[6]

The witness protection programme relocated the Abrahams family to Bloemfontein, where they complained about their living conditions. A request to move to Durban was turned down, given Pagad's presence there. Without the permission of the authorities, Abrahams returned to Mitchells Plain, where he was gunned down in his driveway in April 2001. In a letter to Pagad, provided to the *Cape Times* by his daughter after his death, Abrahams wrote: 'It's been an eternity of misery since I ignited the fire of distraught within myself and my loved ones ... I discovered that [the state's] main objective is to degrade, control and punish.' At his funeral, his daughter Aisha said he felt guilty about turning state witness: 'He said the lives of his Pagad brothers would be at stake and he would not have been able to live with himself.'[7]

The killings of these key witnesses were significant blows to the state's prosecutorial work in getting Pagad's killers behind bars. But, as a byproduct, they had long-term positive consequences. Witness protection at that point fell under the Department of Justice. 'It was being run in a totally ad hoc way, and if it had not been this couple [the Enouses] it would have been someone else,' said a senior NPA prosecutor involved with witness protection.[8] That yet more witnesses had been killed incensed Ngcuka: the Enouses had been persuaded to testify because they believed they would be protected. As the judge in the trial of their murder accused noted: 'There can be no successful prosecution of criminal cases without evidence of state witnesses. Where such witnesses are threatened or harmed in any way, not only do such persons suffer but damage is done to the criminal justice system as a whole.'[9]

If the state was to effectively prosecute key figures within Pagad's violent network, it was clear that people who took the risk of appearing on the stand needed to be protected much more effectively. On hearing of the Enous case, Ngcuka had had enough. He called Chris Macadam, a respected prosecutor then wrapping up at Idoc and about to transfer to the TRC, and begged him to stay and establish an effective witness protection programme. Ngcuka had already made arrangements that this reformed, revitalised programme would fall under the NPA.

Macadam's detailed assessment of what had gone wrong in the Enous case suggested the programme was being run without strategic awareness of the threat Pagad posed. Comparable systems were also studied. Later, Dawood Adam, the former human rights lawyer who was at the meeting on Christmas Day 1999, took over the programme and ran it successfully. Between 2002 and 2019 it provided protection to close on 6000 witnesses. The challenges of managing the programme remained, but the safety of witnesses dramatically improved.[10] An independent comparative study a decade after its establishment concluded that the NPA witness protection programme 'provides an excellent operational example of how to protect witnesses in extremely precarious security environments'.[11]

Tragic and brutal as the Enouses' murders were, they may not have died in vain. No more witnesses died after the protection programme was overhauled and placed under new management.

Evidence 'at all costs'

After the Keg and Swan episode there was a cohesive effort by the Scorpions and police investigators to get suspects into court. By October 2001 there were more than 500 cases under investigation involving suspected members of Pagad, with 81 trials pending based on hundreds of charges. These included 47 for murder, 56 for attempted murder, one for possession of explosives, 11 for possession of an unlicensed firearm, 13 for armed robbery and two for conspiracy to commit murder. Seventy suspected Pagad members were arrested.[12] Led by the Scorpions, the trials had a clear focus on putting behind bars those who had driven the violence of the past few years.

The US State Department, which placed Pagad on its terrorism exclusion list in late 2001[13] and no doubt watched events in Cape Town closely after the 11 September attacks of that year in New York and Washington, DC, noted in a report that 'urban terrorism [had] decreased significantly in the Western Cape' and that 'there have been no incidents of urban terror since late 2000'.[14] By 2003, the State Department reports were even more laudatory: 'The activities of Pagad have been curtailed severely by a successful law enforcement and prosecutorial effort against leading members of the organisation for crimes linked to urban bombings and murder.'[15] This was true at a high level but in the courts the picture often remained distinctly mixed: cases were old and the investigations and evidence were tainted. The Scorpions, cooperating with Booysen's investigators, had to work with what they had.

At the top of the Scorpions' wish list was Abdus-Salaam Ebrahim.

The state's case against Pagad's leader had run into trouble early on. It hinged, as we have seen, on the media providing evidence in the form of footage that showed Ebrahim was present when Rashaad Staggie was murdered. Once the trial was under way, the judge ruled that the provenance of the video material had to be proven. As Ngcuka had anticipated, that rickety bridge now had to be crossed. Willie Viljoen, the prosecutor assigned to the case, applied to the United Kingdom – under provisions for international cooperation in criminal matters – to obtain video footage from Reuters. That was granted by a London judge in June 2001 and the NPA team had good reason to celebrate.[16] Ebrahim would shortly be brought to justice.

However, the NPA failed to anticipate the strong, and indeed understandable, backlash from the media, who objected to being used as toys in a game of law enforcement. An application by Reuters to interdict the use of the footage in the case was brought before the Western Cape High Court. It was an unpleasant experience for Viljoen as Reuters, which owned the footage, brought the case not on the grounds of press freedom, as might have been expected, but by challenging the honesty and integrity of the prosecutor. The crux of the matter was that Viljoen and Jan d'Oliveira, the deputy NDPP, had undertaken to inform Reuters should such an application be made, but had not done so. For this, they and the NPA received a powerful slap on the wrist from two respected judges, Jeanette Traverso and Dennis Davis, who said the NPA representatives 'were determined to obtain the video material for purposes of the Ebrahim trial at all costs. It seems that they were satisfied that whatever the means, they could justify the end.'[17] It was an adequate description of the desperation that had come to define the NPA's efforts. (Illustrating the extent of the court's unhappiness, the judges also said the behaviour of Viljoen and d'Oliveira 'warranted investigation at the highest level' and copied their ruling to Ngcuka, the justice minister and the president.[18])

Viljoen was shattered by the judgment. The media had begun to refer to him as 'Mugabe'. He asked Ngcuka to be removed from the case. 'I refused at first but then I saw that we needed to do it. Willie was withdrawn and we had to replace him. But he knew that file backwards with lots of detail, so it was a loss for us. He had worked on the case for years,' said Ngcuka.[19]

Having lost their legal tussle with Reuters, the NPA turned to the SABC, which also had tapes of the crowd and Staggie's murder. Promises were made but the tapes never materialised. The Scorpions then raided the premises of the South African Broadcasting Corporation (SABC), Reuters and Associated Press but the timing couldn't have been worse: 19 October was International Press Freedom Day. The Scorpions, who hadn't been aware of the significance of the date, predictably took a beating in the press and Ngcuka was given the unenviable title of 'mampara of the week' by South Africa's *Sunday Times*. While the clumsy raid failed to turn up any tapes, it underlined the determination of the fledgling Scorpions; but it seemed Ebrahim would escape justice.

Then, out of the blue, Ngcuka received a call from Snuki Zikalala, a senior executive at SABC News. Zikalala, an ex-MK combatant, was a controversial figure given his tendency to soft-soap the ANC in SABC news coverage. But he was concerned about the violence. 'What do you need?' he asked Ngcuka. The tapes were handed over. 'Go defend our country,' Zikalala said.[20]

In March 2002, over two years after he was arrested and amid unprecedented security measures, Ebrahim's case finally reached a conclusion. He had been in prison during this period, uncertain of his fate, and Abdullah Salie had replaced him as leader of Pagad. Salie was a relative unknown (he has been described to me as a 'pseudo leader') and never developed the public profile Ebrahim commanded. 'Salie was only a seat-warmer for Abdus as he had to rush to prison to get his actions endorsed before he could act,' is how a prominent member described things.[21] So, Ebrahim remained effectively in control; he knew too much to relinquish power. Salie was an effective communicator but could never shake the influence of the overbearing Ebrahim. Later, he was expelled from Pagad by Ebrahim (a clear sign of where the real power lay) after a speech in a Johannesburg mosque that was found disagreeable, and experienced family tragedy.[22]

Ebrahim was found guilty of public violence based on images from the SABC tape. He was acquitted, however, on the charge of murdering

Staggie. Judge John Foxcroft said Ebrahim 'should have foreseen that violence would break out' that day in Salt River.[23] He was sentenced to eight years in prison.

The escape artist

If convicting Ebrahim was challenging, it was nothing like the process of getting Ebrahim Jeneker behind bars. Jeneker was arrested in April 1999 but went on trial only two years later, on 10 April 2001. He was not granted bail and spent this time in prison. Predictably, the Scorpions threw the book at him: he faced 138 charges including 9 of murder, 10 of attempted murder, 23 of robbery, 1 of attempted robbery, 3 of theft, 8 of malicious damage to property, 1 of housebreaking, 4 of kidnapping, 1 of serious assault, 42 of illegal possession of firearms and ammunition, 9 of the illegal pointing of a firearm, 26 of illegal possession of a machinegun and ammunition, and 1 of illegal possession of explosives. It was an unprecedented list of crimes and it became known as the 'Jeneker series'.

The trial ran for 149 days and 184 witnesses testified, some appearing multiple times. 'The court,' said Judge Deon van Zyl, whose home was broken into as proceedings got under way,[24] 'recognises the legion of problems and harassment the prosecution's investigating team had to encounter. Certain witnesses, through intimidation or otherwise, were not capable or willing to give evidence.'[25]

Many of the cases under which Jeneker was charged had been poorly investigated over the years. Captain Kobus Roelofse, a long-time SAPS detective who worked under Knipe and later the Scorpions (and who two decades later worked for the Zondo Commission probing state capture), joined the investigating team at a late stage to assist in pulling things together properly. Roelofse, said the judge, 'acquitted himself effectively and showed admirable professionalism'. 'Unfortunately', his honour noted scathingly, Roelofse 'had to rely on the incapable or unsatisfactory work of police investigators. This necessarily had a negative impact on the quality of providing proof of evidence.'[26]

Jeneker escaped twice from court holding cells during the trial, leading to dramatic engagements with the authorities on the streets of Cape Town. In October 2001, seven months into the hearing, he and six other Pagad suspects slipped from the Western Cape High Court cells in the city centre. The prisoners were being served lunch by a court orderly when they overpowered him and took his firearm. They jumped over the wall surrounding the cells and fled on foot down Queen Victoria Street before turning into Wale Street, then St George's Mall and Adderley Street. The men were pursued by the police and shots were exchanged in the crowded lunchtime city centre as the escapees hijacked a vehicle and fled. The vehicle was spotted near Athlone and the police converged on the area in force. Jeneker was found hiding behind boxes in a garage wearing only one shoe. The lost shoe led the police to the fugitive: it was found on the road by an alert officer who noted that the insole was still warm. Believing the wearer was close by, the policeman called for backup.

A year later, in September 2002, and a few months before judgment was due to be passed in December, the ever-resourceful Jeneker escaped again. He and two other Pagad members had been left alone in a holding cell with the door wide open. A set of duplicate keys was used to unlock their shackles and leg irons. It looked highly suspicious. In a bizarre rewind, the three then disappeared into the city using the same route as the year before. The court complex erupted in chaos. National police commissioner Jackie Selebi happened to be there at the time and cleared the scene. Red-faced, the authorities were ordered to mount a massive operation, deploying units of the SAPS elite Special Task Force. Jeneker was arrested several days later, again in Athlone.

A senior detective told me Jeneker was in serious danger of not being taken alive that day: he was South Africa's most wanted man and Selebi was fuming. The officer who arrested him told me that Jeneker had a .38 revolver, the Quran and a prayer mat with him. He was taken down roughly and his lip was bleeding. Showing perspicacity, the detective delayed calling the Special Task Force as he thought they would kill Jeneker. There was now a long list of people who would have liked to eliminate one of Pagad's most prolific assassins, but the detective concluded it was difficult not to respect the man: 'Jeneker knew what he was standing for ... he was prepared to die. I didn't agree with him, and we couldn't prove he killed [detective Bennie] Lategan, but he was a real leader of his people.'[27]

In both escapes, inside help was suspected and several police officers were prosecuted or transferred. In the second case, senior police investigators and the NIA had briefed police management about a planned escape by Jeneker, and at least two other escapes were foiled. One of those who escaped with Jeneker in 2001, however, told me the decision to attack the orderly was taken on the spur of the moment. Jeneker was reported to have stated simply: 'I am sick and tired of this now. I am going home. When the policeman puts the food on the floor and you are picking it up, that's when we act.'[28] The full truth about the escapes never emerged.

In the end it was the killing of a female gang boss that brought down Ebrahim Jeneker. Of all the charges, it was those related to the murder of Adiela 'Mama Africa' Davids that stuck. Davids was the crime boss who, with her daughter and niece, was gunned down in her Manenberg hair salon in 1999 (see Chapter 4). At the trial, a witness testified that one of the masked killers with a machinegun passed a comment before squeezing the trigger: 'He said that they had already warned Adiela twice and that they had now come to shoot her dead because she did not want to listen.'[29] The parting message was, 'Let this be a lesson to you and others': it was a classic line from the Jeneker playbook.

After the poor police work in other cases, this time the evidence was carefully marshalled by Kobus Roelofse. Jeneker's fingerprints were found on the machinegun used in the crime, a weapon he deposited afterwards with Alimah Lodewyk (whose husband, ironically, had strong gang connections) for safekeeping. There was also clear evidence that Jeneker had stored a bag of jewels from Davids's salon at the Lodewyks' house, and his fingerprints were found in both vehicles associated with the murder and robbery. The defendant relied heavily on an alibi defence, claiming he was somewhere else when the crime was committed, but he was unable to prove this.

One fascinating aspect of the trial documentation is correspondence between Jeneker while he was in prison and Alimah Lodewyk, who was under state protection. (It was little wonder the NPA was concerned about the insecure state of the witness protection programme.) Lodewyk outlined in a letter to Jeneker the evidence she had given the police. Jeneker, in turn, provided her with advice that might help his case: 'Very important – it is alleged that I brought a "bag" there on Tuesday 13th May ... when you left the house [in] the morning the police were already outside in the road and I had not got any access to the house. Mention how many people got access to the house. If you mention it in your statement the two statements will contradict each other. It will make it difficult for the police in court to have a strong case.'[30] Judge Van Zyl said Jeneker acted as a 'grand legal adviser'.[31]

In the end, the police's case was strong enough despite Jeneker's coaching of the witness. He and his co-accused, Abdullah Maansdorp, each received three life sentences. Jeneker was sentenced to an additional 116 years for related offences. He was released in November 2020 after serving 21 years and rearrested in June 2022 for breaking his parole conditions.

Bombs away

The murder of the Enouses was also ultimately solved through good police work. As it turned out, an alert and efficient police reservist in Gouda, Andries le Fleur, saved the day. Around the time the murders were being committed, he came across an unattended pick-up truck and noted the registration number. Once the two bodies were found, the number was passed on to the investigating officer, Captain Eddie Clark, one of Booysen's new appointees. It was an important breakthrough. (Just how dangerous the struggle against Pagad had become is illustrated by the fact that Le Fleur immediately went into witness protection.) The vehicle was registered in the name of Samir Orrie, brother of Haroon Orrie, one of the accused in the attempted bombing of the Keg and Swan. Before long a third brother, Phadiel, was also drawn into the case.

On 28 December, Samir Orrie was stopped while driving the vehicle in Athlone and Clark was summoned. Orrie's subsequent statement to Clark was ruled inadmissible as it was made 'in violation of the constitutional duty to inform him that any statement he made could be used against him in later proceedings'. In the judge's words, Clark's engagement with Orrie 'compromised the accused in some way'.[32] While Clark 'left a favourable impression as a witness' it was another sign that the detectives still had not come to grips with the new constitutional order and that prosecutorial guidance was crucial.[33] Orrie walked free.

Traces of blood were found on a curtain in the Enouses' safe house and in Samir Orrie's bakkie. There was again a tussle in court over the fact that there was a 'measure of confusion regarding which blood sample had been taken from which accused'[34] and the state had to make an additional application for fresh samples, which was naturally opposed. The judge granted the application and DNA results showed it was Phadiel Orrie's blood inside the house and in the bakkie seen in Gouda. He was convicted of the murders and sentenced in September 2004 to two terms of life imprisonment.

Despite these convictions, the state was unable to bring to trial or convict anyone for any of the major bombings of civilian targets. Planet Hollywood, the Blah Bar, Bronx, Sea Point and Mano's bombings are all still open files. This speaks to a major failure on the part of the state. Most other bombing cases also remain unsolved, invariably because of investigative shortcomings.

One was linked to a raid on the home of Nazier and Said Mhatey immediately after the Christmas Day meeting in 1999. The brothers were originally charged with possession of a pipe bomb and a grenade found in their house in 1996, and it was this case docket which was presented to Ngcuka (and which later shocked Selebi, given that no action had been taken). In the 1999 raid, bomb instruction manuals and cellphones that were being mechanically adjusted were found and more charges were added. They led to nothing. In October 2000, magistrate Jack Redelinghuys (who tried several cases related to Pagad, replacing the murdered Theron in the Lansdowne bombing case) acquitted the brothers of possession of explosives. He 'lashed out at the police for their poor investigation of the Mhatey case and for not doing anything about it for three years' and concluded that after finding the explosives in December 1996 the original investigating officer 'did nothing as far as we know'.[35]

Another abortive case involved the NIA agent in the Grassy Park cell, Martin (later Mansoor) Manuel (who warned David Africa of the impending attack on his home). He was the state's key witness in the case of the August 1998 bombing of the Wynberg Synagogue by the Grassy Park cell, which included imam and cell leader Moegsien Barendse as one of the accused. A senior member of the Grassy Park cell told me they never suspected Mansoor was working for the state, even though neighbours warned them that people from outside the area often visited his house. The trial began in 2001 but the state's case crumbled. Manuel testified that he and one of the accused assembled the bomb but the court regarded him as an unreliable witness because he had been involved in multiple illegal activities, again highlighting the challenge of using state agents to infiltrate Pagad then give evidence. A leading member of the Grassy Park cell, smiling at his good fortune, told me: 'The judge said that the state witness was so untruthful that he should actually be charged himself, but he was never charged. He has disappeared up until today, he is totally missing.'[36] Barendse was in custody for five years awaiting the completion of the trial.

A third disappointing trial involved the Keg and Swan case, where charges were laid against Faizel Waggie, Haroon Orrie and brothers Shahied and Naziem Davids. The case went to court in January 2001 with the state adamant that the murder of the Enouses would not cause it to collapse. But progress was slow and then stopped. Charges were provisionally withdrawn in October 2003. All accused spent considerable time behind bars awaiting trial. The case was quietly closed in March 2008, seven years after the event. There were clearly concerns about Petros's affidavit, the only evidence that could have conclusively linked the flowerpot bomb to the accused.

In the end, the one bombing that was successfully prosecuted was that of Lansdowne police station in 1998. Incredibly, despite both men having been arrested at the scene and eyewitness testimony from the courageous police officer who chased them (see Chapter 7), Ismail Edwards and Faizel Waggie were only tried in 2001 after spending 20 months on bail, during which they committed other acts of violence. They were each sentenced to 15 years for the bombing and another 15 years on three charges of attempted murder. Edwards received another 25-year sentence for the attempted murder of a drug dealer.

The wave of arrests and prosecutions, including the Abdus-Salaam Ebrahim trial, ripped the heart out of Pagad and the bombings stopped. Despite multiple police mishaps, as in the case of the Keg and Swan, the violent network was extensively damaged and penetrated by the state. The failure to successfully bring to justice key members of the bombing network remained upsetting after all the effort, but it was also due to the fact that much of the investigation and collection of evidence in the earlier cases was too compromised to bring cases to court (as the prosecution of Jeneker showed). Desperate intelligence efforts, as in the case of Mansoor and the Keg and Swan, all too often failed, perhaps reinforcing Knipe's old bugbear about the difficulty of converting covert intelligence into evidence. Yet this kind of crime intelligence work, in Ngcuka's assessment, ultimately degraded and broke Pagad's violent core. It wasn't perfect, by any means, but it achieved its objectives: go after the leadership and as far as possible break the links that hold the bombing and assassination networks together. The role of informants may have had limited evidentiary value but they were an asset in being able to shape the course and targets of investigations leading up to a trial. They could also provide dramatic opportunities for 'red-handed' arrests, as ideally would have been the case at the Keg and Swan. And even if only two bombers were brought to justice, many other Pagad members were tried and sentenced.

The story of the campaign against Pagad, however, cannot be fully told without adding two last dimensions; a 'peace negotiation' between its imprisoned leaders and the state's intelligence agency, and the ultimate rupture in the organisation after a series of internal disputes. Both raise issues about the illegal economic underpinning of the movement.

15

THE PRICE OF PEACE

After the Keg and Swan arrests and prosecutions, large numbers of Pagad supporters found themselves in prison. Abdus-Salaam Ebrahim and Ebrahim Jeneker had been awaiting trial but now many others were going through the criminal justice system. Prison was a psychologically defining experience for them, and the hard reality of so many members being locked away had an impact on the organisation as a whole. The dynamics were changing in the face of the state's pressure and Pagad, it seemed, was ready to talk.

It had been involved in talks with government representatives before. In the early days, before Ali 'Phantom' Parker was expelled, he reached out to the state. And in September 1997, a round of talks began with the police, in the shape of Arno Lamoer.[1] The first meeting was tense but an agreement was hammered out that Pagad would stop marching for three months and let the police get on with their job.[2] Those discussions were abruptly halted. It is unclear why the government withdrew but at the time there was a growing recognition of the violence emanating from Pagad.[3]

There had also been an independent effort to find a negotiated solution. This was the initiative of a group of civil society activists led by Irvin Kinnes, brave and opinionated in equal measure, who tried to engage with senior leadership of the gangs and Pagad. But the time for talking had passed and no civil society effort would work if the state had rejected engagement. For the activists, it was a bitter pill to swallow. Deeply committed to the new democratic order, they had been working to show how gangsterism and corruption were harming the police, and now a series of violent encounters were sweeping aside these well-meaning efforts. 'Violence begets violence and the process moved out of our hands,' said a committed civil society leader, Moosa Kaprey, who was responsible for talking to Pagad as part of the intervention.[4]

Now, several years later, after hundreds of bombings and countless deaths, younger Pagad operatives who had been involved in extensive violence decided fresh negotiations were needed.

The secret channel to the state

It began in prison with two streetwise Pagad members who had been on the front line of the violent struggle. Zain Cornelsen, chosen as the 'emir' by Pagad and Muslim inmates in Cape Town's Pollsmoor prison, had lost friends to drugs and joined Pagad as its campaign gained momentum. Ultimately convicted of escaping with Jeneker from prison, he was widely respected by younger members and generally regarded as not to be messed with.[5] Naziem Davids, a wiry, quieter, more intellectual man, was also involved. Davids, who was arrested with Faizel Waggie after the Keg and Swan incident, was responsible for looking after Ebrahim in prison. He and Cornelsen appear to have felt an engagement with the state was now overdue, primarily to improve the conditions under which Pagad members were being held in correctional services institutions across the country.

Cornelsen took the first step: 'Even though it was not really my style, I exposed myself to the National Intelligence Agency by approaching them in a manner that we could negotiate something, which was better than nothing.'[6]

He and Davids spoke to the head of the prison, who gave them access to Arthur Fraser, then head of the NIA in the Western Cape. 'We spoke with the NIA because they seemed to be the most sincere in the pit of snakes that we faced when we wanted to negotiate our freedom,' said Cornelsen.[7] Achieving freedom may have been presumptuous after all the violence, but many in Pagad still regarded their fight as just. Cornelsen and Davids also entertained ideas about infiltrating the NIA themselves, although this was perhaps bravado.

The NIA could not negotiate with Pagad without political authority, and the agency sought the president's permission. Mbeki gave the nod but within the parameters of a clearly prescribed mandate, the contents of which have never been made public. As it became clear in the government that talks with Pagad were in the offing, resistance began to build. The state was split between hawks and doves. The police, taking their lead from their boss, were vehemently opposed: Pagad was being defeated on the streets and this was no time for talking, Selebi emphasised, banging his fist on the table.

In police intelligence circles, however, there was support for the talks. Petros and Fraser were in constant communication and the old ANC intelligence network had a good feel for how negotiations might be leveraged to their advantage. The bombs may have stopped after the Keg and Swan incident, but it was an eerie silence and there was no guarantee violence would not resume. The state was also uncertain whether it had all the bombers behind bars. There seemed little to lose and much to gain.

That the NIA, and not the police or the NPA, was the point of entry for the imprisoned Pagad members is significant. One possible reason for choosing it is that the NIA was seen as close to the top of the government, with more of a strategic remit. In contrast, the sole objective of the gumshoes in police intelligence seemed to be to put Pagad men behind bars. Pagad members were aware of these different interests and the transformational challenges facing the intelligence system, so the choice was smart: Cornelsen and Davids knew the role of the NIA was to use information and strategic positioning as a form of leverage. What they hoped to achieve was their comrades' freedom in exchange for undertakings to end the bombings.

The idea of negotiations also seemed to emerge among Pagad members outside prison. The NIA had begun a round of consultations with representatives of the Muslim community in the Western Cape in late 2000, aiming to craft a more strategic response to the violence. For the deputy director-general of the agency at the time, Barry Gilder, it was clear that the wider community, while opposed to how Pagad had transformed into a hyper-violent outfit, 'squarely laid the blame for the ... violence at the door of the South African state for its failure to effectively partner with the community in the struggle against gangsterism'.[8] It was equally clear that the extreme violence had undermined support for Pagad among the Muslim community. The organisation had lost crucial legitimacy. Through a Qibla contact, the NIA began to talk to Pagad leaders outside prison. They denied involvement in the bombings, Gilder told me.[9]

In a parallel process to the one Cornelsen and Davids initiated, Gilder and Fraser approached Abdus-Salaam Ebrahim through their external Pagad contact. Yusuf Patel, a senior NIA member related to Nizaam Shaik (also arrested after the Keg and Swan incident) by marriage, introduced the two sides in this process, Ebrahim told me. 'They wanted to meet just after I went to prison. They wanted us to make an agreement that some of us must leave prison and others should stay. They wanted us to renounce violence. I told them to go to hell.'[10] So the idea died but the young lions' approach provided another opening.

According to Gilder, the government had clear objectives: stop the bombings and draw Pagad into a process of community support and engagement around tackling crime. But what were the strategic interests of Pagad? The young operatives' first concern was the conduct of Crime Intelligence. Police agents, they said, were preying on the vulnerability of Pagad members in prison, hoping to get them 'to sing like nightingales', as one prisoner put it.[11] Another jailed member reiterated this: 'For some members, speaking to the police and getting into the witness protection programme became an option and we needed to plug that hole. I think that's why it became important for us to enter into this negotiation process so that our guys could see some action was being taken in support of them.'[12]

One reason the men in prison were becoming so vulnerable, in the assessment of Cornelsen and Davids, was that they had no hope of leaving. The time many of them had spent awaiting trial stretched on, with bail hearings unsuccessful and cases postponed. This was partly the outcome of Scorpions prosecutors turning the screws but also the result of a more careful assessment of case files by the NPA under Ngcuka. The results, as we have seen, were not always successful, but the overall strategy was clear – keep people in prison as long as possible, even if cases are weak.

Jailed members were also being approached to join the prison Numbers gangs and this worried Cornelsen and Davids, who were aware of gang culture and its sophisticated recruitment methods.

'Prison', my Pagad interlocutors said, 'broke the spirit of many men'.[13] Negotiations were a way to restore their confidence because they introduced a process and a possible outcome. In essence, the peace talks gave hope and they unified the men around a common objective. It was an astute judgement in the context of a criminal justice system that was slowly but surely gaining the advantage.

But there was another major driver for the talks: the state of their leader. Many of the men in prison had begun to lose faith in Ebrahim, as I heard from multiple sources. Pagad's boss seems to have taken to prison badly and lost his strategic outlook. 'Abdus-Salaam had no agenda at this point. ... he showed absolutely no direction and thus it was up to people like Zain that was forced to take the reins,' a Pagad member who spent time in prison told me.[14] Ebrahim was also seen fraternising freely with low-level gangsters in prison and many felt this did not befit his status as the leader of their movement.

In prison there was time and opportunity aplenty for cross-pollination. Many men, comparing notes, concluded that Pagad was going in the wrong direction and that its 'targeting strategy' (basically, who should be killed) became deeply flawed when it started identifying opponents of its leadership or innocent people, including Muslims (to portray the Muslim community as under attack).

Ebrahim was initially opposed to the talks: 'Abdus was a reluctant participant. You could almost say he was pushed into this ... or should I say forced into it,' a jailed Pagad member explained.[15] At one point Cornelsen became so angry, someone in prison with him told me, that he lifted Ebrahim bodily and thrust him against a wall, exasperated at his loss of focus and his inability to stand up for the men; Cornelsen told others later that he came to regret this, but faced with a revolt among his prison-based constituency, Ebrahim subsequently agreed to join the discussions.

The talks got under way under strict secrecy in Goodwood Prison in Cape Town in late 2001. The NIA team was led by Gilder and included Patel and Fraser; in the Pagad camp were Ebrahim, Cornelsen and Davids.

A high-level gentlemen's agreement seemed to cover the way the negotiations were conducted. Too many difficulties seemed to stand in the way of a written agreement and neither side pushed for one. In any case, if such a document had leaked there would have been a public outcry. Hennie Bester, then the provincial minister for community safety, told me he was unaware of the negotiations; had he known, he would have regarded the strategy as a mistake in that it would lend 'credence or voice' to a group widely seen as 'villains'.[16]

'The initial negotiation process,' said Cornelsen, 'allowed us to speak with Muslim community leaders who visited us in prison and we were also able to speak to other important people who gave us insights. Where our situation initially seemed fatalistic, all of a sudden there were rays of light shining through the storm clouds.'[17] The NIA shared their interpretation of Pagad and members of the organisation were briefed on this. This was important for Cornelsen and Davids as it showed they were not being coopted or using the discussions to their advantage, which might have reinforced the narrative that they were also penetrating the NIA.

The government parties emphasised that they wanted the bombs to stop. They also wanted an end to fights with gangs in prison and escape attempts. The Pagad representatives asked for confidence-building measures in the form of the release of some of their prisoners awaiting trial. The agreement seemed to be that this would be done as part of the regular process of bail applications and prosecution reviews. There was no suggestion that once cases went to trial the NIA could influence their outcome. In the words of a Pagad participant, 'they were not going to let the public out there know that they negotiated deals with us, because we were seen as a terrorist organisation at the time. Each guy that was released went through the system; that is, he had to appear in court and go through the entire procedure before he was released ... and they were set free because either there was not enough evidence against them or there were technical aspects to the investigations into their cases that were botched.'[18]

In the eyes of the imprisoned group, the fact that some releases did occur in this way built confidence. A request was granted that all Pagad prisoners be moved to Goodwood and Malmesbury prisons. This gave families easier access, addressing a key grievance, and allowed Pagad prisoners to be together. The NIA apparently pitched the idea of a joint computer system on which crimes could be monitored, with the proviso that the information would also be available to the NIA. This smacked of a wink and a nod for Pagad activities against the gangs, and as far as I know nothing came of it.

Spy-organised negotiations are always likely to include secret measures, and it would surprise no one (least of all the Pagad representatives) to know the proceedings were taped by the spooks. Furthermore, when the NIA negotiators realised the Pagad representatives were writing notes to each other, they developed a technical means to determine what had been written.

The sensitivity of these negotiations was underlined by another factor: there was considerable suspicion of the NIA in the provincial government, which was paranoid about being spied on. The NIA, in turn, believed the Western Cape government was overstepping its mandate in collecting information. (Its director-general, Niël Barnard, was after all the former head of the pre-1994 National Intelligence Service.)

Although he took part in the talks, Abdus-Salaam Ebrahim maintained his vehement opposition to the process. 'The people who were booked out of prison,' he told me, 'were those that were part of the [post-2010] G-Force. Some of them were desperate to come out of prison. National intelligence was talking to them in prison. The enemy was Abdus-Salaam. [He often refers to himself in the third person.] [Some Pagad members] wanted to work with us but they also wanted a satanic right to rob people. They were protected by intelligence.'[19]

Peace dividend?

The prison talks did not peter out so much as reach a set of conclusions bolstered by confidence-building measures. Cornelsen and Davids felt they were being shifted aside and negotiations seemed to continue outside prison too. A direct engagement then took place between Ebrahim and the NIA without the younger men, and there were suspicions that he may have made a secret deal with the state.[20]

The discussions between Ebrahim and the NIA apparently focused on the sensitive issue of handing in the organisation's weapons, primarily

R5 rifles stolen from the state which the NIA representatives felt strongly should be returned. Nizaam Shaik was tasked to collect these. Some weapons were handed over but in the fraught environment that was now developing, members excluded from negotiations felt they were being targeted for their firearms.

It is difficult to assess the success of the secret peace talks. Gilder conceded: 'I still do not know for sure to this day whether or not the bottom line to the Pagad leadership indeed brought an end to the bombings.'[21] However, most police and prosecutors I spoke to did not believe the NIA effort had any influence.

This is for two reasons. First, by the time the talks began the bombings had in any event stopped. So the claim that a negotiation process ended them was disingenuous. The last attempted bombing was outside the Keg and Swan in November 2000 and negotiations began several months later. It is possible to argue that in the run-up to a negotiation it was better for Pagad to cease its bombing campaign, as more violence would have jeopardised any chance of engagement. It is also likely that given the level of penetration and law enforcement action, Pagad could no longer mount attacks anyway as the core group of bombers were in prison or custody. In this period, though, targeted killings of gangsters continued, albeit at a much slower rate.

The second reason, as we have seen, is that law enforcement and intelligence operations were in any event continuing. The Scorpions, the police and the prosecutors assessing the cases knew that even if they thought they had the right people in the dock, the evidence they had was often not sufficient to win a clear conviction. That meant releasing people as part of a 'deal' was a process that would have to occur anyway, so there was little to be lost and goodwill to be gained. For Pagad, however, such releases allowed the imprisoned leadership to show they were trying to secure freedom for their members. A formal negotiation process also allowed a clearer recognition of the group's identity.

The assessment of Pagad's own participants follows these two lines of reasoning but is interesting in another respect. The peace talks did not end the bombing, as, by then, the organisation was already effectively crippled, they say, but reduced the possibility that the bombers would turn state witness. In the final analysis, the negotiations were a good thing. They were not contentless, nor did they concede too much. They allowed a recalibration of government and Pagad views.

However, another angle to the state's engagement with the Pagad leadership is more unpalatable and harder to assess: did the NIA pay individual leaders to refrain from violence? I have heard whispers that this happened but it is almost impossible to confirm. One former senior police intelligence official who is in a position to know such things told me: 'The NIA adopted an all-inclusive approach to Pagad and tried to win people from Pagad over. Some people in the top structure of Pagad are still on the payroll. People were being paid to keep quiet and not make trouble. Sometimes the police were investigating people and the same people were being handled by another investigating agency.'[22] Ebrahim told me the NIA did not offer to pay him or Pagad. However, he said an NIA representative once proffered a 'document' which seemed to be a draft contract that mentioned the amount of R33 million. Ebrahim refused to discuss it, he said.

If this is true, it seemed a new form of an old political economy of extortion. Was a price paid for peace? It is unlikely that we will ever unequivocally know whether the state paid members of Pagad; but financing its war chest, or satisfying the personal ambition of some members to reap financial gain for what they saw as their noble efforts, was in line with how the Pagad business model developed. It may have also contributed to its downfall.

16

STAGGIE'S GOLD CHAIN

A source recounted a story that gives some insight into how Pagad members viewed money and valuables as part of the 'exchange' they believed they were justifiably engaged in. He is a man with a reputation for violence equal to Ebrahim Jeneker's, but who has remained under the radar. He has a bull neck and hard eyes, and speaks slowly and carefully. Bull Neck said he had a friend in Pagad who was part of the lynch mob when Rashaad Staggie was killed. Amazingly, his friend snatched the chain around Staggie's neck as he was being assaulted, shot and set alight. It was apparently an expensive gold item. He kept it as a trophy and sometimes wore it on special occasions. They had been reminiscing about the old days and the chain was a symbol of their work, said my source.[1]

Taking your opponents' jewellery is standard practice in gang warfare. 'When you hit another gang, you grab their gold,' is how someone who follows gang culture explained it to me. Bling represents success, so confiscating it represents conquest. It is also a form of emasculation.[2]

Taking Staggie's chain also says something about Pagad that is crucial to understand. Besides the symbolism of the victor collecting his dues, taking the spoils of war is also seen as righteous. Pagad members believed that taking belongings from drug dealers was legitimate, rather than theft. (According to court documents, Jeneker, as we saw, took jewellery from Adiela Davids after murdering her in her salon.)

Pagad's internal governance rules made it clear that all seized booty was to be handed in to the central administration, in effect to Abdus-Salaam Ebrahim. (This was explained to me as being justified in terms of the Surah Al-Anfal, a chapter in the Quran that covers the right to take the spoils of war on the battlefield.) Ebrahim would then disburse them to finance the work of Pagad. How the proceeds of the guns, drugs, cash and cars taken from druglords were used to finance the organisation was up to Ebrahim, and this became a growing point of tension. In this sense Pagad became a business, partly financed by amassing a treasury of underworld spoils at the centre.[3]

The feeling among the rank and file at the coalface of the violent campaign was that gangsters had acquired their profits illegally, so there was no reason not to help themselves to their items. Many Pagad interviewees also envied the trappings of gangsters' flashy lifestyles and cast themselves in the role of honest soldiers fighting for a just cause but with nothing to show for it. So, despite the organisational policy of handing what was taken to the top, individual members kept money and valuable items. Stealing Staggie's chain is an early case in point, and in interviews several told me they had done the same.

As Pagad became an armed force, it became able to trade in its capacity for violence, effectively monetising its 'muscle'.[4] This included extortion activities which began by competing with local security outfits. 'Abdus was initially pissed off that people were paying neighbourhood watch and private security firms a monthly fee when that was supposed to be Pagad's domain … he wanted people's donations to go towards Pagad instead of security companies,' one of the organisation's hardmen told me.[5] Contracting out violent capacity naturally developed into Pagad members being hired to conduct armed robberies, with the spoils shared. Targeted killings were also abused by the rank and file to settle personal vendettas. I know of one case where an individual was added to the 'targeting list' because he had refused to pay for a stolen car.

Illicit finance helped Pagad wage its campaign for several years, but ultimately it contributed to a process of internal weakening and fragmentation, making the organisation even more vulnerable at a time when the state was finally turning the screws. For this reason and others, things began to fall apart at the centre.

A failed pledge

The dispute between Cornelsen and Davids on one side and Ebrahim on the other over the prison peace process – and maintaining the cohesion of Pagad's imprisoned fighters – had a longer-term consequence: the decisive split in the organisation. Like all civil wars, it is hard to describe how strongly held the views are in the opposing parties, and they coalesce around Ebrahim himself. Enmity runs deep and almost always comes up immediately in conversations on both sides.

Ebrahim was convicted again in 2006 on an additional charge of public violence and eventually released in September 2008. (Charges in 2013 relating to the murder of several Tanzanian drug dealers were dropped.)[6] A sizable cohort of Pagad members were released in 2010, but instead of being greeted as soldiers who had served their time for the organisation they are reported to have been summoned to Ebrahim's house for a bizarre ceremony. In what was described to me as 'a cult-like ritual', the men were ordered to sit in a circle with Pagad's working committee and apologise to Ebrahim for the way they had treated him in prison. 'He felt that we had challenged his authority,'[7] said one of the ex-convicts.

Later, the group was given a hit list which included members of the Muslim clergy, police, lawyers and others. The group that was released from prison, some of Pagad's most practised killers and loyal members, seem to have had enough, however. Prison transformed them in important ways, they said, and Ebrahim had little hold over them now. One member who was close to him in prison said: 'I do not feel that he acted appropriately as a leader in prison. I witnessed his mental downfall and I am certain that he suffered a nervous breakdown. He became super-paranoid and his decision-making processes became clouded.'[8]

This group decided to leave Pagad, although Ebrahim insisted to me that they were 'expelled'. They formed a new group and debated what they should call themselves. The initial idea from prison peacemaker Naziem Davids was 'Peace', but it was rejected. Boeta Yu, who carried great authority in the group, intervened in his rasping voice and argued that the organisation could not be called Peace because 'there was still no peace in our communities and we needed to bring awareness of what we were struggling for'.[9]

The name G-Force was chosen, based on the idea that unlike its early days, Pagad was now considered to be an entirely Muslim organisation. The new name, it was agreed, would attract a more diverse membership and send the message that this was a no-nonsense outfit. It also drew on the name of Pagad's internal G-Force, used when the organisation was at its most feared. G-Force, constituted in 2013, tried to reconcile with Pagad by signing a memorandum of understanding but it was rebuffed.

If the NIA had planned an influence operation when it undertook to negotiate with Pagad, it could not have hoped for a better outcome: a split organisation with a strong degree of enmity between the two parts. Pagad also now had low levels of public support. It is unlikely that this was entirely the result of the NIA talks, although the spooks were sufficiently well versed in influence operations to have given it a push. Whatever the case, the agency's analysts must have watched with fascination (and with informers in both factions) as the group unravelled.

The split that divided Pagad can be attributed in part to the peace negotiations but it was also shaped by deeper factors. One of these was that the ex-prisoners who left believed there was a class divide between them and Pagad's working committee. 'I feel that Pagad's top order is elitist,' said one. Members from impoverished communities were unlikely to make it into leadership positions. 'It is always individuals who come from nice houses and a higher social bracket that are on the working committee.'[10] This grievance was no doubt accentuated by the reality that many of the men had made considerable sacrifices for Pagad and now wanted recompense.

Another factor, in my opinion, was that many from the most violent group suffered from PTSD in the form of flashbacks. In some cases, they regretted what they had done. In the cooldown period of imprisonment, when they saw their leader up close, many became conflicted about their past activities.[11] Some no longer wanted to live like that.

Unsurprisingly, one of the key disputes that emerged was about money. After spending many years in prison, the new G-Force members saw it as their right to 'tax' drug dealers to raise funds as compensation. Some had also developed links with criminal networks in prison and several admitted doing contract hits. Aslam Toefy said: 'I wanted to see whether I could bring them back, but they were still robbing and doing all these activities.' Ebrahim added: 'We told them we would not meet with anyone who met with gangsters or worked with them.'[12]

A person who has talked extensively to Pagad told me: 'Members who left were taught a system of how to make money. When they began to use it to benefit only themselves, they became a threat and were expelled.'[13]

Motivated by the same impulse that drove the Pagad member to snatch Staggie's gold chain, some members went rogue. The chain was a harbinger of what was to come: a system of fighting crime that masked violent criminal accumulation.

The two Pagads

As a result of the split, today there are two Pagads. Although one side vehemently argues that the splinter group, the new G-Force, is not Pagad, it is still sometimes referred to as such in the press. The rump group continues to make statements that decry gang-related crime but it has little support in the Muslim communities of the Western Cape. It retains a lineage to the violent bombing campaign. Its national coordinator is Haroon Orrie, one of the men arrested on the day of the failed bomb attempt on the Keg and Swan and the brother of Phadiel Orrie, who was convicted for the murder of the Enous couple, potential witnesses to the bomb makers.

Haroon Orrie, addressing a February 2023 Pagad rally during the Cape Town Pride Festival, said: 'Gun rights, homosexuality, prostitution and alcohol, drugs, theft, gambling, incest, you name it. This is the golden calf that the people are worshipping today in this country. So how do we expect to prosper and thrive as a nation if we go against the instruction of the divine creator?'[14]

G-Force remains active and meets often. Some of its members are engaged in the criminal economy, in line with Ebrahim's accusations. Moegsien Barendse, once the head of the Grassy Park cell which intended to attack David Africa's home, is its head. Its members include Naziem Davids and Faizel Waggie, so those arrested for the Keg and Swan bombing attempt are now present in both factions of the organisation. The relationship between Barendse, who is said to fear for his life, and Ebrahim can best be described as poisonous.

The pervasive, orchestrated violence has long since stopped but the pipe bombs are not entirely silent. I began the book with an account of a bomber, Mogamat Lakay, who died in Grassy Park in August 2021 when the device he was carrying – intended for gang boss Desmond Swartz – detonated in the car. The attempted bombing of Swartz came after the murder of Yassiem Adjouhaart, who with Mungalee was a member of the Pagad Five arrested in the Karoo on their way to the Cape. Fate did not smile on Adjouhaart: he was one of the youngest Pagad members arrested after developing a reputation for extreme violence and killing several gang members. He later developed PTSD, resumed using drugs and mixed with gangsters. His body was found bound and brutalised in Zeekoevlei, a shallow lake in the Cape Flats, courtesy of the same gangsters. Revenge, as they say, is a dish best served cold.

Barendse was arrested in relation to the December 2022 killing of a scrap dealer and his two sons were later charged with the murder. After his sons were taken into custody, Barendse allegedly threatened witnesses. It is unclear in this case whether Barendse, a brick maker, targeted the dealer for business or G-Force reasons. A community worker in the know told me it is believed Barendse has connections in the gang world, a sign, if one is needed, of the greying of the line between the remnants of Pagad and the underworld.

The attempted bombing of Swartz, which neither group claimed credit for, was intended to show that Pagad still means business. Assassinations of gang bosses and associates still occur. As is the case with Swartz, no one claims responsibility, and they are few and far between. Both Pagad groups remain conscious of how they are perceived. The official Pagad, in particular, is deeply sensitive to how it is portrayed. It continues to deny that it was involved in the four-year bombing campaign, producing convoluted arguments about who may have been responsible ('provocateurs' is the term favoured by Ebrahim), including agents of the state. Pagad, in its two parts, is a husk of its former self.

THE AFTERMATH

Today, it is easy to forget how much community popularity Pagad commanded at the height of its campaign against gangs and drugs. If you speak to older people in the Muslim community, some still talk about the movement in hushed tones of admiration and respect. But they also realise that things went badly wrong. Pagad all but vanished after the arrests and jailing of its key members. Occasional killings of gang bosses continued, as one or two hitmen remained active, but for the most part the movement fell quiet. The release from prison of many Pagad members and the activities of G-Force in particular, have raised the organisation's profile again in the last few years. Killings may continue but it is hard to distinguish between gang crime and vigilantism. In effect, they have merged and become the same thing.

Opportunities lost

The period from 1998 to 2001, the years forming the main chapter of Pagad's violent campaign and the state's response to it, was one of the most significant for criminal justice reform in South Africa's modern history. Old ways of doing things were cast aside, and crisis bred opportunity and innovation. A key group of reformers emerged, notably Bulelani Ngcuka and Percy Sonn, and in some respects George Fivaz. Many other brave and committed players from the new and old orders also played key roles.

Was the way the state dealt with the Pagad threat perfect? Not at all. Nobody assessing this period would say things ran smoothly. But out of it emerged a shared vision and a determination that ultimately prevailed. With the organised crime challenges South Africa currently faces, it is worth reminding ourselves of that. Too often we despair when we should remember that the country has faced down serious security challenges in the recent past. Pagad, in my view, is the most important case. It was an urban terrorism campaign of some significance, germinating in a community in need of security then mutating into widespread violence. It is remarkable that so few people have written about it – at least not in a comprehensive way that covers all the people and events.

One reason for that is certainly that people remain afraid of Pagad; the killings and bombings left their mark, something that became clear as I worked on this book. Victims are afraid to speak out. Former police officers still fear the assassination squads. But it is time to air the room, to put fear aside, understand what happened and discuss how to prevent a recurrence. This is particularly important in the context of a state that has been weakened, with politics divided and often corrupted, and when organised vigilantism is again rearing its head and crime bosses often have more power and authority in local communities than elected officials.

One of the remarkable things about the Pagad story is how well the politics was managed. Steve Tshwete bluntly pointed to the perpetrators without accusing a community. Hennie Bester remarked to me how the Pagad campaign could have seriously damaged the social cohesion of the province; instead, national and provincial politicians and different political parties worked together to ensure that it didn't. Civil society, particularly religious groups, also played crucial roles, and for this credit should go to organisations representing the Muslim community in Cape Town. Muslims, Christians and Jews prayed together and condemned the violence. It was a completely different response from the one that often characterised the 'war on terror' after the 9/11 attacks.

That is not to say politicians and the police were not compromised by Pagad, most notably in the early days. Jessie Duarte's comment to Ayob Mungalee – that targeting gangsters was acceptable – provides a case in point. There is also ample evidence that the police cooperated with Pagad by providing police radios or details of gangsters to facilitate the work many felt they could not do through the justice system. There were probably incidents where police investigators turned a blind eye – the thinking being along the lines of, 'it's only another gangster' – and no doubt that is a reason some investigations were so poorly conducted.

We should also remind ourselves, in an era when the default position is sometimes to remember with misplaced fondness the old SAP's 'expertise', that the new order of democratic policing needed new thinking. And in a space of a few years, as outlined here, South Africa was not found wanting. Bureaucracy was pushed aside and leaders came to the fore. Expertise was drawn on when it was needed and international experts were consulted. Solutions were crafted. The team that eventually defeated Pagad was made up of former rivals, people from the old and new political orders, but they found ways to combine expertise and approaches.

Today, in contrast, faced with the enormous challenge of mafia-like organised criminal activity, South Africa's systems and responses seem sclerotic, bureaucratic and politicised, characterised by factional feuding and lack of leadership. We have misplaced something, and if we are to face the challenge of organised crime we need to rediscover it: a capacity to draw on all the expertise we have, to find credible leaders willing to take risks rooted in the rule of law. We lost the opportunity to sustain the solutions that the counter-campaign against Pagad taught us. In the perilous time we now face, we need to grasp them again.

Many paid the ultimate price in the campaign against Pagad. Bennie Lategan, a detective of promise, was gunned down in cold blood. Piet Theron, a magistrate, was targeted in a hit for doing his job without fear or favour. Seven witnesses to Pagad's criminal activities paid with their lives: Mogamat Zahied Abrahams, Samir January, Nathier Brown, Ebrahim Gallie, Ashraf Saban, and Yusuf and Fahiema Enous. Scores of other people were threatened and several fled the Western Cape and the country.

Despite their contribution to the ultimate, albeit qualified, success, there are many tragic figures who emerged wounded by the Pagad story and the state's response.

Bulelani Ngcuka resigned as NDPP in 2004. He endured a vicious whispering campaign about his role as an alleged spy for the apartheid state. A judicial commission of inquiry found him innocent. Just as his innocence was established, he was felled by the intricate politics around his decision not to prosecute then deputy-president Jacob Zuma for bribe-taking. For several years, exhausted and bitter, he all but disappeared off the radar. More than anyone else since 1994, Ngcuka had the personality, competence and energy to take a problem by its horns and solve it. He did that in the case of Pagad. He recognised that when people lose hope, much of law enforcement is symbolic. His approach was not the empty news of ministers visiting victims, but high-profile action and arrests, something that did not endear him to his detractors.

Percy Sonn's vision, determination and willingness to take on the established interests of the police made Idoc possible. The Scorpions followed from that, and under Ngcuka they made a significant difference to South Africa's law enforcement dynamics.

Leonard Knipe is a conflicted figure in all of this. Emerging from the apartheid police with his reputation largely intact and his conflict with the Security Branch well documented, he nevertheless failed to rise to the challenge. He could have embraced change but in the end it was the quieter, little-known station detective Riaan Booysen who stepped in and delivered. From the old-order police, many who were doubted – including several figures from the old Security Branch (Lategan among them) and the 'men in black' – served the new state well in this moment of early crisis.

A tragic figure is undoubtedly Arno Lamoer. Pagad made his name and may well have broken it too; his corruption conviction rested on a link to a man with Pagad connections. Lamoer could have been national commissioner of police and he would have done an exceptional job. He would have been a unifier. It was not to be.

Some ANC intelligence figures were central to this story. Mzwandile Petros, his mistakes notwithstanding, was an outsider who rose to the task. David Africa, perhaps the key intellectual figure on the ground and at the centre, shaped state understanding and the secret response. Anwar Dramat, always eager to be out of the public eye, did his duty. They are flawed heroes, no doubt, but heroes all the same in the face of Pagad.

Jackie Selebi, once a bright light, proved to be as destructive a force to policing in South Africa as can be imagined. Corrupted by organised crime, he moved fast and broke things. We suffer the consequences still. His conflict with Ngcuka was kept under wraps but it undercut the formation of a new law enforcement system suitable for a complex and evolving democracy rooted in the rule of law. Had they worked together, things might have been different. Selebi embodies a crucial missed opportunity.

The role of the NIA is hard to assess, given its secret mandate, but the evidence suggests a committed and innovative response, including being ready to talk to Pagad. In this, Arthur Fraser emerged as an instrumental figure. Should it ever be shown that the agency paid Pagad leaders to end the bombing, it would legitimately be a scandal.

In his role as an informant for the state, Ayob Mungalee personified many of the contradictions at the heart of the Pagad story. He believed in the organisation's objectives of hunting down the gangsters destroying communities, but he was absolutely opposed to the bombing of state and civilian targets. His stance was unequivocal and he demonstrated this by spying for the state at the risk of being killed by his own movement. The state did not try to protect him but threw him to the wolves. It is tragic that he was killed by avenging gangsters.

Mission not accomplished

What of those who took part in Pagad's campaign? They told me how desperate they felt: drugs were exploding on the streets and in the schools of their communities, and the state did not care. Worse, it was an active participant in facilitating the drug trade. But Pagad became a killing machine and, like Dr Frankenstein's monster, the protagonist turned into the antagonist. Pagad bred a group of killers who became criminals themselves.

As the book recounts, I accept the view that Pagad was created as a front by Qibla to advance its cause. It drew on the aspirations of communities across Cape Town to respond to the challenge of drugs and crime. It mutated in two steps: the first was an assassination campaign targeting the gang bosses and their minions; the second (among a smaller and more hardcore ideological group) was the bombing of civilian and state targets. There is no evidence of external connections: Pagad was a homegrown terror outfit.

In my view, a great burden of responsibility for what happened should rest on the shoulders of Abdus-Salaam Ebrahim. While he was convicted for a comparatively minor crime (public violence), by all accounts, as Bulelani Ngcuka concluded at the Christmas Day meeting, he did much to shape Pagad's campaign. Ngcuka acted in the country's best interests in his determination to go after him. Structural and other factors drive and shape the path of history but decisions made by people determine events.

The small core group of bombers have remained unidentified for years. They were the ones who organised the attacks on civilian and state infrastructure. I know that at least one, and maybe more, regret their actions. At least two survivors asked me if they could talk with the bombers. They should answer in the positive and stand up and be counted. Keeping up the mantra that the bombing is disconnected from Pagad and the work of some outside force is nonsensical; the public has long seen through this veil of mendacity. Bruce Walsh, badly injured in the Planet Hollywood bombing, told me that after deep introspection he had forgiven the perpetrators, but had two questions for them: what were your objectives? And did you achieve them?

The biggest tragedy that emerges from this story is that despite the removal of hundreds of gangsters and scores of powerful gang bosses, gangs and other forms of organised crime have grown since the Pagad era. In this sense, Pagad failed in its mission. And so has the South African state.

The killings, like pruning a tree growing wild, resulted in stronger growth and the emergence of new and powerful criminal leaders. This is the legacy of the Pagad campaign. It is perhaps the biggest lost opportunity that a wider, peaceful mobilisation around gangs and crime in the early years of the new democracy might have brought greater and more sustainable benefits. Vigilantism eats its children. In the absence of an effective state, those who may have legitimate reasons for attacking criminals, as comparative evidence shows, become criminals themselves. Violence begets violence and the temptations of the profits of criminal markets can become irresistible.

The Scorpions embodied all the hopes of the new state: clean, clinical and focused in their execution, with an emphasis on directing all their efforts to ensuring criminals faced trial under the rule of law. The police alone, despite all the power and influence they wielded in pre-1994 South Africa, were ill-prepared for this job. The intelligence operatives, while their actions were crucial and courageous, had only one task in the end: to provide information and to shape the environment so arrests could be made and justice delivered through the presentation of evidence before an objective and unthreatened judiciary. In this context, a body like the Scorpions was crucial, not only because it was effective but because it was the only way to enact state enforcement in a democratic environment respectful of the rule of law. It is for this reason that the disbandment of the Scorpions in 2009 has proved to be a tragic lost opportunity.

Citizens' constitutional rights to peace and freedom were the result of the hard-won struggle. If there is a lesson from the tragic events and figures of this story, it is that only a state that works together, with clear, committed leadership, can solve the country's enormous security challenges, many of which are concentrated in the areas where gangs and crime bosses continue to hold sway.

NOTES

Preface

1 Strictly speaking, the term 'black widow' refers to the small firecracker used as a fuse, but the name came to encompass the most basic pipe bomb device.
2 Some bombs were most likely not reported and it is difficult to piece together the number of cases from the available documentation, much of which is not accessible or has been lost.

Prologue

1 Interview, Cape Town, January 2022.
2 Interview, Cape Town, February 2022.
3 Interview via Zoom, August 2021.
4 Interview, Cape Town, January 2022.
5 Interview via Zoom, August 2021.
6 Interview, Cape Town, February 2022.
7 Quoted in Sheila Croucher, 'South Africa's Democratisation and the Politics of Gay Liberation', *Journal of Southern African Studies*, Vol. 28, No. 2, 2002, p. 321.
8 Ibid., p. 330.
9 See, for example, Glen Elder, 'Somewhere, over the Rainbow: Cape Town, South Africa as a "Gay Destination"', in Lahoucine Ouzgane and Robert Morrell (eds), *African Masculinities: Men in Africa from the late Nineteenth Century to the Present*, London: Palgrave, 2005.
10 Quoted in Gustav Visser, 'Gay Men, Leisure Space and South African Cities: The Case of Cape Town', *GeoForum*, No 34, 2003, p. 129.
11 Delaney died in December 2017 at the age of 95.
12 Interview, Cape Town, January 2022.
13 Interview via Zoom, May 2021.
14 Interview via Zoom, May 2021.
15 Interview via Zoom, May 2021.
16 Interview via Zoom, August 2021.
17 Interview via Zoom, May 2021.
18 Interview, Cape Town, January 2022.
19 Interview via Zoom, May 2021.
20 Interview, Cape Town, January 2022.
21 Interview via Zoom, May 2021.

Chapter 1

1 Quoted in Dean E Murphy, 'Unsolved Bombings Stir Fear in S Africa', *Los Angeles Times*, 27 December 1999, https://www.latimes.com/archives/la-xpm-1999-dec-27-mn-48053-story.html.

2 Ibid.

3 'Mostert still a suspect in Cape Town bombings', *The Star*, Johannesburg, 9 December 1999.

4 Communication from UK Ambassador Lyall Grant to London, 'Bomb Attack in Cape Town: Offer of Help from SO13', DCT051/334/001/98, 26/08/1998. Obtained from the then Foreign, Commonwealth and Development Office Information Management Department under a Freedom of Information Act request, February 2022.

5 Our meeting was in January 2022.

6 Fanie Schoeman died soon after reaching hospital, and Brian Duddy died later in hospital.

7 Interview via Zoom, June 2023.

8 I applied under the UK Freedom of Information Act 2000 for any information held by the Foreign and Commonwealth Office in relation to the Planet Hollywood bombing. A series of communications between different officials was provided.

9 Fax from Andrew Turner, BHC Cape Town, to Andrew Page AD (S), 13 October 1998, CS5051/001/98.

10 Interview via Zoom, February 2022.

11 Interview via Zoom, March 2022.

12 Interview via Zoom, March 2022.

13 Quoted in Chené Blignaut, 'When love conquers terror', *Fair Lady*, 29 March 2000, p. 27.

14 Editorial, *Femina*, September 2000, p. 14.

15 Renate Meyer, 'Between Waking and Dreaming: Living with Urban Fear, Paradox and Possibility', in Sean Field, Renate Meyer and Felicity Swanson (eds), *Imagining the City: Memories and Cultures in Cape Town*, Cape Town: HSRC Press, 2007, p. 89.

16 Rory Bester, *Fresh: Dorothee Kreutzfeldt*, Cape Town: Bell-Roberts, 2002, pp. 23 and 25.

17 Anastasia Maw, '"The Quickest Way to Move On is to Go Back": Bomb Blast Survivors' Narratives of Trauma and Recovery', in Sean Field, Renate Meyer and Felicity Swanson (eds), *Imagining the City: Memories and Cultures in Cape Town*, Cape Town: HSRC Press, 2007, p. 85.

18 The portraits were published in *Femina*'s September 2000 issue.

19 Toni Younghusband, 'Heartbreak of a bomb survivor', *Femina*, February 2001, p. 40.

20 Anastasia Maw, '"The Quickest Way to Move On is to Go Back": Bomb Blast Survivors' Narratives of Trauma and Recovery', in Sean Field, Renate Meyer and Felicity Swanson (eds), *Imagining the City: Memories and Cultures in Cape Town*, Cape Town: HSRC Press, 2007, p. 87.

21 Interview via Zoom, March 2022.

22 Anastasia Maw, '"The Quickest Way to Move On is to Go Back": Bomb Blast Survivors' Narratives of Trauma and Recovery', in Sean Field, Renate Meyer and Felicity Swanson (eds), *Imagining the City: Memories and Cultures in Cape Town*, Cape Town: HSRC Press, 2007, p. 90.

23 Ibid.

24 Thabo Manetsi interviewed by Renate Meyer, Centre for Popular Memory, Department of Historical Studies, University of Cape Town (undated).
25 Anastasia Maw, '"The Quickest Way to Move On is to Go Back": Bomb Blast Survivors' Narratives of Trauma and Recovery', in Sean Field, Renate Meyer and Felicity Swanson (eds), *Imagining the City: Memories and Cultures in Cape Town*, Cape Town: HSRC Press, 2007, p. 89.
26 Interview, Cape Town, January 2022.
27 Interview, Ian McMahon, Cape Town, February 2022. Russell Shapiro said something similar.
28 Interview, Cape Town, March 2022.
29 Mike Davis, *Buda's Wagon: A Brief History of the Car Bomb*, London: Verso, 2017, p. 11.
30 Ibid., pp. 4–12.
31 Ibid., p. 123.
32 Monde Dlakavu, 'The handiwork of cowards', *Cape Argus*, 21 August 2000, p. 1.
33 Personal communication, Cape Town, February 2022.
34 That is the distance recommended by the US Treasury Department's Bureau of Alcohol, Tobacco and Firearms. The same distance is recommended in the SAPS training material.
35 Interview, Cape Town, March 2022.
36 Monde Dlakavu, 'The handiwork of cowards', *Cape Argus*, 21 August 2000, p. 1.

Chapter 2

1 This point is well made by Bill Dixon and Lisa-Marie Johns in 'Gangs, Pagad and the State: Vigilantism and Revenge Violence in the Western Cape', Centre for the Study of Violence and Reconciliation, *Violence and Transition Series*, Vol 2, May 2001. This remains one of the best analytical overviews of Pagad and the state's response.
2 Interview via Zoom, August 2021.
3 There is substantial literature about the challenges, lessons and failures of police reform in South Africa. One of the most original and important is Jonny Steinberg, 'Policing, State Power, and the Transition from Apartheid to Democracy', *African Affairs*, 2014, Vol 113, No. 451, pp. 173–191.
4 Speech by Minister F S Mufamadi, 'Opening address: Confronting Crime Workshop', Cape Town, 9 September 1995.
5 This was the result of several factors. A number of community activists clustered around the office of the National Institute for Crime Prevention and the Reintegration of Offenders (Nicro) and the outspoken Western Cape Anti-Crime Forum, which uniquely combined a response to gangs in Cape Town with a focus on police reforms. The city was also home to the Institute of Criminology at the University of Cape Town, which had long had a focus on police reform and where an influential ANC-aligned adviser on police reform, Janine Rauch, had worked. For a neat summary of the role of the Institute of Criminology see Anine Kriegler, 'Balancing Harms and the Role of Courts in Psychoactive Substance Policy Reform: Lessons from a Cannabis

Case', in Thembisa Waetjen (ed), *Opioids in South Africa: Towards a Policy of Harm Reduction*, Cape Town: HSRC Press, 2019, p. 41.

6 The principles of doing so could be boiled down to the following: recruit sources on the ground, analyse the information obtained, brief decision makers, and where possible try to shape events through public actions (arrests) or secret means (the planting of stories or spreading of rumours).

7 Interview via Zoom, July 2021.

8 Ibid.

9 Interview via Zoom, August 2021.

10 A surprising number used their pension payouts to open restaurants. But secret police officers and entrepreneurs are different things, and many of these ventures failed.

11 Dutton, who insisted on partnering with black officers, had a distinguished career that culminated in his work for the Zondo Commission of Inquiry into State Capture. He died in January 2022.

12 Interview, former senior Murder & Robbery detective and commander, Cape Town, May 2022.

13 Interview, former senior Murder & Robbery detective, Cape Town, September 2021.

14 Interview, former senior Murder & Robbery detective and commander, Cape Town, May 2022.

15 Interview, Cape Town, May 2022.

16 For example, among insiders Nick Acker is often mentioned as a key figure in the Cape detectives. He was provincial commander for detectives in the early 1980s when the successes of Murder & Robbery units were at their peak. He created a system that produced good detectives and is still spoken of with reverence by old-timers.

17 Truth and Reconciliation Commission, Day 2 – 18 February 1997, 'Submissions, Questions and Answers: Leonard Knipe', p. 51 (of the printed version), https://www.justice.gov.za/trc/hrvtrans/gug/knipe.htm.

18 Ibid., p. 22 (of the printed version).

19 Interview, Pretoria, January 2022.

20 Jeremy Vearey, *Into Dark Water: A Police Memoir*, Cape Town: Tafelberg, 2021, p. 19

21 Williams had his own ghosts, though, having faced accusations in the febrile atmosphere of the ANC that he had been a former government spy. There is no evidence of this but he remained bitter about it. When he was called on by the ANC to assume the post, he agreed only reluctantly.

22 During Jacob Zuma's presidency, Dramat's investigation of corruption cases landed him in hot water, and he was pushed from the police with a golden handshake after accusations that he had illegally ensured the rendition of several Zimbabwean suspects without following due process. A senior official told me that 'this was nothing but a dredged-up excuse to get rid of him to disrupt the investigations' into the Zuma regime. Interview, Pretoria, October 2021.

23 In the latter post, Petros courted controversy about allegations that he had manipulated crime statistics to bolster his image.

24 The most public example is Vearey, who, never one to keep his opinions to himself,

was later suspended from the police after a distinguished career for publicly insulting the national commissioner.

Chapter 3

1 I know his name but refrain from using it in order to protect him and his family; the meeting has never been made public.
2 This story was recounted to me by Fivaz in two interviews in July and August 2021.
3 See Bill Dixon and Lisa-Marie Johns, 'Gangs, Pagad and the State: Vigilantism and Revenge Violence in the Western Cape', Centre for the Study of Violence and Reconciliation, *Violence and Transition Series*, Vol 2, May 2001 (unpaginated).
4 One of the founders of the Call of Islam was Ebrahim Rasool, who went on to be ANC premier of the Western Cape and played an important role in the campaign against Pagad. The formation of the Call of Islam was closely linked to the political developments of the time, with Rasool and his colleagues seeking to link the Muslim community with wider South African society and in opposition to the actions of the apartheid state. For that reason, the organisation labelled itself 'Muslims Against Oppression'. The Call of Islam was unashamedly South African in outlook.
5 Chris Saunders, 'Pan-Africanism: The Cape Town Case', *Journal of Asian and African Studies*, Vol 47, No 3, p. 296.
6 Rania Hassan, 'Identity Construction in Post-Apartheid South Africa: The Case of the Muslim Community', PhD thesis, University of Edinburgh, 2011, p. 68.
7 I made several attempts to contact Cassiem for an interview but was unable to secure one.
8 Farid Esack, 'Three Islamic Strands in the South African Struggle for Justice', *Third World Quarterly*, Vol 10, No 2, 1988, p. 488.
9 Several people have suggested that Cassiem and Qibla's role in the fight against apartheid did not achieve the attention it deserved because they operated outside of mainstream opinion. See Ursula Günther and Inga Niehaus, 'Islam, Politics and Gender During the Struggle in South Africa, 1976–1990', *Journal for the Study of Religion*, 2002, Vol 15, No 2, pp. 87–88.
10 This was said to be because the PAC accepted financial contributions from Iraq during the Iran-Iraq war. Qibla remained loyal to Iran. See HE Chehabi, 'South Africa and Iran in the Apartheid Era', *Journal of Southern African Studies*, Vol 42, No 4, 2016, p. 708.
11 See Sindre Bangstad, 'Hydra's heads: Pagad and Responses to the Pagad Phenomenon in a Cape Muslim Community', *Journal of Southern African Studies*, Vol 31, No 1, March 2005, pp. 200–201.
12 Rania Hassan, 'Identity Construction in Post-Apartheid South Africa: The Case of the Muslim Community', PhD thesis, University of Edinburgh, 2011, p. 69.
13 Interview with a businessman with close ties to Qibla, Cape Town, August 2021.
14 Interviews, Pretoria, August and September 2021.
15 The classic study of this is Don Pinnock, *The Brotherhoods: Street Gangs and State Control in Cape Town*, Cape Town: David Philip, 1984.

16 Wilfried Schärf, 'Organised Crime Comes of Age: During Transition to Democracy', in Raashied Galant and Fahmi Gamieldien (eds), *Drugs, Gangs, People's Power: Exploring the Pagad Phenomenon*, Cape Town: Claremont Main Road Masjid, 1996, p. 55. This little-known volume is an excellent overview of several key issues around Pagad's formation.

17 Mark Shaw, *Hitmen for Hire: Exposing South Africa's Underworld*, Johannesburg: Jonathan Ball, 2017, p. 105.

18 See, for example, data in S Pasche and B Myers, 'Substance Misuse Trends in South Africa', *Human Psychopharmacology*, 27, 2012, pp. 338–341.

19 Document provided to the author, 'Pagad impact', September 2021. I do not have any doubt as to the authenticity of the source.

20 Wilfried Schärf, 'Organised Crime Comes of Age: During Transition to Democracy', in Raashied Galant and Fahmi Gamieldien (eds), *Drugs, Gangs, People's Power: Exploring the Pagad Phenomenon*, Cape Town: Claremont Main Road Masjid, 1996, p. 59.

21 The Firm ultimately excluded two of the most powerful gangs, the Americans and the Sexy Boys.

22 Not to be confused with the prison gang of the same name.

23 Wilfried Schärf, 'Organised Crime Comes of Age: During Transition to Democracy', in Raashied Galant and Fahmi Gamieldien (eds), *Drugs, Gangs, People's Power: Exploring the Pagad Phenomenon*, Cape Town: Claremont Main Road Masjid, 1996, p. 54.

24 For example, comments made at a meeting with members of the Pagad executive, September 2021. But such comments also came in informal discussions with people who had never had an affiliation to Pagad.

25 Shamil Jeppie, 'Introduction', in Raashied Galant and Fahmi Gamieldien (eds), *Drugs, Gangs, People's Power: Exploring the Pagad Phenomenon*, Cape Town: Claremont Main Road Masjid, 1996, p. 13.

26 Irvin Kinnes, 'From Urban Street Gangs to Criminal Empires: The Changing Face of Gangs in the Western Cape', Monograph No. 48, Institute for Security Studies, 2000.

27 Christopher Clohessy, 'Thoughts on Pagad', in Raashied Galant and Fahmi Gamieldien (eds), *Drugs, Gangs, People's Power: Exploring the Pagad Phenomenon*, Cape Town: Claremont Main Road Masjid, 1996, p. 74.

28 Interviews with gang members active at the time, 2020 and 2021. See also Wilfried Schärf, 'Organised Crime Comes of Age: During Transition to Democracy', in Raashied Galant and Fahmi Gamieldien (eds), *Drugs, Gangs, People's Power: Exploring the Pagad Phenomenon*, Cape Town: Claremont Main Road Masjid, 1996, p. 53.

29 Farid Esack, 'Three Islamic Strands in the South African Struggle for Justice', *Third World Quarterly*, Vol 10, No 2, 1988, p. 484.

30 Comments made as part of a wider discussion with some members of the Pagad executive, Cape Town, September 2021.

31 Clohessy has been described as a Catholic priest who teaches Shia Islam. See,

for example, https://web.archive.org/web/20191001232929/https://twitter.com/The_IPH/status/1179176389087510528.

32 Christopher Clohessy, 'Thoughts on Pagad', in Raashied Galant and Fahmi Gamieldien (eds), *Drugs, Gangs, People's Power: Exploring the Pagad Phenomenon*, Cape Town: Claremont Main Road Masjid, 1996, p. 69.

33 Keith Gottschalk, 'Vigilantism v. the State: A Case Study of the Rise and Fall of Pagad, 1996–2000', Institute for Security Studies paper, No. 99, February 2005, p. 1.

34 Interview, Cape Town, February 2022.

35 This is according to the court testimony of police officer Gavin Haupt, who had arrived at the scene. See 'Court, Pagad men visit Staggie lynching scene', News24, 16 May 2001, https://www.news24.com/news24/court-Pagad-men-visit-staggie-lynching-scene-20010516.

36 I have spoken to several people who were present that night. The accounts of what happened vary. The best overview of what happened is from a video taken of the murder. For a summary, see: https://lostmediawiki.com/Lynching_of_Rashaad_Staggie_(found_on-aired_death_footage_of_South_African_gang_leader;_1996).

Chapter 4

1 Several estimates have been provided for the numbers present. They vary from 350 to 3 500.

2 I have not been able to determine whether gangsters were in fact present, although I doubt it. Nevertheless, given the uncertainties of the time, the caution on the part of the police was warranted.

3 Interview via Zoom, July 2021.

4 Interview with former police intelligence analyst, via Zoom, July 2021.

5 Bill Dixon and Lisa-Marie Johns, 'Gangs, Pagad and the State: Vigilantism and Revenge Violence in the Western Cape', Centre for the Study of Violence and Reconciliation, *Violence and Transition Series*, Vol 2, May 2001.

6 Marianne Merten, 'Murdered Pagad leader was an informer', *Mail & Guardian*, 23 July 1999, https://mg.co.za/article/1999-07-23-murdered-Pagad-leader-was-informer/.

7 Shamil Jeppie, 'Introduction', in Raashied Galant and Fahmi Gamieldien (eds), *Drugs, Gangs, People's Power: Exploring the Pagad Phenomenon*, Cape Town: Claremont Main Road Masjid, 1996, p. 13.

8 Sindre Bangstad, 'Hydra's Heads: Pagad and Responses to the Pagad Phenomenon in a Cape Muslim Community', *Journal of Southern African Studies*, Vol 31, No 1, March 2005, p. 199.

9 Christopher Clohessy, 'Thoughts on Pagad', in Raashied Galant and Fahmi Gamieldien (eds), *Drugs, Gangs, People's Power: Exploring the Pagad Phenomenon*, Cape Town: Claremont Main Road Masjid, 1996, p. 70.

10 Bill Dixon and Lisa-Marie Johns, 'Gangs, Pagad and the State: Vigilantism and Revenge Violence in the Western Cape', Centre for the Study of Violence and Reconciliation, *Violence and Transition Series*, Vol 2, May 2001.

11 'Pagad now part of the crime problem says police chief', *Cape Argus*, 20 December 1996.
12 Bill Dixon and Lisa-Marie Johns, 'Gangs, Pagad and the State: Vigilantism and Revenge Violence in the Western Cape', Centre for the Study of Violence and Reconciliation, *Violence and Transition Series*, Vol 2, May 2001.
13 See Lisa Vetten, 'Invisible Girls and Violent Boys: Gender and Gangs in South Africa', *Development Update*, Vol 3, No. 2, 2000, Centre for the Study of Violence and Reconciliation.
14 At least one property was sold well below market value after her death to another gang boss. See Marianne Merten, 'Gang boss faces further asset seizure', *Mail & Guardian*, 9 March 2001, https://mg.co.za/article/2001-03-09-gang-boss-faces-further-asset-seizure/.
15 Interview via Zoom, June 2022.
16 See 'Part Five: Africa', in *Crime, Law and Social Change*, Vol 36, Nos. 1–2, 2001, p. 258.
17 Interview via Zoom, June 2022.
18 Chiara Carter and Marianne Merten, 'Gangster's fast life, hard death', *The Mail & Guardian*,13 November 1998, https://mg.co.za/article/1998-11-13-gangsters-fast-life-hard-death/.
19 The letters of Mongrel's name each stood for some representation of what the gang was about: 'M' was for '*mingenade*' (no mercy); 'G' was for '*geweld*' (violence).
20 Interview, social worker with long engagement with gangs, by telephone, June 2022.
21 See, for example, this 2018 presentation on gang intervention work in Avian Park, Worcester, funded by the Western Cape government, in which the Junior Cisko Yakkies are named, https://www.westerncape.gov.za/assets/day_2_session_2_gangs_stefan_snel.pdf.
22 Personal communication, June 2022.
23 Ibid.
24 Personal communication, former gang general, June 2022.
25 The quote is from *Pagad – The Gangsters' Enemy*, http:www.journeyman.tv/film/532.
26 Alex Dodd, 'The Women of Pagad', in Raashied Galant and Fahmi Gamieldien (eds), *Drugs, Gangs, People's Power: Exploring the Pagad Phenomenon*, Cape Town: Claremont Main Road Masjid, 1996, p. 64.
27 'Part Five: Africa', in *Crime, Law and Social Change*, Vol 36, Nos. 1–2, 2001, p. 258.

Chapter 5

1 Interview, Cape Town, September 2021.
2 Toefy told me in front of other members that he stepped back from Pagad because of illness. Discussion with members of the Pagad executive, Cape Town, 30 September 2021.
3 The exchange was part of an initial discussion with some members of Pagad's executive committee, Cape Town, September 2021.
4 Quoted in Anneli Botha, 'People Against Gangsterism and Drugs (Pagad): A Study of Structures, Operations and Initial Government Reactions', MA thesis, Rand

Afrikaans University, March 1999, p. 48.
5 This summary is nicely captured in Heinrich Matthee, 'Muslim Identities and Political Strategies: A Case Study of Muslims in the Greater Cape Town Area of South Africa', PhD thesis, University of Kassel, 2008, p. 154.
6 Anneli Botha, 'People Against Gangsterism and Drugs (Pagad): A Study of Structures, Operations and Initial Government Reactions', MA thesis, Rand Afrikaans University, March 1999, p. 49.
7 Ibid., p. 50. See media reports at the time: T. Younghusband, 'Now it's the people against Pagad', *The Sunday Tribune*, 17 November 1996; and T Younghusband, 'New twist on Pagad', *The Sunday Tribune*, 22 December 1996.
8 See 'Police, Pagad clash: 1 dead', *The Citizen*, 4 November 1996, and 'Pagad demo death row', *The Citizen*, 5 November 1996.
9 Interview, Vienna, September 2021.
10 Interview, Cape Town, May 2022.
11 He hinted at this directly and it was confirmed by other members of Pagad.
12 Interview, Cape Town, May 2022.
13 Interview, Cape Town, May 2022.
14 An overview of the structure can be found in Henri Boshoff, Anneli Botha and Martin Schönteich, 'Fear in the City: Urban Terrorism in South Africa', Institute for Security Studies, September 2001, https://issafrica.org/research/monographs/monograph-63-fear-in-the-city-urban-terrorism-in-south-africa-henri-boshoff-anneli-botha-and-martin-schonteich.
15 'Briefing Summary: Current situation – Pagad and Gangsterism', Picoc, Western Cape, undated but likely completed around October 1997.
16 Interview, Cape Town, October 2021.
17 Interview, Cape Town, October 2021.
18 Interviews, Cape Town, February 2022.
19 Interview, Cape Town, May 2022.
20 Interview, Cape Town, February 2022.
21 Quoted in Henri Boshoff, Anneli Botha and Martin Schönteich, 'Fear in the City: Urban Terrorism in South Africa', Institute for Security Studies, September 2001, https://issafrica.org/research/monographs/monograph-63-fear-in-the-city-urban-terrorism-in-south-africa-henri-boshoff-anneli-botha-and-martin-schonteich, chapter 2 (unpaginated).
22 Interview, Cape Town, February 2022.
23 Quoted in Estelle Ellis, 'Pagad man names amir in Staggie video', *Cape Argus*, 20 September 2001.
24 Heinrich Matthee, 'Muslim Identities and Political Strategies: A Case Study of Muslims in the Greater Cape Town Area of South Africa', PhD thesis, University of Kassel, 2008, p. 157.
25 Interview, Cape Town, October 2021.
26 Interview, Cape Town, February 2022.
27 Interview, Cape Town, October 2021.

28 Interview, Cape Town, May 2022.
29 Interview, Cape Town, October 2021.
30 Damian Daniels, 'Pagad's true colours revealed', *Mail & Guardian*, 28 August 1998, https://mg.co.za/article/1998-08-28-Pagads-true-colours-revealed/.
31 'Briefing Summary: Current situation – Pagad and Gangsterism', Picoc, Western Cape, undated but probably completed around October 1997.
32 Interview, Cape Town, October 2021.

Chapter 6

1 Interview, Cape Town, September 2021.
2 In researching this chapter, I interviewed several people who know or are close to Jeneker, or who worked with him. I also obtained court and other documentation from Jeneker's various run-ins with the law, which while often too detailed for inclusion here, provided some insight into his personality. In my estimation, the interviewees were reliable witnesses, and in some cases eyewitnesses, to events and Jeneker's personality.
3 In three instances, law enforcement officers declined to speak to me when I mentioned Jeneker.
4 By telling this story, I am not trying to justify the actions of Jeneker and his compatriots, but only trying to explain their motivations.
5 Interview, Cape Town, September 2021.
6 Interview, Cape Town, October 2021.
7 Translated from Afrikaans. Transcript of Jeneker's testimony, Supreme Court of South Africa, The Cape of Good Hope Provincial Section, *The State v Abdullah Maansdorp, Ismael Maansdorp and Ebrahim Jeneker*, case number SS. 121/99, 5 June 2002, 11.45 am.
8 Interview, Cape Town, October 2021.
9 Interview, Cape Town, September 2021.
10 Cornelsen would later be charged with a spate of crimes, including murder and sedition, although he was ultimately convicted for escaping from prison with Jeneker. He spent 14 years behind bars.
11 Interview, Cape Town, September 2021.
12 Interview, Cape Town, September 2021.
13 Interview, Cape Town, October 2021.
14 Interview, Cape Town, September 2021.
15 Personal communication, Cape Town, September 2021.
16 Interview, Cape Town, September 2021.
17 Interview, Cape Town, September 2021.
18 Interview, Cape Town, September 2021.
19 Joseph Aranes and Ashley Smith, 'Sedicka: Pagad man in court', *Cape Argus*, 10 December 1998.
20 Quoted in 'Cops testify at start of urban terror trial', 3 May 2001, IOL, https://www.iol.co.za/news/south-africa/cops-testify-at-start-of-urban-terror-trial-66177

21 Personal communication, Cape Town, September 2021.
22 A card shared by Boeta Yu from Jeneker writing in Worcester Prison, 3 August 2013.
23 John E Douglas, Ann W Burgess, Allen G Burgess and Robert K Kressler, *Crime Classification Manual*, Hoboken, NJ: Wiley, 2013 (3rd edition), p. 115.
24 See Ronald M Holmes and Stephen T Holmes, *Serial Murder*, London: Sage (3rd edition), 2010, pp. 123–137. It is worth adding here that the use of typologies for serial killers has also been criticised.
25 But of course such factors characterise the lives of many people who do not turn into serial killers or mass murderers. See the classic study, Peter Vronsky, *Serial Killers: The Method and Madness of Monsters*, pp. New York: Berkley Books, 2004, pp. 267–285.
26 Ronald M Holmes and Stephen T Holmes, *Serial Murder*, London: Sage (3rd edition), 2010, p. 95.
27 A good overview is to be found in James Alan Fox, Jack Levin and Emma E Fridel, *Extreme Killing*, London: Sage (4th edition), 2010, pp. 31–32.

Chapter 7

1 From sources, it does indeed seem the family is no longer involved.
2 Interview, Cape Town, July 2022.
3 Personal communication, local community worker, Cape Town, July 2022.
4 Interview, Cape Town, March 2022.
5 Interview, Cape Town, July 2022.
6 Interview, Cape Town, June 2022.
7 Interviews, current and former members of Crime Intelligence, Cape Town, August and September 2021; personal communication with people close to the process of bomb making, Cape Town, June 2022.
8 Interviews, current and former members of Crime Intelligence, Cape Town, August and September 2021; personal communication with people close to the process of bomb making, Cape Town, June 2022.
9 Interview, Cape Town, June 2022.
10 Interviews, former Pagad members, Cape Town, June and July 2022.
11 I discussed this with a well-known and knowledgeable gun dealer. He was also of the view, however, that gunpowder was not the best substance to make pipe bombs.
12 Abrahams turned state witness and was murdered by Pagad in April 2001.
13 Interview, Cape Town, June 2022.
14 Interview, Cape Town, February 2022.
15 Interview, Cape Town, May 2022.
16 Interview, Cape Town, June 2022.
17 Interview, Cape Town, June 2022.
18 Francis, who was also facing other charges at the time, was acquitted on a technicality. See Jeanne van der Merwe, 'Arms charge dropped in Pagad trial', IOL, 20 February 2001, https://www.iol.co.za/news/south-africa/arms-charge-dropped-in-Pagad-trial-59823.
19 Lynnette Johns, 'Cop tells court how he caught

"bombers"', IOL, 24 July 2001, https://www.iol.co.za/news/south-africa/cop-tells-court-how-he-caught-bombers-71160.

20 Interview, Cape Town, June 2022.
21 Interview, Cape Town, June 2022.
22 Interview, Cape Town, February 2022.
23 Joseph Aranes, 'Muslim "targets" issue appeal for support: We bear brunt of reprisals', *Cape Argus*, 5 December 1997.
24 An information campaign targeting the wider Muslim public was also assisted by what were apparently right-wing bomb attacks in early 1997 on mosques in Rustenburg and Worcester by a group calling itself the Boere Aanvals Troepe, which also used pipe bombs.
25 Interview, Cape Town, October 2021.
26 Affidavit of Yusuf Enous, Bellville CA 76-11-2000, 19 November 2000 (in the possession of the author).
27 In October 2001, Waggie was convicted for the bombing of Lansdowne police station in August 1998. See 'Pagad bombers get 30 years', News24, 19 October 2021, https://www.news24.com/news24/Pagad-bombers-get-30-years-20011019.
28 Affidavit of Yusuf Enous, Bellville CA 76-11-2000, 19 November 2000 (in the possession of the author).

Chapter 8

1 This chapter draws on interviews with former members of the bomb squad.
2 Bombings by right-wing groups on the eve of democracy involved commercial explosives that were widely used in the mining industry.
3 Personal communication, February 2023.
4 A woman joined the bomb squad for a short time. 'She is often overlooked when the boys reminisce,' says a former member. Personal communication, March 2023.
5 Personal communication, former member of the bomb squad, February 2023.
6 Interview, former member of Security Branch and later the bomb squad, October 2021.
7 'Bomb disposal hero set Cosatu and Khotso bomb blasts: TRC hears', Sapa, 31 July 1998. The citation is drawn from a description of the award. See https://en.wikipedia.org/wiki/South_African_Police_Cross_for_Bravery.
8 Ibid.
9 'TRC to consider police amnesty applications for 1980 bombings', Sapa, 14 July 1998.
10 Truth and Reconciliation Commission, Amnesty Hearing, 31 July 1998, Pretoria, George Francois Hammond, AM 5452/97.
11 The *Government Gazette* of 28 March 2002 (No. 23257), for example, provided amnesty for two limpet mine explosions in Johannesburg in July 1980.
12 Many found jobs elsewhere in the world, including in UN missions desperate for the skills required to lift landmines in the post-conflict contexts of the late 1990s.
13 Interview, Cape Town, January 2022.
14 Insiders say the standard of the courses has since dropped.

15 Here is a direct quote from a WhatsApp exchange, for example: 'Every time we did this, we knowingly exposed ourselves. It's a rush knowing that actions have real consequences ... most bomb techs don't want to die, they want to live, they want to preserve life, all lives. But if the device were to bite, you'd rather die than be disabled'. Personal communication, March 2023.
16 Several old-order police involved say they never got the credit for what was a professional and difficult undertaking that protected the new constitutional order.
17 Soldiers from these units, in particular, were said to have provided training to Pagad.
18 Interview, Cape Town, January 2022.
19 The unit never carried dockets but opened sub-files on explosions, bomb threats, suspicious items, explosives recoveries and incidents of arson. These then became part of wider investigations.
20 Interview, Cape Town, October 2021.
21 Interview, Cape Town, January 2022.
22 How this occurs is described in a recent book about the career of a bomb forensic investigator in the UK. Cliff Todd, *Explosive: Bringing the World's Deadliest Bombers to Justice*, London: Headline, 2022, p. 183.
23 A statement of this sort cropped up in almost all interviews when discussing bomb-making.
24 Interview, Cape Town, October 2021.
25 Interviews, Cape Town, October 2021.
26 Interview, Cape Town, October 2021.
27 Interview, Cape Town, October 2021.
28 Interview, Cape Town, January 2022.
29 Personal communication, March 2023.
30 Personal communication, March 2023.
31 Interview, Cape Town, October 2021.
32 Having reviewed hundreds of newspaper articles on the bombings in which investigators were widely quoted, I never found a case of a bomb tech speaking to the press, even off the record. There is little press coverage of the bomb disposal function outside TRC coverage. One exception is an undated feature piece (probably from around May 1994) about the response to right-wing bomb attacks. See Trish Beaver, 'Beepers which prevent booms', *Weekend Argus*, undated press clipping.
33 Those I spoke to are quick to point out that many played a role, each contributing something unique. They are equally quick to name Frank Gentle as an important presence.
34 Personal communication, March 2023.
35 There is no trace of Frank Gentle online, in contrast to his detective colleagues.
36 Interview, Cape Town, October 2021.
37 I have a picture of him from a card produced for his funeral: he is a handsome man with short hair and greying temples, speaking animatedly into a microphone. At the bottom of the card is a sketch of a grenade.
38 Personal communication, ex-member of the bomb squad, March 2023.

39 Most of the team subsequently left the police, moving abroad to work for the UN and NGOs performing humanitarian explosive work across the world. Some emigrated to Australia and New Zealand, leaving policing behind. Others found employment in foreign police services.
40 This appeared to be the modus operandi in the June 2000 Sea Point bombing.
41 Online interview, March 2022.
42 The photos I have seen attest to the enormous amount of work involved.
43 Interview, Pretoria, January 2021.
44 Terence Strong, *The Tick Tock Man*, London: Simon and Schuster, 1994.
45 Another recommendation was a book written by British counterterrorist bomb disposal expert Major Chris Hunter called *Eight Lives Down* (London: Bantam, 2007), which details the thought processes and experiences from a bomb tech's point of view. It is hair-raising stuff.
46 Interview, Cape Town, January 2022.

Chapter 9

1 Interview, Pretoria, January 2021.
2 Interview, Cape Town, September 2021.
3 Interview via Zoom, July 2021.
4 See Marianne Merten, 'Controversial Knipe promoted to Pretoria', *Mail & Guardian*, 23 April 1999, https://mg.co.za/article/1999-04-23-controversial-knipe-promoted-to-pretoria/.
5 Interview, Cape Town, February 2023.
6 Schalk Visagie, *Under Fire in South Africa*, Pinelands: Christian Liberty Books, 2019.
7 The name of the outfit was later changed to the Crimes Against the State unit, lest Pagad feel it was the only organisation in the spotlight.
8 Schalk Visagie, *Under Fire in South Africa*, Pinelands: Christian Liberty Books, 2019, p. 207.
9 Ibid., p. 244.
10 Ibid., p. 245.
11 'Timeline of Events_Pagad' (undated).
12 Personal communication, Arno Lamoer, July 2021.
13 Act 32 of 1998.
14 Under section 28 of the act.
15 Martin Schönteich, 'Lawyers for the people: The South Africa Prosecution Service', Institute for Security Studies, 2001, https://issafrica.s3.amazonaws.com/site/uploads/Mono53.pdf. The relevant sections are in chapter 3, 'Controversy surrounding the new act'.
16 Martin Schönteich, 'A Story of Trials and Tribulations: The National Prosecuting Authority, 1998–2014', *SA Crime Quarterly*, 50, December 2014, p. 7.
17 Sonn was forced to issue a public apology after he got drunk at a 2003 Cricket World Cup game between India and the Netherlands.

18 A now senior UN official, who worked extensively with Sonn at the time, providing support to South Africa's process of criminal justice reform, recalled several conversations with him along these lines. Personal communication, April 2023.
19 Interview, Bulelani Ngcuka, Johannesburg, January 2022.
20 Quoted in Marion Sparg, *Bulelani Ngcuka: The Sting in the Tale*, Cape Town and Johannesburg: Jonathan Ball, 2022, p. 170.
21 Interview, Bulelani Ngcuka, Johannesburg, January 2022.
22 Ibid.
23 Ibid.
24 Schalk Visagie, *Under Fire in South Africa*, Pinelands: Christian Liberty Books, 2019, p. 253.
25 The details of Lategan's assassination are drawn from the judgment in the case. See in the Supreme Court of South Africa (Cape of Good Hope Provincial Section), in the case between *The State and Ismail Edwards and Ebrahim Jeneker*, SS.145/2001, 22 April 2003. I have had the judgment officially translated and the page numbers in a later footnote in this chapter refer to the translated version.
26 Interview, Cape Town, January 2021.
27 Case SS145/2001 (author's translated version of the judgment), p. 3.
28 Ibid., p. 8.
29 Ibid., p. 11.
30 Ibid.
31 These details are drawn from Schalk Visagie, *Under Fire in South Africa*, Pinelands: Christian Liberty Books, 2019, pp. 258–288.

Chapter 10

1 When I met Mungalee, he came across as open and thoughtful. He was also frail, suffering from diabetes (as a result of which he had just had a toe amputated). By contrast, pictures in the media after his arrest show a strapping, confident man in his prime. Mungalee talked openly about what happened to him. The contents of this chapter are drawn from engagements with Mungalee, mainly in September 2022, and interviews with individuals who were in the intelligence community at the time.
2 Interview, Johannesburg, September 2022
3 Interview, Johannesburg, September 2022.
4 Staff reporter, 'Pagad in Jo'burg fracas', *Mail & Guardian*, 26 June 1997, Johannesburg, https://mg.co.za/article/1997-06-26-Pagad-in-joburg-fracas/.
5 Interview, Johannesburg, September 2022.
6 Interview, Johannesburg, September 2022.
7 These are portrayed in Barry Gilder, *Songs and Secrets*, Johannesburg: Jacana, 2012.
8 See Mark Shaw, 'Spy meets Spy: Negotiating New Intelligence Structures', in Steven Friedman and Doreen Atkinson (eds), *South African Review 7: The Small Miracle – South Africa's Negotiated Settlement*, Johannesburg: Ravan Press, 1994.
9 Interview, Johannesburg, September 2022.

10 Richards showed up again in a picture taken in President Jacob Zuma's office in 2012, alongside Zuma and George Darmanovic, a controversial Serbian underworld figure with links to South African intelligence who was murdered in 2018. See 'Exclusive: Zuma's mystery meeting with SA spook murdered in Serbia', News24, 10 May 2018, https://www.news24.com/news24/exclusive-zumas-mystery-meeting-with-south-african-spook-murdered-in-serbia-20180510.

11 Interview, Johannesburg, September 2022.

12 Full disclosure: I acted as Duarte's adviser for municipal and metropolitan policing at the time. Duarte died in July 2022.

13 Interview, Johannesburg, September 2022.

14 'Pagad threatens to kill drug dealers', *Mail & Guardian*, 30 June 1997, https://mg.co.za/article/1997-06-30-Pagad-threatens-to-kill-drug-dealers/.

15 Interview, Johannesburg, September 2022.

16 Interview, Johannesburg, September 2022.

17 Mungalee said he did not want to give the name of the informant as, to his knowledge, it had never been made public.

18 Memorandum provided to an officer in the SAPS, Cape Town, 12 August 1999.

19 Affidavit of Cornelia Susaré Margaretha Bezuidenhout, signed 10 October 1999 in Cape Town.

20 Interview, Johannesburg, September 2022.

21 Things were also complicated by the fact that Mungalee's wife was unhappy with what he was doing. She felt he was not telling her everything that was going on – which of course he was not. The number of people coming in and out of the house made her suspicious.

22 Affidavit of Cornelia Susaré Margaretha Bezuidenhout, signed 10 October 1999 in Cape Town.

23 Hannes de Wet, 'NIA still in the dark about police move to name agent', Sapa, Pretoria, 25 February 1999.

24 The original quote was in Afrikaans and the translation is mine. See Petra Cillié, 'Oudsthoorn. 'n Agenthanteerder van die Nasionale –' *Die Burger*, 27 February 1999. (The heading of the article is obscured in the copy I have and I was not able to source the original.)

25 Personal communication, January 2022.

26 Personal communication with someone present, December 2021.

27 Fraser went on to become the controversial head of the State Security Agency, where he allegedly established a parallel intelligence network, a claim he disputes. Later, as head of correctional services, he released Jacob Zuma on parole in circumstances challenged by the Constitutional Court. More recently, in June 2022, he laid a criminal complaint against President Cyril Ramaphosa over the Phala Phala incident.

28 There is a surprising lack of reporting on what happened to the others. One of the five told me about the successful appeal.

29 Never afraid of the public eye, Mungalee made accusations that the police were involved in gun-running between Gauteng and the Western Cape. He was later also

accused of murder, although he argued it was a police set-up. Greta Bezuidenhout acted as a character witness. He was acquitted.

30 'Mufamadi, Nhlanhla meet after police blew cover of NIA agent', Sapa, 25 February 1999.

31 De Wet Potgieter, *Black Widow White Widow: Is Al-Qaeda operating in South Africa?*, Johannesburg: Penguin, 2014, p. 21.

Chapter 11

1 Interview, Johannesburg, September 2021.

2 This can become even more perverse when the leadership structure is thoroughly controlled by the state's intelligence assets. Something like this may have been occurring with right-wing groups at the time, with the joke being that the leadership structure was different intelligence agencies' assets talking to each other.

3 It is noteworthy how many of the characters in this story intersect somehow with events in Manenberg: Lamoer, Jeneker, Africa and others.

4 Brookbanks is credited with building links to former members of the ANC Department of Intelligence and Security in 1994. He was also central in establishing and managing the provincial intelligence coordination structure, Picoc.

5 This section draws on several interviews with people close to the process. I was told the story by someone in the unit. Personal communication via Zoom, July 2021.

6 Interview, Pretoria, September 2021.

7 Interview via Zoom, July 2021.

8 Someone who was present told me that Africa said to his colleagues, 'How can I be anti-Islamic given my ideological background and that I am married to a Muslim woman?' Interview via Zoom, February 2022.

9 Interview, Pretoria, January 2021.

10 A good overview with a mention of the reports is to be found in Mary Braid, 'South Africa's guilty secret', *The Independent*, 2 November 1997, https://www.independent.co.uk/arts-entertainment/south-africa-s-guilty-secret-1291659.html.

11 Interview, Cape Town, January 2021.

12 Interview via Zoom, August 2021.

13 Interview, Pretoria, January 2021.

14 Jeremy Vearey, *Into Dark Water: A Police Memoir*, Cape Town: Tafelberg, 2021, p. 51.

15 Interview via Zoom, August 2021. Another informant was recruited shortly afterwards.

16 Interview, Pretoria, September 2021.

17 It seems to be the only place where Denel (once a division of Armscor) made grenades. See CM Rogerson, 'Defending Apartheid: Armscor and the Geography of Military Production in South Africa', *GeoJournal*, Vol 22, No 3, November 1990, p. 246.

18 In Chapter 5, we noted how Pagad operatives were frustrated by the fact that their newly acquired grenades were not detonating properly, one of the reasons they turned to making pipe bombs.

19 Andy Duffy, 'Cops face probe of Pagad link', *Mail & Guardian*, 21 November 1997, https://mg.co.za/article/1997-11-21-cops-face-probe-of-Pagad-link/.

20 Marianne Merten, 'Murdered Pagad leader was informer', *Mail & Guardian*, 23 July 1999, https://mg.co.za/article/1999-07-23-murdered-Pagad-leader-was-informer/.
21 Quoted in Andy Duffy, 'Cops face probe of Pagad link', *Mail & Guardian*, 21 November 1997, https://mg.co.za/article/1997-11-21-cops-face-probe-of-Pagad-link/.
22 Interview, former senior police officer, Cape Town, January 2021.
23 Marianne Merten, 'Murdered Pagad leader was informer', *Mail & Guardian*, 23 July 1999, https://mg.co.za/article/1999-07-23-murdered-Pagad-leader-was-informer/.
24 Only one was named publicly. Inspector Wymar O'Reilly said he would use the court to tell his side of the story. See Andy Duffy, 'Cops face probe of Pagad link', *Mail & Guardian*, 21 November 1997, https://mg.co.za/article/1997-11-21-cops-face-probe-of-Pagad-link/.
25 Interview via Zoom, August 2021.
26 Interview via Zoom, July 2021.
27 Interview via Zoom, August 2021.
28 Interview, Cape Town, January 2021.
29 Interview, senior police intelligence official at the time of the Pagad bombings, Johannesburg, September 2021.
30 Interview, Johannesburg, September 2021.
31 Schalk Visagie, *Under Fire in South Africa*, Cape Town: Christian Liberty Books, 2019, pp. 218–220.
32 A senior police officer recounted to me what occurred and I verified details from others, including Pagad sources.

Chapter 12

1 There had been many blasts earlier that year: 166 pipe bomb blasts were recorded in 1999 alone, with no single prosecution; see Marion Sparg, *Bulelani Ngcuka: The Sting in the Tale*, Cape Town and Johannesburg, Jonathan Ball, 2022, p. 216.
2 See Jean Redpath, 'The Scorpions: Analysing the Directorate for Special Operations', Institute for Security Studies, Monograph 96, Pretoria, March 2004, p. 13, https://issafrica.org/research/monographs/monograph-96-the-scorpions.-analysing-the-directorate-of-special-operations-jean-redpath.
3 Interview, Johannesburg, January 2022.
4 Talk around this incident may be one reason why Abdus-Salaam Ebrahim later claimed that Mbeki had instructed judges to be tougher on Pagad. This was nonsense.
5 Interview, Johannesburg, January 2022.
6 Quoted in Steven Mann, 'Scorpions, more police to hunt Western Cape bombers', *Mail & Guardian*, 25 December 1999, https://mg.co.za/article/1999-12-25-scorpions-more-police-to-hunt-western-cape-bombers/.
7 Interview, Cape Town, March 2022.
8 Quoted in Karen Helen Geyer-van Rensburg, '"It Was a Brilliant Time": An Investigation into the Experiences of the Founder Group of the Directorate for Special Operations', MBA thesis, Rhodes University, January 2004, p. 47.
9 The words are according to Bulelani Ngcuka. Interview, Johannesburg, January

2022. A similar narrative was provided by another person present. Interview, senior prosecutor, Cape Town, September 2021.

10 *Reuters Group Plc and Others v Viljoen and Others 2001 (2) SACR* p. 522.

11 An attempt was made earlier in the Staggie case to subpoena journalists as witnesses. The media threatened to take the case to the Constitutional Court; Minister of Justice Dullah Omar, sensitive to such an issue given the role of the press during apartheid, agreed that they should not testify.

12 Interview, Bulelani Ngcuka, Johannesburg, January 2022.

13 Quoted in Marion Sparg, *Bulelani Ngcuka: The Sting in the Tale*, Cape Town and Johannesburg, Jonathan Ball 2022, p. 214.

14 Interview, former police general from Crime Intelligence, Pretoria, September 2021. Many senior police also admired how Selebi pushed back against what was termed 'civilian oversight', bizarrely telling a meeting where I was present that there was 'no longer any need for civilian oversight, as I am a civilian'.

15 Marianne Merten, 'Controversial Knipe promoted to Pretoria', *Mail & Guardian*, Johannesburg, 23 April 1999, https://mg.co.za/article/1999-04-23-controversial-knipe-promoted-to-pretoria/.

16 Interview, Cape Town, January 2022.

17 Interview, former senior police officer, Cape Town, September 2021.

18 Recounted to me by a detective who was present, Cape Town, January 2022.

19 They included men such as Eddie Clark, Paul Hendricks and Clive Ontong, who later made their names. Several are now members of the Hawks, aka the Directorate for Priority Crime Investigation, the SAPS unit that ultimately replaced the Scorpions.

20 Interview, Cape Town, September 2021.

21 Interview, senior detective, Cape Town, January 2022.

22 'Seventh Pagad witness dead', News24, 9 April 2001, https://www.news24.com/news24/seventh-Pagad-witness-dead-20010409.

23 Jeremy Lovell, 'Tshwete declares war on Pagad', IOL, 13 September 2000, https://www.iol.co.za/news/south-africa/tshwete-declares-war-on-Pagad-44058.

24 'South Africa warns group after fatal attack on judge', *The New York Times*, 10 September 2000, https://www.nytimes.com/2000/09/10/world/south-africa-warns-group-after-fatal-attack-on-judge.html; Marianne Merten, 'Back to detention without trial?' *Mail & Guardian*, 15 September 2000, https://mg.co.za/article/2000-09-15-back-to-detention-without-trial/.

25 Recounted to me by someone who was present, interview via Zoom, August 2021.

26 Tony Roshan Samara, *Cape Town After Apartheid: Crime and Governance in the Divided City*, Minneapolis: University of Minnesota Press, 2011, p. 120.

27 Interview, former senior police officer, Vienna, September 2021.

28 Interview via Zoom, August 2021. He recounted this story to me.

29 While not named here the identity of 'Curly Toes' is known to the author.

30 Interview, Pretoria, January 2022.

31 Marianne Merten, 'NIA agent linked to Pagad attacks', *Mail & Guardian*, 1 October

1999, https://mg.co.za/article/1999-10-01-nia-agent-linked-to-Pagad-attacks/.

32 After the Green Point bombing, Ngcuka received a pledge from MTN and Vodacom that SIM cards would not be sold without the buyer providing an identity number. This later became normal practice under the Regulation of Interception of Communications and Provision of Communication-Related Information Act.

Chapter 13

1 Personal communication, April 2023.

2 A bomb blast at Bishop Lavis police station in November 2002 did not seem to be connected to the Pagad bombing campaign.

3 'Police tightlipped on bomb arrests', *Mail & Guardian*, 5 November 2000, https://mg.co.za/article/2000-11-05-police-tightlipped-on-bomb-arrests/; 'Cops outsmarting bombers', News24, 3 November 2000, https://www.news24.com/news24/xarchive/archive/cops-outsmarting-bombers-20001103. Bester reiterated this to me 20 years later. Interview via Zoom, March 2022.

4 Interview, September 2021.

5 I have pieced together the story of the flowerpot bomb from multiple interviews, press reports and several documents. Most participants know, or could tell me, only part of the story.

6 In 2009, Stefaans Brummer and Sam Sole got close to the whole story, including the bugging of the car. See Stefaans Brummer and Sam Sole, 'Did top cops rig Pagad case?', *Mail & Guardian*, 21 August 2009, https://mg.co.za/article/2009-08-21-did-top-cops-rig-pagad-case/.

7 Interview, September 2021.

8 Interview, September 2021.

9 This was Ebrahim Gallie, a witness in the trial of Ebrahim Jeneker.

10 Interview, Cape Town, September 2021.

11 Interview, Cape Town, September 2021.

12 Personal communication, March 2023.

13 Interview, Cape Town, September 2021.

14 I have a copy of the affidavit.

15 Mzwandile Petros, affidavit (undated).

16 Stefaans Brummer and Sam Sole, 'Did top cops rig Pagad case?', *Mail & Guardian*, 21 August 2009, https://mg.co.za/article/2009-08-21-did-top-cops-rig-pagad-case/.

17 Interview, Cape Town, September 2021.

18 Stefaans Brummer and Sam Sole, 'Did top cops rig Pagad case?', *Mail & Guardian*, 21 August 2009, https://mg.co.za/article/2009-08-21-did-top-cops-rig-pagad-case/.

19 Ibid.

20 Bill Blumenthall, 'Failed Cape bomb a filthy deed, says Tshwete', IOL, 3 November 2000, https://www.iol.co.za/news/south-africa/failed-cape-bomb-a-filthy-deed-says-tshwete-52172.

21 Stefaans Brummer and Sam Sole, 'Did top cops rig Pagad case?', *Mail & Guardian*, 21 August 2009, https://mg.co.za/article/2009-08-21-did-top-cops-rig-pagad-case/.

22 Media release by Acting Provincial Commissioner: Western Cape Deputy Provincial Commissioner Zelda Holtzman, 3 November 2000.
23 Stefaans Brummer and Sam Sole, 'Did top cops rig Pagad case?', *Mail & Guardian*, 21 August 2009, https://mg.co.za/article/2009-08-21-did-top-cops-rig-pagad-case/.

Chapter 14

1 See Lucy Nthepa Mphaphuli, 'Experience and Challenges of Witnesses in the Witness Protection Programme in South Africa: Guidelines for Coordinated Service Delivery developed from a Social Worker Perspective', PhD thesis, University of South Africa, November 2020, pp. 178–181.
2 Interview, Pretoria, January 2022. In court, the brother of Yusuf Enous made the same point: Terri-Liza Fortein and Dan Bennett, 'South Africa: Key witness stood out like a sore thumb', *Cape Argus*, 11 September 2003, https://allafrica.com/stories/200309110573.html.
3 In the High Court of South Africa (Cape of Good Hope Provincial Division), *The State v Mogamat Phadiel Orrie, Sentence, SS32/2003, 18-10-2004*, p. 3.
4 Fatima Schroeder, 'Pagad man guilty of murdering witnesses', IOL, 15 October 2004, https://www.iol.co.za/news/south-africa/pagad-man-guilty-of-murdering-witnesses-224164.
5 In the High Court of South Africa (Cape of Good Hope Provincial Division), *The State v Mogamat Phadiel Orrie, Sentence, SS32/2003, 18-10-2004*, p. 3.
6 Interview, Cape Town, June 2022.
7 Judy Damon, 'Shot witness had "planned return to Pagad"', IOL, 9 April 2000, https://www.iol.co.za/news/south-africa/shot-witness-had-planned-return-to-pagad-63920.
8 Interview, Pretoria, January 2022.
9 In the High Court of South Africa (Cape of Good Hope Provincial Division), *The State v Mogamat Phadiel Orrie, Sentence, SS32/2003, 18-10-2004*, p 4.
10 Lucy Nthepa Mphaphuli, 'Experience and Challenges of Witnesses in the Witness Protection Programme in South Africa: Guidelines for Coordinated Service Delivery developed from a Social Worker Perspective', PhD thesis, University of South Africa, November 2020, p. 65.
11 Chris Mahony, 'The Justice Sector Afterthought: Witness Protection in Africa', Institute for Security Studies, 2010, p. 110, https://issafrica.s3.amazonaws.com/site/uploads/Book2010WitnessProt.pdf.
12 I have several matrices of the hundreds of cases that were under investigation at that time. These consolidated numbers are from the US Department of State, Country Report on Human Rights Practices, Bureau of Democracy, Human Rights, and Labor, 4 March 2002 (under 'South Africa', in the section 'a. Arbitrary or Unlawful Deprivation of Life', https://2009-2017.state.gov/j/drl/rls/hrrpt/2001/af/8404.htm.
13 'Pagad on US terror list', News24, 8 December 2001, https://www.news24.com/news24/pagad-on-us-terror-list-20011208.
14 US Department of State, Annual Report on International Religious Freedom

for 2002 – South Africa, 7 October 2002, https://2009-2017.state.gov/j/drl/rls/irf/2002/13854.htm (See Section III, Societal Attitudes).

15 US Department of State, Annual Report on International Religious Freedom for 2003 – South Africa, 18 December 2003, https://2009-2017.state.gov/j/drl/rls/irf/2003/23753.htm (see Section III, Societal Attitudes).

16 I made a Freedom of Information request to the UK Home Office (ref. 68157) to obtain more details of the London case and received a reply in June 2022. This was to the effect that the file could not be located and it would be too costly to access it.

17 *Reuters Group plc and Others v Viljoen and Others 2001 (2) SACR* p. 536.

18 Ibid.

19 Interview, Johannesburg, February 2022.

20 As recounted to me by Ngcuka. Interview, Johannesburg, February 2022.

21 Interview, Cape Town, January 2022. The fact that there was no real leadership change was to be a key complaint of some members, who felt Ebrahim should have relinquished complete control to a new leader who could have taken things forward. As will be seen in the next chapter, when the NIA wanted to negotiate with Pagad it reached out to Ebrahim as the man in charge and responsible for the violence.

22 His brother, Ebrahim Salie, was a prominent assassin for Pagad, having killed several gangsters. He escaped justice, being acquitted in a case where the police investigation was poorly conducted. A partner, Mansoer Leggett, was convicted. Tragically, Abdullah Salie's gun was picked up by Ebrahim's six-year-old relative, and while playing with it he shot and killed Ebrahim's six-month-old baby. Ebrahim later died in a fall from Table Mountain when the two brothers were out walking together.

23 See Estelle Ellis, 'Pagad chief found guilty of public violence', IOL, 6 March 2002, https://www.iol.co.za/news/south-africa/pagad-chief-found-guilty-of-public-violence-82914.

24 It was determined that this had nothing to do with the case, but it was a reminder of the vulnerability of judicial officials.

25 In the Supreme Court of South Africa (Cape of Good Hope Provincial Section), In the case between *The State and Abdullah Maansdorp, Ismael Maansdorp and Ebrahim Jeneker*, SS 121/99, Judgment, 17 December 2002, para. 7, pp. 3–4 (the original judgment is in Afrikaans; page numbers are from a translated copy in the author's possession).

26 Ibid.

27 Interview, Cape Town, September 2001.

28 Interview, Cape Town, August 2022.

29 In the Supreme Court of South Africa (Cape of Good Hope Provincial Section), In the case between *The State and Abdullah Maansdorp, Ismael Maansdorp and Ebrahim Jeneker*, SS 121/99, Judgment, 17 December 2002, para. 90, p. 28 of translated version.

30 Ibid., para, 123, p. 39 of translated version.

31 Ibid., para. 50, p. 50 of translated version.

32 In the High Court of South Africa (Cape of Good Hope Provincial Division), in the

matter between the *State and Mogamat Phadiel Orrie and Mogamat Samir Orrie, SS 32/2003*, Judgment, 14 October 2004, p. 22 (1st judgment).

33 Ibid., p. 11.

34 In the High Court of South Africa (Cape of Good Hope Provincial Division), in the matter between the *State and Mogamat Phadiel Orrie and Mogamat Samir Orrie, SS 32/2003*, Judgment, 21 November 2003, p. 2 (2nd judgment).

35 'Pagad "hitman" gets 25 years', IOL, 3 October 2000, https://www.iol.co.za/news/south-africa/pagad-hit-man-gets-25-years-49598.

36 Interview, Cape Town, January 2021.

Chapter 15

1 On Pagad's side were Ebrahim, as national coordinator and head; Abida Roberts, the hard-talking national secretary; and Salie Abader, head of security. On the government side were Omar Valley, the provincial head of the community safety secretariat; Simon Mpempe, a gruff old-school police officer from provincial headquarters; and Lamoer. The meeting was facilitated by Craig Arendse from the University of Cape Town.

2 As a way to build confidence, Pagad provided information and the police ensured it was acted upon, with firearms subsequently being seized in Manenberg. Lamoer was hopeful, feeling strongly that maintaining contact was important and that this approach might work – or at least keep the sharp edges off Pagad.

3 Senior crime intelligence people had concluded by this point that Pagad would become increasingly violent and there were early attempts by prosecutor Willie Viljoen (unsuccessful before the arrival of Bulelani Ngcuka) to see whether Ebrahim could be charged.

4 Interview, Cape Town, February 2023.

5 This is the opinion of several in Pagad whom I spoke to.

6 Personal communication through an intermediary, May 2023.

7 Interview, Cape Town, January 2022.

8 The quote is taken from a written speech provided to me by Barry Gilder, 'The Pagad experience' (undated), p. 4. The paper is available online at https://www.academia.edu/43072944/The_PAGAD_Experience, and is described as a 'Paper presented to the 2008 South African Institute of International Affairs (SAIIA) conference on "Radicalisation"'. He makes similar points in his memoir, *Songs and Secrets: South Africa from Liberation to Governance*, Johannesburg: Jacana, 2012, pp. 305–324.

9 Interview via Zoom, February 2022.

10 Interview with Ebrahim and other Pagad representatives, Cape Town, February 2022.

11 Interview, Cape Town, February 2023.

12 Interview, Cape Town, February 2023.

13 Interviews, Cape Town, January and February 2022.

14 Interview, Cape Town, February 2022.

15 Personal communication, May 2023.
16 Interview, via Zoom, May 2022.
17 Interview, Cape Town, January 2022.
18 Interview, Cape Town, January 2022.
19 Interview with Ebrahim and other Pagad representatives, Cape Town, February 2022.
20 The other Pagad participants saw the NIA's Patel as crucial in drawing Ebrahim aside to be negotiated with as the head of the organisation, even if the outcomes of that process were not clear. (In the hothouse of Pagad politics their suspicions were bolstered by the family link between Nizaam Shaik and Patel, both seen as close to Ebrahim.)
21 Barry Gilder, 'The Pagad experience' (undated), p. 5.
22 Interview, Pretoria, January 2022.

Chapter 16

1 Personal communication, February 2023.
2 Personal communication, May 2023.
3 Charitable giving was a source of financing too, which is why Mungalee, who was well connected to Johannesburg's rich Muslim business community, was so important to Ebrahim.
4 The literature on organised crime is full of cases where armed formations, in the absence of an effective state, moved into the vacuum to establish territorial governance through taxing and extortion.
5 Interview, Cape Town, February 2023.
6 This was for his role in an attack on the home of Mogamat Madatt, a prominent gang boss, drug dealer (he pioneered the sale of 'tik' in the Cape) and taxi boss from the Americans gang.
7 Interview, Cape Town, February 2023.
8 Interview, Cape Town, February 2023.
9 Personal communication via an intermediary, May 2023.
10 Personal communication via an intermediary, May 2023.
11 Interview, Cape Town, January 2022.
12 Interview with Toefy, Ebrahim and other Pagad representatives, Cape Town, February 2022.
13 Personal communication, May 2023.
14 Mwangi Githahu, 'Pagad leader launches attack on LGBTQIA+ community amid Pride Month celebrations', IOL, 16 February 2023, https://www.iol.co.za/capeargus/news/pagad-leader-launches-attack-on-lgbtqia-community-amid-pride-month-celebrations-9a1a8b35-ac0d-48e1-8875-b864144e09bb.

THE PAGAD STORY: TIMELINE OF SELECTED EVENTS

11 May 1996: Pagad leads a mass march to parliament, protesting about drugs in Cape Town communities.

4 August 1996: Mob killing by Pagad members of Hard Livings gang leader Rashaad Staggie in Salt River.

11 August 1996: Inauguration of Pagad at a rally at Vygieskraal Stadium in Rylands. About 10 000 people attend.

3 November 1996: Mass meeting of Pagad members at the Victoria & Alfred Waterfront develops into a confrontation with the police. Achmat Najaar, brother of an Islamic Council of South Africa member, is killed.

23 October 1997: Launch of Operation Recoil.

12 January 1998: Launch of Operation Saladin.

20 January 1998: Moeneeb 'Bowtie' Abrahams, a prominent member of the Hard Livings gang, is shot dead in Manenberg.

25 January 1998: Bombing of Lansdowne police station.

March 1998: Prominent gang bosses Katy-Ann Arendse and Faried 'Keusie' Davids are shot dead in Heideveld (exact date unknown).

26 June 1998: Bombing of Mowbray police station.

13 July 1998: Bombing of the Rondebosch East home of Ebrahim Moosa, a prominent religious studies academic.

1 August 1998: Establishment of the National Prosecuting Authority (NPA).

6 August 1998: Bombing of the Bellville office of the police task team leading investigations into Pagad.

25 August 1998: Bombing of Planet Hollywood restaurant at the Victoria & Alfred Waterfront. Two people are killed and 24 injured.

November 1998: Ismail April, aka Bobby Mongrel, leader of the Mongrels gang, is shot dead at his Grassy Park home (exact date unknown).

11 November 1998: Neville Heroldt, aka Jackie Lonte, leader of the Americans gang, is shot dead in Athlone.

November 1998: Ernie 'Lapepa' Peters, leader of the 28s gang, is shot and dies in hospital.

18 December 1998: Bombing of the Wynberg Synagogue.

1 January 1999: Car bomb explodes at the Victoria & Alfred Waterfront.

14 January 1999: Assassination of Bennie Lategan, a leading detective investigating Pagad-related bombings.

23 January 1999: Launch of Operation Good Hope.

28 January 1999: Bombing outside Caledon Square police station. Eleven people are injured.

30 January 1999: Bombing of Woodstock police station.

2 February 1999: Arrest of the 'Pagad five', including Ayob Mungalee, near Laingsburg.

19 February 1999: Attempted assassination of Schalk Visagie, a prominent detective who investigated Pagad.

10 April 1999: Adiela Davids, a leading member of the Americans gang, and two other women are killed at a Grassy Park hairdressing salon.

1 September 1999: Formal establishment of the Directorate for Special Operations (the Scorpions).

5 November 1999: Bombing of the Blah Bar in Green Point.

28 November 1999: Bombing of St Elmo's pizzeria in Camps Bay injures 48 people.

24 December 1999: Bombing outside Mano's restaurant in Green Point injures seven police officers. The bomb is detonated remotely via cellphone.

25 December 1999: Impromptu high-level security gathering chaired by NPA chief Bulelani Ngcuka determines a focused strategy to bring down Pagad.

29 December 1999: Arrest of Abdus-Salaam Ebrahim and his wife at their Lansdowne home.

12 January 2000: Bomb attached to a motorcycle explodes outside Wynberg Magistrates' Court.

1 April 2000: Launch of Operation Crackdown.

10 June 2000: Car bomb explodes outside New York Bagels and Sitdown in Sea Point, injuring three people.

18 July 2000: Bomb explodes in a bin at Cape Town International Airport.

11 August 2000: Car bomb explodes at Constantia Village shopping centre.

19 August 2000: Car bomb detonates outside Bronx nightclub in Green Point. The bomb does not explode properly due to a technical deficiency.

29 August 2000: Car bomb detonates in Heerengracht during peak-hour traffic. The bomb fails to explode properly but six people are injured.

7 September 2000: Piet Theron, a magistrate presiding over cases involving Pagad and urban terror, is shot dead at his home in Plumstead.

8 September 2000: Car bomb explodes outside Obz Cafe in Observatory.

12 September 2000: Bomb explodes during a Democratic Alliance rally in Gatesville, injuring seven people. Western Cape premier Gerald Morkel is there but is unharmed.

3 November 2000: Intelligence-driven operation leads to the discovery of a bomb outside the Keg and Swan pub in Bellville. The device is defused and two Pagad operatives, Faizel Waggie and Naziem Davids, are arrested.

26 December 2000: Assassination of Yusuf Enous, a prospective witness in a trial involving Pagad members involved in planting the Keg and Swan bomb; his wife, Fahiema, is also killed.

9 April 2001: Zaid 'Pang' Abrahams, a prolific Pagad pipe bomb maker who turned state witness, is shot dead at his home in Mitchells Plain.

19 October 2001: Faizel Waggie and Ismail Edwards are convicted for their role in the Lansdowne police station bombing and three attempted murders.

6 March 2002: Abdus-Salaam Ebrahim, Abdurazak Ebrahim and Moegsien Mohamed are convicted for public violence over the killing of Rashaad Staggie in 1996.

17 December 2002: Ebrahim Jeneker and Abdullah Maansdorp are convicted of multiple charges, including three murders.

ACKNOWLEDGEMENTS

This book has been several years in the making. It simply would not have been possible without the help of many people along the way. This is particularly true of my colleagues at the Global Initiative Against Transnational Organized Crime. I owe them a special thanks and many are mentioned individually below.

I am deeply indebted to Alastair MacBeath, who skilfully trawled an enormous media archive on Pagad over several months. This has been crucial in shaping the story. Rukshana Parker was a talented and enthusiastic research partner who put up with my often hasty requests with aplomb. Rukshana, better than most, helped me understand why Pagad was formed.

Rumbi Matamba, Chwayita Thobela and Michael McLaggan provided valuable support, including hunting down people and case files and responding to queries and legal questions as the deadline approached. Two old friends always find a way: Jenni Irish-Qhobosheane helped me access some hard-to-get interviewees and came along to the discussions too. Peter Gastrow opened some important doors, and then, with his standard good humour, attended the meetings. He also read and commented on a draft.

As deadlines neared, and with no possibility that I could meet them, Tuesday Reitano suggested I take a month off to finish the manuscript. She took on the job of managing the Global Initiative during that time, while also reading parts of the developing manuscript. After so long, a simple thank you does not cut it any more – it is just as it is.

Theresa Hume made the logistical arrangements, without which I would never have left home. Karen Yap carved out time so I could write.

In Cape Town, two people in particular have been central to this book. The first, after some thought and discussion with him, I have decided not to name, but he was able to access the otherwise unreachable elements of Pagad and Cape Town's gangland. He opened doors, arranged meetings and held many discussions himself that shaped my thinking. I am grateful, good sir. Lyndsay Johannisen was able to answer difficult questions at short notice. ('No problem, I think he is dead, but I will try to phone him ...') The book would not have been possible without them.

I am grateful to the many people who spoke with me during the research. Several participants who asked me not to use their names were particularly instrumental in providing information. This included former state officials who helped beyond the call of duty. They deserve much credit, explaining in multiple interviews exactly how things unfolded, even if it did not always shed a positive light on their own actions. That takes some courage.

Mark Ronan has edited my work now for many years, often under tight deadlines. He does so with a critical, detailed eye. I have taken up several of his evenings and weekends talking about this book and its structure. Mark, I am grateful: a very big thank you. Designer Pete Bosman commissioned the maps and helped with the photos.

Jeremy Boraine has been a kind and considerate publisher, commissioning the book with a raised eyebrow about why I was setting out to write this story while I nattered on about its importance. Gill Moodie took over later and has been a pleasure to work with. Dave Chamberlain smoothed the text. Caren van Houwelingen expertly pulled things together. I couldn't ask for a better publisher than Jonathan Ball.

My parents have been a source of support and inspiration for so long, always inquiring how 'the book' was going, even when it wasn't. My immediate family continues to put up with me and my pursuits. They are an unending source of amusement and discussion, mostly at my expense – 'is researching crime a viable career?' – and a reminder of what life is about. I love them very much.

I was deeply moved by speaking with several survivors of the Pagad bombings, who pieced their lives back together after months of hospitalisation. No book is enough to honour them and their quiet courage, but I have tried. My renaissance man, uncle Peter Spargo, died while this book was being researched. I still feel his presence under the mountain. This book is dedicated to the survivors and to him.

INDEX

Page numbers in italics indicate photos or maps.

MARK SHAW is the author of *Hitmen for Hire* and *Give Us More Guns*. He is also director of the Global Initiative Against Transnational Organized Crime. Shaw was previously the National Research Foundation Professor of Justice and Security at the University of Cape Town and worked for ten years at the United Nations Office on Drugs and Crime. He has held a number of positions in the South African government and civil society, where he worked on issues of public safety and urban violence in the post-apartheid transition.

www.ingramcontent.com/pod-product-compliance
Lightning Source LLC
Chambersburg PA
CBHW072114270326
41931CB00010B/1551

9781776191512

Save Our WBASD High Schools

The Big Toxic School!

Wilkes-Barre Area's Tale of Corruption, Deception, Taxation & Tyranny

A struggle for safe, enduring neighborhood schools.
We can't wait until there are no WB high schools and the tax burden is unsustainable.

In this book, you will learn about the actions taken by a democratically elected board of directors whose job is to manage the affairs of the Wilkes-Barre Area School District. Unfortunately, in this book and through other sources, you will also learn that though this board was duly elected by the people, they lied about their intentions. In fact, they misrepresented themselves by agreeing, if elected, to represent the people and provide for the needs of the people above all else. We will cite quotations from citizens subject to the board's dictates. You will see that this board has chosen to follow a corrupt course of action rather than follow the known wishes of the people of the area which they serve.

The essence of the issue in dispute is whether perfectly maintainable and well-built and historically relevant neighborhood school structures in the City of Wilkes-Barre should be abandoned, discarded, and torn down so that the board can build its idea of a Taj Mahal School on top of a toxic mine dump, in a community outside the city expected to give up its high schools for this folly. The three WB City High Schools currently meet the needs of the students and the taxpayers of the City of Wilkes-Barre. Coughlin, GAR, and Meyers.

The current board believes it has served the people well. Yet, they have no maintenance plan and have had no plan for the upkeep of school buildings for over fifty years if ever. They have no qualified staff to provide maintenance work in any of the $300,000,000 worth of properties, which are "owned" by the school district. Why is this so important?

If the board had the proper team of in-house builders, and maintainers, and a plan for them to do their jobs regularly, keeping the properties maintained, there would not be an urgent need today to replace the three historically relevant high schools in Wilkes-Barre City with an abomination built outside the city limits on a toxic mine shaft. The board, over the citizens objections, plans to tear down these historical structures because the board itself did not perform its trustee role in maintaining them. The board failed and they are preparing to fail again. The board's dream school shall not be built because the people can do better than the decisions of a myopic school board. Despite grave warnings, this board has chosen to place the health of students at risk. What esteemed body working for the public good would subject those learning or working in Mine Shaft High from breathing in the toxic fumes from the designed school built on top of a hazardous waste dump.

More and more citizens of the Area believe we were duped into believing the words of the Consigliere that putting poor Wilkes-Barre Area citizens in debt up to a half billion or more dollars after the State's contribution, was the only solution to having children well-educated in this area. How long do we think it will be that the foreclosure teams from the county and other taxing bodies would be coming for all the properties of the elderly who won't be able to pay the taxes required for the board's Taj Mahal. Folks, there is no need for this monstrosity and there are a few names you need to know who will change the school board to represent the people instead of the outside interests of board members. These names are Terry Schiowitz, Robin Shudak, Jody Busch, Beth Anne Owens, and Debra Formola. Folks, reading this book is a must. Tell your friends to download it free.

BRIAN W. KELLY

 Editor: Brian P. Kelly

The Big Toxic School!
Wilkes-Barre Area's Tale of Corruption, Deception, Taxation & Tyranny

Author Brian W. Kelly

Published by: LETS GO PUBLISH!
Editor Brian P. Kelly
Email: info@letsgopublish.com
Web site www.letsgopublish.com

LETS GO PUBLISH

Library of Congress Copyright Information Pending
Book Cover Design by Brian W. Kelly

Acknowledgments are available for viewing at www.letsgopublish.com **at the bottom of the main menu..**

ISBN Information: The International Standard Book Number (ISBN) is a unique machine-readable identification number, which marks any book unmistakably. The ISBN is the clear standard in the book industry. 159 countries and territories are officially ISBN members. The Official ISBN for this book: **978-1-947402-86-7**

The price for this work is: **$14.95 USD**

10 9 8 7 6 5 4 3 2 1

Release Date: August 2019